"Finally! A user's manual for those struggling with ADD *and* addiction. This superb book provides insight into addictive behavior and its link to ADD, as well as the latest understanding of how the brain functions. Must reading for patients, providers, and anyone helping those with ADD and addiction."

—Dwaine McCallon, M.D., medical director, Buena Vista Colorado Correctional Facility; assistant chief medical officer, Colorado Department of Corrections

"Wendy Richardson knows what she's talking about. *The Link Between ADD and Addiction* is a clear, easy-to-read book that grabs your attention and offers readers the help they need to live happy and successful lives."

—Lynn Weiss, Ph.D., best-selling author of *ADD in Adults* and *Give Your ADD Teen a Chance*, counselor, and national speaker

"*The Link Between ADD and Addiction* explains the complicated interaction between ADD and addiction in a clear and accessible way that brings the subject matter alive. Filled with numerous examples and anecdotes, this book will help anyone who struggles with ADD and addictive behavior."

—Kate Kelly, RN, MSN, ADD coach, and coauthor of *You Mean I'm Not Lazy, Stupid, or Crazy?!*

THE LINK BETWEEN

A.D.D. & ADDICTION

GETTING THE HELP YOU DESERVE

WENDY RICHARDSON, M.A., LMFCC
CERTIFIED ADDICTION SPECIALIST

P.O. Box 35007, Colorado Springs, Colorado 80935

OUR GUARANTEE TO YOU

We believe so strongly in the message of our books that we are making this quality guarantee to you. If for any reason you are disappointed with the content of this book, return the title page to us with your name and address and we will refund to you the list price of the book. To help us serve you better, please briefly describe why you were disappointed. Mail your refund request to: PiñonPress, P.O. Box 35002, Colorado Springs, CO 80935.

Library of Congress Catalog Card Number: 97-5122
ISBN 1-57683-004-7

Cover illustration: Jeff Jackson/Lindgren & Smith

Some of the anecdotal illustrations in this book are true to life and are included with the permission of the persons involved. All other illustrations are composites of real situations, and any resemblance to people living or dead is coincidental.

This publication is designed to provide accurate and authoritative information in regard to the subject matter covered. It is sold with the understanding that the author and the publisher are not engaged in rendering legal, medical, or other professional service. If medical advice or other expert assistance is required, the services of a competent professional person should be sought. The exercises and checklists in this book are not designed to substitute for professional evaluations or psychotherapy.

Richardson, Wendy, 1954-
    The link between ADD and addiction : getting the help you deserve / Wendy Richardson.
        p.   cm.
    Includes index.
    ISBN 1-57683-004-7 (paper)
    1. Attention-deficit disorder in adults. 2. Substance abuse. 3. Compulsive behavior. I. Title.
RC394.A85R53   1997
616.85'89—dc21   97-5122
                                         CIP

Printed in the United States of America

2 3 4 5 6 7 8 9 10 / 05 04 03 02 01 00 99

CONTENTS

The Link Between ADD & Addiction
is dedicated to my father,
Robert Andrew Willis.
For it was after his death
that I came to understand
the impact of untreated ADD and addictions.
Through this understanding,
I learned to love and forgive him,
and accept the many gifts he gave me.
Thanks, Pop.

ACKNOWLEDGMENTS

I want to thank my friend and colleague Dr. Lynn Weiss for her mentorship and support. I very much appreciate my agent, Mary Kelly, for her devotion, wisdom, and guidance. Thank you, Mary, for creating a writer out of a therapist. I also want to thank Traci Mullins of Eclipse Editorial Services for understanding "the link" so well that she skillfully guided me through the writing and publication process, which resulted in this book becoming a reality. I also want to express my appreciation to all the people at Piñon Press for their kindness and enthusiasm about this book.

Special appreciation goes to poet David Thorn for his creative and organizational talents that contributed to the flow and tone of this book. Thank you, David, for understanding and accepting my unique writing style and working with me to pull the book together. Your encouragement and permission to write from within myself helped me trust my own voice as a writer.

This book could not have been written without the help of my husband, Eric. First, thank you, Eric, for your impeccable proofreading skills and thoughtful suggestions. Also, thank you for your fathering, cooking, and laundering skills, as well as the myriad responsibilities you undertook to keep our household afloat. Special thanks to Lindsey and Tyler for their love and patience while Mom was "writing on her book."

I also want to express my appreciation to the following people for their personal or professional contributions: Chris, David Carberry, David E. Comings, M.D., Cynthia Del Peloso, Frank Giuliani, Pharm. D., David Leland, Kate Kelly, D. Steven Ledingham, Matt, Dory Keefer-Naumes, M.A., Dwaine McCallon, M.D., Timothy F. Myers, M.D., Nancy Ratey, Ed.M., John J. Ratey, M.D., Jim Reisinger, M.B.A., Jerry Seiden, Lynne Sheehan, Rob Willis, and Colin Wright, Ph.D.

This book would not be what it is without you!

∽∾

CHAPTER ONE

THE BOTTOM LINE

You Can Have a Better Life

Do you ever feel like your life is moving so quickly that it passes you by in a blur of color? Do you stop long enough to ask yourself, "Where has the time gone?" "Where was my mind?" "How could I have missed that?" Are you able to be still and listen for the answers to these important questions, or have you spent years frantically chasing a life you've never been able to catch?

Only in the past few years have I been able to slow down enough to listen. I've always wanted to get right to the point—show me the bottom line! Then off I would go chasing something else. I've missed much in my life because I've been driven to find answers yet haven't been able to listen once I found them. For most of my life, I suffered from undiagnosed and untreated Attention Deficit Disorder. And that was only half of my problem.

For those of you who like to cut to the chase, here's the bottom line:

If you think you have Attention Deficit Disorder or addictions, this book will help you.

How?

I wrote this book to help you find answers to your problems with ADD and/or addictions. I have no magic fairy dust to sprinkle or magic wand to wave. What I offer you here are information, encouragement, and practical suggestions to help you cope effectively with your ADD and addictions. Take what works for you. Reread parts as often as you want to. Allow yourself to skip parts if they're not helpful.

I find the stories people have volunteered to share with you powerful and enlightening, but if you're not a story person, feel free to skip them. You can always come back to them if you like. It's not important that you digest every word and concept in this book. There will be no test!

I wrote this book to help you accept all of who you are, including your ADD and addictions. My number one suggestion is this: *Give yourself permission to read at your own pace, in your own style.*

Perhaps you don't suffer from untreated ADD or addictions, but you work with or love someone who does. This book is for you, too. With the information I provide, you will be better able to understand and, perhaps, offer constructive support and encouragement to your loved one, coworker, or friend.

WHAT'S IN STORE

In the next chapter you will learn about the link between ADD and addictions. Then, in Chapter Three, you will learn about ADD traits in adults.

Chapter Four talks about the biological and genetic components of ADD and addictions.

Chapter Five gives you the opportunity to find out if you should be evaluated for ADD.

Chapter Six looks at the assets many people with ADD

have. Focusing only on the "problem" of ADD is unfair and insufficient.

Chapter Seven helps you look honestly at your relationship with alcohol, drugs, food, and certain behaviors and evaluate how you're using them.

Chapter Eight explains why and how you or someone you love may be using drugs, alcohol, or food to self-medicate the troublesome symptoms of ADD.

Chapter Nine discusses self-medicating ADD with compulsive behaviors such as gambling, spending, overworking, sex, and Web browsing.

Chapters Ten and Eleven provide suggestions for treating ADD, with and without medications.

Chapter Twelve addresses ADD and addiction relapse issues.

Chapter Thirteen explains why people with ADD sometimes have trouble following a Twelve Step program for addiction recovery. I offer practical suggestions to work Twelve Step programs when you have ADD.

Chapter Fourteen gives suggestions for working with five powerful feelings—fear, anger, grief, guilt, and shame. These emotions are common among people who have ADD and/or addictions, and we'll discuss how processing them effectively is essential for sustained and gratifying recovery.

This book is the truth as I know it today. It is based on the research and opinions of many experts in the ADD and addiction fields who provide new information daily. This book is also based on my personal and professional experience and the experiences of other people who have ADD and addictions. They have volunteered to share their truth with you. Together we provide you with knowledge, tools, experience, strength, and hope for a better life. Addictions are never cured, and neither is ADD. We can, however, learn to treat these problems and find serenity and fulfillment in our lives.

In the next chapter, people with ADD and addictions

tell you their stories. You may relate to some of these stories and find them painfully familiar. By reading them, you will better understand the link between ADD and addictions and be able to look at your own life with compassion and acceptance.

CHAPTER TWO

OUR STORIES AND MAYBE SOME OF YOURS

The Link Between ADD and Addictions

Did you struggle in school because you got bored or had a hard time paying attention? Was it hard for you to control yourself and act in the ways adults wanted? As an adult, are relationships difficult for you? Do your impulses carry you from project to project, relationship to relationship, town to town, country to country, before you realize what you're doing? Are you ever distracted by the screeching of your mind as it skids to a stop when you're trying to recall a friend's name or your own address? Do you feel like you're working far below what you could or would like to be doing?

At one time I could answer yes to most of those questions. My life was run ragged by my untreated ADD. For years I tried to treat my ADD with alcohol and drugs. Now it's been many years since I've taken a drink or used drugs. I don't think about using drugs and alcohol much anymore. They're no longer an option, because living in the solution to both my addictions and my ADD is an ongoing part of my reality.

Reality is different for each of us. No one knows exactly how you feel. But if you have ADD and have been dealing with addictions, I understand what life may be like for you. I know what it's been like for me in the past, and what it's like for me today. I wake up in the morning with ADD and I go to bed with it at night. My ADD goes everywhere with me, including my trips to Hawaii or Disneyland with my family.

If you have ADD and addictions, we both know how difficult and painful life can be. You, too, have experienced the shame and humiliation of being out of control. Your life has probably not been easy. In fact, it may have been a relentless series of struggles for as long as you can remember. I'd like to share with you how I came to understand the link between ADD and addictions and hopefully provide you with some answers to your own struggle.

GATHERING THE PIECES OF THE PUZZLE

I had been working as a therapist in the substance abuse field for ten years when I read my first book about Attention Deficit Disorder in children. Everything the book said described my clinical experience of my substance-addicted clients, except for the part about how children outgrow ADD during puberty. Many of my clients had five-, ten-, twenty-plus years of recovery from drug or alcohol abuse, and yet in some ways they were like kids with ADD. More accurately, they were like adults with ADD. However, anyone who knew anything about medicine and psychology in the 1980s knew there was no such thing as an adult with ADD.

Fortunately, I didn't know any better. I began behaviorally treating my substance-abusing and recovering clients' ADD symptoms. I helped them to broaden their attention spans so they could sit through therapy and Twelve Step meetings. I encouraged them to give themselves permission to leave meetings early rather than not attend at all. We worked on impulsiveness. I gave them strategies such as thinking before interrupting others or saying things they later had to make amends for. We worked together to create goals so they could focus their

16

restless energy. Many found relief by joining a spa or athletic club or by playing tennis or running.

Some clients responded well to the behavioral approaches we were using; others did not. Some clients were so distractible and impulsive that they couldn't change their behavior no matter how hard they tried. Some of these people relapsed into addictions. Others switched addictions, substituting food, gambling, compulsive spending, or relationship addictions, for drugs and alcohol. It was clear to me that a big piece of the puzzle was missing in their overall recovery.

I, too, was frustrated, because I knew I could do so much more in my life if only I could pay better attention, follow through with my ideas, and focus my abundance of energy. In some ways my life was out of control. Something was missing, something was wrong. My willpower alone, which was tremendous, could not fix it. I knew that recovering from addictions took more than willpower, but I didn't yet understand that ADD, like alcoholism, was rooted in biology. You can no more will the biological part of ADD away than you can an addiction to heroin.

FINDING THE MISSING PUZZLE PIECE

In the early nineties, I read the first information about ADD in adults. As the months passed, I sought out tapes, articles, and books that not only validated adult ADD, but addressed treatment. I diagnosed myself as an adult with Attention Deficit Disorder. I realized that I had been intuitively treating ADD in my adult clients through behavior management. The missing piece for me and other professionals, as well as the public, has been information about ADD and the brain. I learned that ADD is a medical problem. The brain of a person with ADD functions differently from the brain of a person without ADD.

Through reading and research, I gained more understanding of how medication works to rebalance chemicals in the brain of the person with ADD. I also grasped why therapy, pastoral care, and behavioral changes were not enough for some of my clients. Their difficulties with attention, impulse control, and activity level were rooted in how their brain functioned. They needed to be treated for the biological part of their ADD, as well as how it impacted their social skills, their styles of functioning at work or school, religious practice, relationships, and legal and financial issues.

Medication was, for many of my clients, the missing piece. I realized that medication could play a significant role in treating ADD. I also realized that while medication could be an important piece of the puzzle for many, it would be only a part of the overall treatment program I would consider.

We will talk a lot more about the genetic aspects of ADD and addictions in Chapter Four, and we'll explore treatment strategies in detail in Chapters Ten and Eleven. But first I'd like to introduce you to several people who struggle with ADD and addictions. You might not relate to everything about their stories, but notice what rings true for you.

David Rocks and Rolls

It's 1968 in the Haight Ashbury district of San Francisco. David is a drummer for several nameless bands that warm up the crowds for bands the people really came to hear: Country Joe and the Fish, Quicksilver Messenger Service, and Ten Years After. David shoots heroin, plays music at night, and sleeps all day like a mole in a hole. Even on heroin his high energy drumbeat makes him feel powerful and omnipotent. But in the afternoon when he awakens, he is sick from withdrawal and feels as slimy and helpless as a baby lizard.

David always wanted to be a drummer, but he never intended to become a junkie. As a boy, he had so much energy and rhythm that he banged and tapped on everything in sight, including his body. His parents bought him a drum set when he was seven, and David would bang away for hours. Rock and roll helped him get through high school. David was very bright, but he found school boring and hated to go. However, playing in his funky little band at school dances kept him going. If he dropped out of school, he would no longer be able to play.

In high school David found that taking "uppers" such as benzedrine and dexadrine helped him deal with his high-speed personality during the day. He took "downers" such as seconal or other barbiturates to sleep at night. He snorted cocaine, smoked pot, and drank to slow down his brain, mouth, and body. He was twenty-one when he discovered heroin. Heroin became David's "guide dog" that led him through a world he never saw clearly or felt comfortable in. After thirteen years of rock and roll heroin use, David was playing very few gigs. Heroin and alcohol no longer controlled his moods or energy. He was lethargic when not using drugs and suicidally depressed when he did use them.

Out of desperation, David became involved in a Twelve Step program of recovery, Narcotics Anonymous (NA). Several other musicians he respected were cleaning up their acts, and David followed them into recovery. Sober life was not fun for him. He felt tortured sitting through hour-long Twelve Step meetings, but saw no other option if he wanted to stay clean and sober. He couldn't deal with the drugs and alcohol always being in his face when he played music, so he quit the music business. He returned to school and received a degree in journalism and got a job as a news correspondent.

After a dozen years of recovery, David's untreated ADD led him back to narcotics, this time to prescription painkillers. While loaded, he felt a false sense of well-being and peace; at last his mind and body could take a rest. His drug use was short-lived, because he had learned too much during his recovery to deny what he was doing to himself and his family.

Since recommitting to his recovery, David has been diagnosed with ADD and is now working on treating his ADD along with his addictions. He's become very involved and disciplined in martial arts. Through his devotion to Tae Kwon Do he's able to expend energy and find peace in meditation. He is now more accepting of his toned down high energy style, and accepts how it works for him rather than against him.

Daydream Believer

Michelle was a daydreamer. She quietly daydreamed and fantasized her way through high school. Her grades were never horrible, but her teachers and parents told her she could do better if she would only apply herself. Michelle, though, felt she was applying herself. She was just forgetful. Her mind would time travel and topic travel while reading. For all this, Michelle was intelligent, and in spite of her wandering mind, she was surviving in school.

Michelle was not impulsive. She took forever to make a decision. Even choosing her clothes for the day was laborious and often drove her to tears. Michelle did not cause trouble at home or at school, so no one ever bothered to find out why she appeared to be in another world, or why she was so lethargic.

No one knew how much pain and confusion Michelle was mired in. She didn't volunteer or participate in extracurricular activities, and everyone accepted that she was just a quiet, spacey, lovable airhead.

Michelle was also overweight. She felt bad about herself, her weight, her forgetfulness, and her inability to complete things and focus on a job or career. She would take a bag of potato chips, two or three Snickers bars, and a Pepsi to bed with her. Then, as she experienced the momentary pleasures of the junk food, she would dream of a better life, hoping in some vague way that she could have one. Of course, she had no idea where or how to start actually building this fantasy life.

Michelle learned to drink in high school but never enjoyed being drunk. One night while out with friends, she was introduced to a wonder drug: cocaine. This wondrous new substance did for her what food could not. The first time she snorted coke she had an "awakening." She felt as though someone had turned her brain on for the first time. Suddenly she felt alive. Instantaneously she emerged from the trance she had been trapped in for nineteen years. Michelle could think. She could hold several ideas and thoughts at the same time. She had energy and felt the euphoria that cocaine seductively provides.

The second time she snorted cocaine she locked herself in the bathroom at the party and read a book. Not only was she able to read while on cocaine, she could stay focused and enjoy the story. What a discovery! Michelle would find herself using cocaine, when she could afford it, to read books, clean up her room, and pay her bills—all tasks she was previously unable to complete.

Michelle spent the next three years in love with and devoted to cocaine. Her lifestyle quickly changed. She moved in with a friend who was a cocaine addict. Michelle had led a fairly sheltered life and had no idea what she was getting into. At first the coke was free. It came out at the many parties she now attended. Soon men were treating her to coke, but eventually she was having sex with men so she could get loaded on coke. And she was getting loaded on coke to have sex with men she didn't even like.

Michelle lost weight. And as her use of cocaine continued, she lost control. It took more and more to get high, and even when she used a lot she didn't feel alert, focused, or euphoric. When she wasn't using or when she couldn't get the drug, she experienced a depression she would never have believed possible. She came to know the terror of the cocaine crash, that nightmarish plunge of coming down off the drug.

Inevitably, Michelle was arrested for possession of cocaine. Since she had no prior involvement with the law, she was sentenced to a drug treatment program. She was frightened and confused. How did a nice girl like her turn into an addict? She had lost all self-respect.

At age twenty-two Michelle started a new life. She attended Cocaine Anonymous (CA) meetings regularly and worked the Twelve Steps of recovery. She was determined to stay away from coke and other drugs. And so she did. However, she started overeating again. This shift in addictions was compensated for with help from a therapist and involvement with Overeaters Anonymous (OA). But her self-image was still shot. She was being eaten alive by her shame.

At twenty-five, with three years of recovery from cocaine addiction to her credit, she felt totally miserable and contemplated suicide. Instead of relapsing or killing herself, Michelle went back into therapy. This time she was diagnosed as having biological depression and ADD. Because of her past substance abuse, Michelle was extremely reluctant to take medication to treat her ADD and the related depression. She spent another year going to meetings, feeling miserable, and thinking of ways to end her life.

Her Twelve Step sponsor told her that she had to get professional help. As a last resort, Michelle went back to the psychiatrist who had diagnosed her and agreed to try medication. Her doctor put her on Paxil, an antidepressant, and on a small dose of Ritalin. Within a month, Michelle not only felt less depressed, she was able to concentrate, focus, and read. She was still not performing as well as she was when she first used cocaine, so her doctor increased her Ritalin, and Michelle's ability to concentrate and follow through with things improved.

This doesn't mean that life became instantly easy for Michelle. Like all people recovering from ADD and addictions, Michelle had to work very hard to maintain her recovery. But now she had a chance. Now she was working with a brain that remembered, that could stay focused, that was able to read and hold more than one thought at a time. Medication did not automatically take away

Michelle's low self-esteem, shame, and resentments. However, Michelle now had the opportunity to work through her issues productively and find a better life.

From Jail to College

David C., another person with ADD and addictions, was twenty-eight years old when we met. His rough, tattooed exterior contrasted with his gentle, creative, intelligent interior. Dave had been clean and sober for over two years prior to our meeting. While he had attended AA and NA meetings for the first year of his sobriety, he had virtually stopped attending meetings. Dave wanted to go to Twelve Step meetings, but sitting still through them was torture. His mind would drift and wander, and then he would berate himself for not paying attention.

Dave heard some program members gossiping about him and, like many of us, he was sensitive to what other members said about him. He never felt a part of Twelve Step groups, and after a while he quit going to meetings altogether.

Dave had been seeing a psychiatrist who was treating him for depression. As Dave's depression began to lift, it became clear to his doctor that Dave had ADD. Dave was very fortunate to be seeing a psychiatrist who had expertise in adult ADD. His doctor worked with him for several months, teaching him about adult ADD and encouraging him to try medication. Dave was cautious, fearful, and unwilling to take the psycho-stimulants used to treat his condition.

Dave had good reason to fear the stimulant medications used to treat ADD. He had a history of self-medicating with drugs and alcohol that began around age twelve. He felt that smoking marijuana in the morning helped him be more creative and concentrate more effectively in school. After a few years of smoking marijuana, however, Dave couldn't think clearly, his memory was worse than before, and he didn't care that he was failing school.

Out of love for their son and feelings of desperation, Dave's parents sent him to a therapeutic school for troubled teenagers. Dave said, "This school, which was actually a locked down facility, stripped my identity away. I couldn't even do my art work." Dave graduated at age nineteen with no preparation for college and no skills. He had been institutionalized for four years and no one had ever mentioned ADD.

Dave was only out of the institution for six months when he started using cocaine. At first he snorted or inhaled the drug, but within six months he was injecting it. When I asked Dave what he would do when he shot cocaine, he replied with answers typical of people who are self-medicating.

"I would shoot coke," Dave confided, "so I could draw, read, and straighten up my apartment. I could think more clearly and focus better when I used cocaine. I didn't go out and party with friends or stay up all night. Instead, I would feel calmer, and I would be content to be alone."

Dave, like most addicts, felt that if relatively small doses of coke were good, bigger doses would be even better. As he began injecting higher doses, he felt anxious, jittery, and wired. "Sometimes," he admitted, "I locked myself in my room with a bag of coke and a needle. I would shoot so much cocaine that my heart would pound, my vision would blur, and I would have to grab my dresser to avoid hitting the floor. After this near-death experience, I would shoot up again. I kept this up all night or until the coke was gone."

I asked Dave if he had been flirting with death back then. "Yes," he told me. "Taking it to the point of death was part of the thrill."

"Did you want to die, Dave?"

"No, I really didn't. But I couldn't stop doing what I was doing."

Then Dave discovered heroin, the drug that took the edge off cocaine and his ADD. Soon he was injecting the deadly combination of heroin and cocaine, known as "speed balls," the same combination that killed John Belushi.

Dave went to jail three times on drug-related charges. He spent six months in county jail. While sitting on his bunk one day, Dave had a moment of clarity. It became clear to him that if he didn't stop drinking and using drugs, he would either die or spend the rest of his life locked up.

Over time, Dave accepted how his ADD had been affecting his life. In spite of Dave's willingness and desire to change his ADD behavior, he realized that he could only change so much on his own. Reluctantly, Dave began taking Desoxyn, a stimulant used to treat ADD.

The first time we met after he had begun the medication, Dave had not noticed much difference, except for one thing that surprised him. When I questioned him in greater detail, he told me he had read the latest issue of *Premier*, a film magazine, from cover to cover. Dave's face broke out in a huge grin. "I've never read anything from cover to cover," he said with a laugh.

Dave's life is drastically different today. He has finished his first year of college. He not only completed his coursework and showed up for classes, he received grades he feels good about. Dave is planning to transfer to a university next year. He's taking care of business, showing up for his life in ways he never dreamed were possible. And most important, Dave feels good about who he is. He more easily accepts the creative, intelligent, compassionate man that he is.

Dave's new life is not without pain and problems. He still has a long road to travel. But now he has the ability to follow his path.

Brandon Tells the Truth

I'd like you to meet Brandon. While he and Dave have different lifestyles, they have a great deal in common.

Brandon is a fifty-five-year-old divorced man who has been married three times. He has two grown sons with whom he has little contact.

Brandon came into my office and told me the truth

about himself: He couldn't stay sober. He had been attending Alcoholics Anonymous meetings even while he was secretly drinking. He had been drinking the night before we met, was unshaven, and smelled of alcohol.

He felt terrified. He thought he'd been controlling his drinking, but now he knew he was out of control. He is a high-ranking executive with a computer firm and had been drinking at lunch when he made a pass at an executive from another company. He had jeopardized the integrity of his company.

Brandon saw only one solution to his problems: suicide. I told him that his decision to see me meant that on some level he believed there were other options. He acknowledged that he felt less burdened by his situation by telling me about it.

During that first session, Brandon's mind leapt from subject to subject. He would start out telling me about one thing, then take a strand of that idea and follow it to a totally different place. Even though his speech was rapid and passionate, and he bombarded me with dozens of strands of information from all areas of his life, my ADD brain followed him quite easily. I suspected he also had ADD.

Another professional might have diagnosed him as being in a manic phase. Sometimes people with ADD, especially when under stress, are misdiagnosed as being manic depressive (also referred to as bipolar disorder). ADD differs from manic depression in that ADD is a pervasive part of the person's life and is evident from childhood. Bipolar disorder has a specific onset, can be accompanied by thought disorders or delusions, and is often cyclical.

A chemical dependency specialist may have viewed Brandon's behavior as a result of his drinking. Truly, it is complicated to make accurate assessments when someone has been abusing alcohol and other drugs. There's an element of anxiety during the post-acute withdrawal phase that can cause people to experience restlessness, distractibility, and impulsiveness. Sometimes these symptoms disappear after a period of sobriety. Brandon, however, had a lifelong history of ADD traits and behaviors.

I told Brandon I wasn't sure, but it appeared that he had Attention Deficit Disorder. I explained how people with untreated ADD commonly self-medicate with alcohol and other drugs. I also told him how difficult it was to stay sober if his ADD was not treated. Brandon had been doing all the "right" things in his Twelve Step program. It was his impulsivity and need to self-medicate his restless mind and body that was contributing to his relapses.

Brandon stared at me in disbelief. He wasn't sure what to do with this new information. He agreed that he wouldn't kill or harm himself. He said he would try not to drink, would go to a meeting, and would come back to see me in two days.

Throughout our next eight sessions, Brandon shared his history. During adolescence he'd found himself squeezing life to extract every drop of juice. He loved fast cars and motorcycles. He did anything on a dare. One day, Brandon found something very special that changed his life—alcohol. Not only was alcohol fun, it was magic. When Brandon drank, his mind slowed down. It stopped chattering. He didn't have to keep moving. Brandon didn't feel bad about himself when he was under the influence. He had found the solution to all his problems; however, his solution soon became a problem in its own right.

Brandon's drinking escalated. Gradually, he began to experience various frightening side effects: he blacked out when he drank, lost control of himself, and felt extremely remorseful. He was arrested after a single-car drunk driving accident that left his arms badly scarred. Not long after this, at age thirty-two, Brandon attended his first court-ordered Alcoholics Anonymous meeting. He stayed sober for a short time but then spent the next twenty years relapsing. He maintained periods of sobriety for several months, even years, but he always returned to drinking.

After an evaluation from a psychiatrist, Brandon

decided to take prescribed medication on a trial basis. Within days, he felt like a new person. He was amazed at his ability to think clearly and in a more orderly fashion. "Is this how normal people think?" he asked me. I replied by saying I had no idea how normal people think, but that he might be thinking more clearly.

The next two years were not easy for Brandon. He went to an AA meeting almost every day and came to therapy weekly. He took a good hard look at his past and worked the Twelve Steps in a way he never could before. Today he has changed many of his negative and inaccurate core beliefs about himself. He has more self-confidence. He has also begun repairing the wreckage that resulted from his alcoholism. He now has contact with both his sons and his grandchildren.

Brandon knows he has a long way to go, but now he has a chance—something he didn't have when he was plagued by addictions and untreated ADD.

THERE IS HOPE

Not everyone who has Attention Deficit Disorder uses alcohol and other drugs to self-medicate their ADD symptoms. Everyone with an addictive problem doesn't have ADD. However, of the estimated 8 to 15 million Americans who have Attention Deficit Disorder,[1] 25 to 50 percent use alcohol and other drugs to soothe their ADD symptoms[2,3]. If you are one of these people, you are not alone.

The family I was born into is riddled with ADD and addictions. The family I helped create is riddled with ADD and recovery. We all, my family as well as your family, have a chance to heal. The next generation will be even better prepared than we were to play the genetic cards they've been dealt. There's hope not only for the next generation, but for all of us, right now.

CHAPTER THREE

SCREENS WITH BIG HOLES
What ADD Looks and Feels Like

Having ADD can be like living in a house with window screens that have extra large holes. It's impossible to let fresh air in yet keep out mosquitoes, butterflies, and even sparrows.

The ADD brain can be flooded by input and is sometimes unable to select what comes through its screen. This can lead to distractions as well as heightened sensitivity to sights, sounds, and feelings. This can also cause input overload—too many stimuli coming in from too many directions, with no way to screen out what is wanted from what is irritating. Sometimes input overload is so intense that it blows the screens right off the windows, letting everything and everyone in.

No wonder so many people with ADD have spontaneous rage attacks; their peace of mind is intruded upon by the ticking of someone's watch, the television program as they walk through a room, or the conversation in the next booth at a restaurant. Their bodies are irritated by the tags in their clothes.

People with ADD are sometimes too distracted to process information. Memory is sporadic, even on a good day. Their minds work so fast that information doesn't have time to find a place to settle before more information jumps through the window. When you live with ADD, you are constantly bombarded with input that others may not even notice.

Having ADD is different from having a genetic predisposition for addiction. You either have ADD or you don't. ADD, unlike addictions, doesn't need a trigger to begin. If you have ADD, you were born with it and you will have it for the rest of your life. There are, however, degrees of ADD. Some people's ADD causes greater impairment than others'.

Although it's an oversimplification to say that a person's ADD is mild, moderate, or severe, because of all the related problems that often accompany ADD, let's take a brief look at Judith, Nancy, and Jed. Their stories will demonstrate how people with different degrees of ADD may be affected.

Judith is a high-functioning criminal defense attorney with "mild" ADD. She is eloquent and brilliant in the courtroom and has a reputation as an excellent attorney. She also has a reputation for being scattered and late. Judith has been held in contempt of court for her tardiness and for impulsive outbursts toward judges. She occasionally misses filing dates. Her clients often find her rapidly firing mouth offensive. However, Judith's greatest problems are in her relationships. Men in her life complain that she's somewhere else when she's with them. When they leave her, she doesn't understand why.

Nancy has "moderate" ADD. She owns two businesses. Both are having financial troubles. Nancy can't decide which business to focus on, the coffee shop or photography. She's an excellent photographer, but her photography business is suffering. In one month she missed photographing a wedding and lost the undeveloped film from another.

Nancy is very trusting and has hired employees for her coffee shop who rip her off. She's in trouble with the IRS for not filing or paying taxes for the last three years. Like

Judith, Nancy has serious relationship problems; she is currently getting a divorce from her fourth husband. She's so disorganized she can't put together a list of her assets for her divorce attorney.

Jed, on the other hand, has "severe" ADD. He has spent the past two years in prison for repeated car theft and cocaine possession. Jed did not finish high school. He's intelligent, but the only skills he's developed so far all land him in jail.

Many of Jed's crimes are impulsive. He saw a big beautiful motorcycle once and decided to take it for a ride. He didn't even notice he was riding a Highway Patrol vehicle until the radio started talking to him. Jed doesn't do well within the structure of prison. He is constantly disciplined for not following prison rules. Since Jed doesn't like spending time in solitary confinement, he tries desperately to comply with the rules, but he just can't pay attention and follow through, no matter how hard he tries.

These three examples provide some very rough guidelines of how the degree of severity of ADD might affect a person's life. They do not, however, give us an exact list of predictable behaviors for each level of ADD. ADD doesn't work that neatly. Each person is affected differently. For example, all people with severe ADD do not end up in prison, just as all people with mild ADD do not fail in relationships.

Continuum of ADD Severity

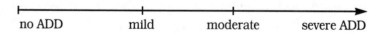

| no ADD | mild | moderate | severe ADD |

FEELING DIFFERENT

ADD is the feeling that you just don't get it, whatever *it* is. ADD can make you feel out of step and out of time. Sometimes you feel like you've been transported to earth from another planet. You watch people express their feelings and you wonder what yours are. You may not be able to put names to your feelings. You may feel as though you're only going through the motions of being human because you don't feel connected with others. Talk about marching to the beat of a different drummer! Having ADD means you question your perceptions. You wonder why life seems so easy for others and is so hard for you.

Have you ever wondered if there was a manual handed out during childhood entitled *Tips to Live in the World*, but you didn't get a copy? Most people appear to be living their lives as if they had this basic instruction manual. But not you.

Maybe others had a brain chip installed in the hospital nursery before Mom and Dad took them home, but for some reason you didn't get yours. This chip, you suspect, helps them remember simple things, process information accurately, complete tasks in an orderly fashion, moderate their impulses, and calm their bodies and minds when they want to.

Have you spent your life feeling that something is different about you? Are you painfully aware that you don't think and act like other people?

You may have been told there's something wrong with you—that you're lazy, stupid, not working to your potential, or just don't care. If you have ADD, you may have spent the greater part of your life feeling different, bad, wrong. The truth is, you *are* different. But different is not bad. It isn't wrong, either. Unfortunately, no one told you this when you were a kid. Like most kids, you believed and accepted unconsciously what was said about you. If important adults and children in your life called you a tyrant, an airhead, a space cadet, stupid, lame, lazy, or bratty, well, over time you came to believe them.

There was some truth in what you were being told. You may not have performed as well on tests as the other kids did. You may not have been able to pay attention in class.

You may have been disruptive, impulsive, and outright aggressive at times, or you may have quietly struggled to learn. But it wasn't because you were bad. It was because your brain functions differently.

ADD is a neurological difference in how the brain functions. We'll talk a lot more about that in the next chapter, but for now suffice it to say that levels of essential chemicals in the brain called neurotransmitters are altered, and the result is some degree of loss of control over attention, impulses, and activity level. Problems with organization, memory, learning, and enhanced sensitivity are also typical for the person with ADD.

WHAT DOES ADD LOOK AND FEEL LIKE?

If you have ADD, you don't always have control over how your brain works. Interestingly, addictions are also characterized by loss of control. Sound familiar? Loss of control over our neurochemistry creates different problems for each of us, but here are some common areas where you will experience pain and difficulties:

- ▶ Attention
- ▶ Frustration level
- ▶ Ability to follow through
- ▶ Activity level
- ▶ Impulsiveness
- ▶ Organization
- ▶ Memory
- ▶ Rage
- ▶ Sensitivity
- ▶ Need for high stimulation
- ▶ Aggression
- ▶ Emotional availability

Problems in the above areas often lead to difficulties with the following:

- Relationships
- Work, school, and career opportunities
- Substance abuse
- Eating disorders
- Depression
- Accidents
- Encounters with the law
- Self-worth
- Physical and emotional well-being
- Finances

Do any of the above sound familiar? You may be thinking, "Yes, but doesn't everyone have some difficulty in these areas? Aren't these just human problems we all have to deal with?"

The answer is, Yes! In fact, ADD involves normal human behaviors which are carried to the extreme. This is why professional and lay people have a hard time differentiating ADD traits from normal human traits. Everyone forgets things now and again. Anyone can be distracted for a while. All of us have moments of impulsiveness. And many of us have high or low energy levels. But having ADD is like having a faulty volume control on an amplifier. The person with ADD has the volume turned up to eleven, even though the amplifier maxes out at ten!

ADD should not be narrowly defined. There are core traits, such as distractibility, restlessness, impulsiveness, sensitivity, rage, and problems with time and organization. However, no one manifests ADD in exactly the same ways as someone else. ADD is as diverse as personality. Some people may be outgoing, funny, assertive, and excitable, while others are shy, quiet, calm, and introspective.

As human beings, we tend to label personality traits as good or bad. We say it's good to be outgoing or it's bad to be shy. However, personality is neither good nor bad; we are simply different. The same is true with ADD.

ADD is riddled with paradoxes. A paradox occurs

when two seemingly contradictory conditions or states exist simultaneously. For example, we are ecstatically happy about our new baby, yet we erupt into tears when we hold her. People with ADD can be extremely active or relatively passive. I find that many people with ADD cross back and forth as they jump from one extreme to another. Here are a few of the many paradoxes of ADD:

- ▶ Oblivious to details/compulsive about details
- ▶ Highly talkative/says very little
- ▶ Aggressive/passive
- ▶ Memory for details from the past/forgets important things in present
- ▶ Disorganized/extremely organized
- ▶ Needs structure/hates structure
- ▶ Risk taker/takes few risks
- ▶ Outgoing/introspective

A person with ADD can be highly focused one moment and completely unfocused the next. This person may take a huge risk one day and be very conservative the next. Some people with ADD are quite contained in one situation, then become impulsive and boisterous in a similar situation. At dinner on Tuesday, Jack is calm, eating quietly with his family. On Wednesday, Jack talks incessantly through the meal, subjecting the family to a barrage of chatter about his day. ADD is predictably unpredictable, ever-changing, unique to the individual, unique to the situation, and unique to a particular moment of a given day.

ADD is frequently accompanied by other conditions and problems. This is especially true in adults. Few people with untreated ADD make it through adulthood without developing other problems, such as substance abuse, eating disorders, anxiety, depression, low self-esteem, or compulsive behaviors. These related conditions make the ADD picture even more multifaceted.

Let's look in detail at the most common traits of adult ADD.

Attention Differences

It's not that people with ADD have a deficit of attention; some have "too much" attention! If you have ADD, you not only have periods of distraction, your life itself is distracting. For example, you may regularly get so distracted that you miss your freeway exit by five miles, or you may go shopping for a pair of shoes and come home having accomplished many errands but having completely forgotten about the shoes.

Your problem involves *focusing* your attention. Like a hungry honeybee, your attention may buzz and bop from flower to flower, to the grass and back to the flower again. However, while the honeybee knows exactly where it wants to go and how to get there, your attention may not always go where you want it to.

Pinball Thinking

Some people with ADD have minds that work like pinball machines. Lights flash. Bells ring. Buzzers buzz. The action is constant. One thought triggers another. A word from that thought sends the pinball racing back through the mazes of sights and sounds.

Pinball thinking can be incredibly fun and entertaining, especially if there's someone to play with. Some people take drugs to experience what people with ADD get all the time. The problem with pinball thinking is that it can't be turned off at will. This makes it next to impossible to think and communicate in a linear fashion. Since we live in a society based on linear thinking, chronic pinballing can be a big problem.

The person without pinball thinking may send a few balls into the machine, push the levers a few times, ring a few bells, flash some lights, and then the ball drops down into the slot. They've finished their thought or action. For the person with ADD, it's as though the brain can't stop pushing those pinball levers, and the balls, bells, and lights are constantly moving, ringing, and flashing. The more stimulated the brain gets, the more pinballing it wants to do.

Hyperfocusing

Distractibility is not the only attentional problem a person with ADD might have. The opposite can happen.

Do you ever get so focused on something that you lose track of time? Do important people in your life say, "Honey, do you realize you've been at the computer for three hours?" or something not as sweet, like, "Here you go again. That computer means more to you than me. Every time you start a simple project I may as well act as if you've gone on vacation."

Some people refer to this as hyperfocusing or overfocusing. I experience it as having my attention captured. My attention is like herds of zebras, gazelles, and giraffes running wild and free on the open plains. It takes something even wilder and faster to capture it, and when it does, I become captivated. Once my attention is captured, I can stay engaged with what I'm doing almost endlessly. Now, my problem is not one of not paying attention; I can't *stop* paying attention to what has captivated me. I think this is why so many doctors and therapists who have ADD can be so attentive to their patients and so disorganized with their paperwork.

Many people with ADD describe periods when their attention becomes so engaged that they can't seem to disengage. The results of having your total attention focused in one place can be awesome. It's amazing what some people with ADD create during these periods of absolute attention. You can get an extraordinary amount done. However, this type of attention can take its toll in relationship problems, exhaustion, fatigue, and sometimes failing health. When your attention is captured, you are elsewhere, which means you are not where you are. Your children or spouse will be talking to you, but what they say doesn't register in your thoughts or feelings.

People who tend to become highly engaged in what they're doing can miss out on life. Over the years they can become isolated and lonely. They may lose their ability to relate with others and, as a result, seek out solitary activities. This can cause tremendous problems in relationships and families. Barbara is a good example of this.

Barbara is fifty-six years old and lives alone. Her children are grown and have their own lives. Barbara's husband left ten years ago because he felt Barbara could not be emotionally present in their relationship. She would disappear into her work or hobbies and not emerge for days. Their lives became separate, and so they separated for good.

Barbara was a very successful clothing designer. She had spent years in her design studio, even after her clothing business was quite successful. Barbara wasn't working for the income, she was working for the enjoyment and complete engagement and escape her work provided. After years of her family begging her not to work so much, Barbara sold her business. She felt that the only way she could stop focusing so hard on her business was to be completely divorced from it.

Barbara mourned the loss of her business but soon became involved in playing the harmonica. She had played this instrument in her younger years and especially enjoyed playing blues. Before long, Barbara was playing the harmonica for hours at a time and was going to blues clubs almost every night. She became so engrossed in playing her harmonica that she would play for six to eight hours a day.

Barbara came in for therapy the week after she missed her daughter's wedding because she had been playing the harmonica. She finally realized that her attention had become uncontrollable.

IMPULSES RUNNING WILD

Impulsiveness expresses itself in two forms—by actions and by words. ADD impulsiveness is often the equivalent

38

of constantly living with your foot in your mouth. Sometimes we find substitutes for our foot. Candy, gum, cigarettes, as well as magazines and trinkets, are intentionally put at checkout stands for people like us.

Our brains lack the ability to think through all the consequences of what we say and do, so we jokingly tell the boss that the new manager has a personality that's dry as a post. We are often funny and offensive. While never intending to hurt anyone, our mouths just keep on flapping. If you have ADD impulsiveness, saying you're sorry has probably become a knee-jerk reaction.

You may also interrupt others. Your mind hears part of what they're saying and immediately responds with your thoughts. Meanwhile, you've cut off the person who was talking and may not even realize you've done it. You may also have a hard time monitoring how much you talk. You may be asked a question where a one syllable answer would suffice. Instead, you barrage your questioner with information that might be interesting but overwhelms them with extraneous details. Or you give expansive answers to questions that haven't even been asked. The information may be brilliant, but your listener is overwhelmed.

You may also impulsively over-expose yourself. Have you ever told the speaker box at the drive-through restaurant about the intimacies or frustrations of your day? Do you tend to tell your life story to anyone who will listen? People with ADD often embarrass themselves by saying more than they really want to.

Impulsiveness of actions is also common among people with ADD. You may impulsively give notice on your apartment with no idea where you are going to move. I know a woman who stopped taking her ADD medication while on vacation and bought two time shares. Fortunately, the contract contained a seven-day grace period and she was able to change her mind!

I have heard many elopement stories from people with

ADD. Jean, who had untreated ADD, lived and worked in San Francisco. She had been sober for several years when she met Jerry at an Alcoholics Anonymous convention. He seemed like a nice guy. They had a good time at the conference and he said he liked kids. Jerry invited her to come live with him. Four days later she and her daughter were traveling across the country in a U-Haul truck bound for Miami. Jerry turned out to be unemployed, not so fond of children, and physically abusive. Two months later Jean packed up her daughter and belongings and headed for California. She stopped in Alabama to visit relatives and decided to stay. She got a job and an apartment, but still hasn't had her ADD treated.

Crime in the Blink of an Eye

Impulsive actions can lead to altercations with the law and incarceration. Dwaine McCallon, M.D. a physician who works in a large correctional facility for men, has found that a large percentage of inmates who commit impulse crime such as car theft, robbery, and spontaneous battery have ADD.[1] A 1994 study found that 25.5 percent of inmates in a male prison population had ADHD.[2] I believe that with further research we will find that the population of prisons has an even higher percentage of inmates with ADD.

I remember working with young people who had been charged with petty theft. Some of these teenagers stole to get attention, to get something they didn't want to pay for, or to get back at their parents. There was a subgroup of petty thieves who looked sincerely puzzled when asked, "Why did you take this wallet when you had one just like it in your pocket?" Frequently they would say, "I don't know. I saw it and just took it." Many of these young people were suffering from the impulse problems of ADD. Other ADD adolescents stole for the thrill of it. Stealing for them was an adrenaline rush that jump-started their ADD brains.

DIFFERENCES IN ACTIVITY LEVEL

Do you have enough energy to power the New York subway system? Are you a fast thinker and an even faster talker? Do you ricochet from project to project? Is your life like a tornado, occasionally touching ground and devastating everything around you? Many people with ADD have an abundance of energy yet lack the ability to focus it in the direction they desire. Are you a toe-tapping, leg-bouncing, nail-biting pacer? If you are, then you know how uncomfortable this energy feels.

A Restless Body

Some people with ADD need to move in order to think. There is a connection between moving their body and their ability to organize thoughts. I refer to this as a Cognitive-Kinesthetic Connection. Children with ADD may move around the classroom because it helps them focus. This behavior is usually distracting to the other students, especially in a classroom of thirty children. So the child is told one more time to sit still. And when she does, her brain shuts down. She can't think unless she is moving.

If this child manages to get an education (which is difficult with untreated ADD), she may choose a career that requires movement. She may use her body by doing physical work or become a teacher who thinks on her feet. She may become a park ranger or a trial attorney who is able to move about as she speaks. However, not everyone with ADD is fortunate enough to find a suitable career. Some cling to the traditional belief that sitting still is important, even if they have to use alcohol or drugs to keep themselves in their chairs.

These children and adults suffer from extreme physical restlessness. Their bodies crave constant motion. It's physically painful to be still for long, and "long" may only be a few minutes. Imagine having your life dictated by your body's need to move. You are powerless to control yourself, and to top it off, you were expected to sit still in school for years. You may have chosen a sedentary career that confines you to a stillness not unlike shackles on your ankles and wrists.

You may run, swim, or play racquetball during lunch or after work, but it's not enough to dissipate your energy, frustration, and anger for having to function in ways that are in conflict with your physical being. You've been this way all your life and may have accepted that there's something "wrong" with you. Other adults seem able to sit still and not feel as though they're shackled to their desks. They aren't constantly chewing their nails, squirming in their seats, tapping out drum beats, playing air pianos, and driving the rest of the office crazy. I heard someone put it so well: "If you think it's a drag being around me, imagine what it's like *being* me."

You come home from school or work and find ways to calm yourself. You may start out as a child by using food and eat your way into a state of oblivion. When you're an adolescent, the world of alcohol and drugs may open its doors. And you know what? It works. You may choose alcohol, pot, cocaine, nicotine, amphetamines, inhalants, or heroin. In the beginning drugs work. You feel calmer, or your restlessness no longer bothers you.

A Restless Brain

Imagine a brain that never shuts up. Do you have a brain that's on the go day and night? Has sleeping always been difficult? Are you awakened by your brain's chattering before the sun comes up? Your restless brain may jumpstart the second you become conscious, and off you go with incessant thoughts, dialogues, songs, music, new ideas, old ideas, memories, connections, disconnections, scenarios, and fantasies. No wonder many people with ADD seek relief through drugs, alcohol, and food.

All of this brain activity can make it difficult to focus and follow through with things as simple as brushing your teeth. A restless brain can be a pain. It comments on everything you think or do. Sometimes it's as though a committee of extremely diverse people all decided to yak at the same time. These "people" are loud, excitable, and rarely shut up. Your gray matter, it seems, has the energy of a playful puppy trapped in the house on a rainy day.

Another way active brains entertain themselves is by deconstructing. They take apart every sound, event, internal or external conversation, movie, piece of music, building, or story. Instead of being able to enjoy the whole experience, restless brains automatically dissect everything and look at new ways to assemble it. If your brain is restless, even watching a movie can be a pain. Your mind is rearranging the scenery, critiquing the dialogue, figuring out all the possible endings, exploring different costume options, or filing through all the actors who could have made the film even better. Oh, please, stop already!

All this brain activity can be exhausting. Restless brains frequently go into overload and crash. And when they crash, it's difficult to remember your child's name, or your name, for that matter. But soon the brain is up and running again, bouncing around in your skull, chattering, interrupting, and deconstructing. No wonder many people with ADD turn to substances or addictive behaviors to calm and quiet their brains.

Less Active ADD
You don't have to be hyperactive to have ADD. ADD affects your activity level in various ways: you may be more active, less active, or have an average level of energy and activity. If you're not highly active, your ADD may have been overlooked. Many professionals still believe that ADD means hyperactivity, and do not understand ADD that only affects attention.

Some people with ADD think and move very slowly. They usually are not impulsive and do not have highly energized bodies and brains. They are the opposite of what you would think of as ADD. They can be very intelligent, yet they process information at different, generally slower, rates, so others view them as intellectually weaker.

It's difficult for them to get out of bed and get going, even after several tall mugs of strong coffee. Once they wake up, they have a hard time figuring out what to do next and may spend their day trying to get started on something. This type of ADD can be painful and shameful, because our culture puts such high value on accomplishing as much as we can as fast as we can. It's hard to live life in the fast lane when your engine won't let you go over forty-five miles per hour.

Did you know that some people with ADD sleep so soundly they need several alarms to wake up? I know a man who sets three alarms one minute apart. The first, a clock radio stationed near his head, is turned up as loud as possible. Next he has his television timed to turn on at full volume a minute later. His final alarm sounds like a bugle and he must get out of bed to turn it off. He has created a functional alarm system to get himself up, but even then it takes him two hours to eat, get dressed, and feel alert enough to start his day.

If you have this type of ADD, you live in a state of perpetual slow motion. You think, walk, and talk more slowly than others. You agonize so long over decisions, such as where to eat lunch, that lunch break is over before you've decided. It's difficult for you to start and complete school or work projects. You may have viewed yourself as lazy; you may feel useless and no good. For those with less active ADD, finding something good about themselves is sometimes harder to do than finding parking at the mall during the holiday season.

Unfortunately, many adults with low energy ADD are not diagnosed. They do not create disturbances, act out, or get involved in high-risk behaviors. Some may be impulsive, but many are only affected in the areas of attention and activity level. Frequently they are diagnosed with depression, which they may also have. Antidepressant

44

medication will treat their depression, but in most cases does not adequately treat their ADD. I have clients with low energy ADD whose lives change dramatically when they take prescribed stimulant medication.

ORGANIZATIONAL DIFFERENCES: FILES OR PILES

Some people with ADD are compulsively organized. They see a pile of anything and immediately create an alphabetical or color-coded system to arrange each item. These people have an affinity for detail to the point of being distracted by it. They make great accountants, professional organizers, editors, and bookkeepers. Some people with this type of ADD will instantly see every typo on a page before they even read it.

At the other end of the ADD organization scale live the people who not only don't see or attend to details, they miss the obvious. These are the men and women who don't notice for two days that their teenager has cut and colored his or her hair green. Even then, they notice only because someone else brings it to their attention. These people are lost in thought, captives of pinball thinking, or preoccupied with getting from point A to point B.

If you live with someone who has this type of ADD, you may find them highly disorganized. Their piles of stuff, which multiply faster than bunnies, may drive you crazy. They organize by the "pile system," so they freak out if you try to put their stuff away. It's interesting to note that most of the time they know exactly which pile each piece of "stuff" is in and how deeply embedded it is. To complicate the picture, they can be detail oriented in some areas while they're completely disorganized in others.

Surviving in our society demands a level of organization that can be difficult and feel demeaning for people with ADD. No wonder they sometimes have rage attacks after spending ten minutes trying to find their car keys, especially when they misplaced them an hour earlier. No wonder they stomp around the house looking for the sunglasses that are hanging around their necks. And they're usually late for work or an appointment when this happens.

Some people with ADD have no frame of reference for such things as calendars, appointment books, desk organizers, and file folders. If they are supplied with these items, they usually aren't able to use them effectively. There are, however, ways to create organizational systems that work for them. For example, using a watch with an alarm can help them arrive on time. We'll discuss more organizational tips in Chapter Ten.

MEMORY: HERE ONE SECOND—GONE THE NEXT

Do you lock your keys in the car after you've misplaced your spare key? Do you sometimes forget your good friend's name, or call your child by someone else's name? Does information slip through the well-lubed, extra-large holes in your brain screen? Don't worry. You probably have ADD, not Alzheimer's disease. This may not sound comforting to you now, but it will as you read on.

Problems with memory are common for people with ADD. Most ADD related memory problems have to do with how information is filed into the memory storage areas of the brain. If we are distracted by brilliant ideas, our child's upcoming birthday party, or what we should eat for lunch, new information doesn't get into our brains in the first place, let alone find a storage area to call home. We find it impossible to remember what never stuck.

LEARNING DISABILITIES

Another important factor to consider is that you can have ADD and learning disabilities (LD). Certain learning disabilities make it difficult to interpret, integrate, store, access, and express information. LD affects other areas of learning, such as reading, writing, and the ability to express yourself with language. Since researchers believe that 40 percent to 80 percent of people with ADD also have LD, it's important to be evaluated for LD under the following circumstances:

- ▶ a childhood history of learning problems
- ▶ difficulty reading and writing
- ▶ your memory is still impaired after you're taking ADD medication
- ▶ you consistently invert letters, numbers, directions, confuse right and left, clockwise and counterclockwise

Can you recite Shakespeare, recall every detail of *The Wizard of Oz*, and remember lyrics to songs you haven't heard for twenty years? This is the flip side of memory for some with ADD. They may forget their shoes, but they can remember how many miles they drove from Dallas to San Francisco in 1968, and sing every song from the Jefferson Airplane eight-track tape they listened to along the way.

Some people with ADD have memory storage for obscure details. They could win a fortune on Jeopardy, if only they could remember to fill out the application to play and send it in on time.

ENHANCED SENSITIVITY

Has anyone ever accused you of being overly sensitive, hypersensitive, or taking things too seriously? You don't have to have ADD to have highly developed senses; some people are just more sensitive to sounds, sights, feelings, and smells. But heightened sensitivity seems especially common for many people with ADD. They hear, see, feel, and smell things others may not. They may also experience their senses with more intensity than others. Having highly developed senses can be a tremendous asset; however, as

47

we'll see, problems can occur when highly developed senses interfere with daily functioning.

The senses I'm referring to are auditory, visual, and kinesthetic. With or without ADD, most people have a dominant way in which they take in information and perceive the world around them.

Auditory

People with highly developed auditory abilities take in the world mainly through their ears. I will often have a family in my office with an adolescent who is there for "intentionally" not paying attention, being lazy, or ignoring instructions. During a session, I will stop and ask the teenager, "What do you hear right now?" The answer is often similar to one young man's response. "Well," he said, "I hear the birds outside, the cars on the road, a dog barking, a siren went by a few minutes ago, and it sounds like the air conditioner is on." I turn to the parents and ask, "Do you hear all of what your child just reported?" The answer is usually no, unless the parents are also auditorily sensitive. I then explain that this is part of why their child has a hard time paying attention. Remember, it's not that people with ADD have a deficit of attention; sometimes, they simply pay too much attention. It's hard to follow instructions, communicate, or listen when your brain fails to automatically screen out sounds that are not essential at that moment.

Visual

Visually oriented people take in information and perceive the world primarily through their eyes. People with ADD can be visually distracted. A young woman was in my office to talk about her relationship with her husband. In the middle of telling me how he didn't think she listened to him, she said, "Did you get a new book?" I impulsively glanced at the bookshelf with its over two hundred books and said, "Yes." She didn't miss a beat and went back to talking about her husband. Meanwhile, I was still looking at the bookshelf, realizing that she had noticed the one nondescript book that hadn't been on my shelf during her last session two weeks earlier.

I asked her if this might be what her husband was referring to when he felt she wasn't listening. "Yes," she responded. "It drives him nuts. I'm really not trying to change the subject; I just notice things."

This woman made her living as an artist. She was famous for her incredibly detailed drawings. Her visual vigilance served her well in her work, but it distracted her when relating with others.

Kinesthetic

People who are more kinesthetic, or feeling oriented, take in information through their body and emotions. They learn more by doing than by following directions. They tend to engage the world in physical ways. Kinesthetic people can be highly intuitive and may make decisions based on how something feels to them.

Frequently, people with ADD are emotionally sensitive. They experience the world through how they feel and pick up on the feelings of others. There are several reasons for this. One reason is that important information may be missed or misinterpreted by the person with ADD. Depending on how attentive your ADD brain happens to be at the moment, information communicated to you may not register in your mind.

Our minds will frequently fill in gaps when we miss something. Unfortunately, sometimes these gaps are filled with misinformation—sometimes with what we wish we had heard or what we are used to hearing. If you're used to hearing that you don't listen well, are forgetful, talk too much, then your mind may fill in the gaps in communication with these expected phrases. In this way, we can perpetuate old beliefs about ourselves, even when new and potentially different information has been given to us.

Another reason for emotional sensitivity may be a result of the screening mechanism of the ADD brain. Some people with ADD have difficulty screening and prioritizing information. People with this type of ADD may not miss anything, not a word, a sigh, or the most subtle body language. Imagine if you absorbed almost all information from a conversation. Then imagine that most of this information carried the same weight.

For example, your supervisor gives you a performance evaluation. She tells you how well you're doing in your work. She points out two areas, following procedures and arriving to work on time, that could be improved. She says you are a valuable asset to the company. She tells you that you're one of the hardest workers she has ever met. To top it off, she gives you a smile, handshake, and a hefty raise in pay.

When you return to your office, a colleague asks you how your review went. What do you think your response will be? If you can't prioritize or rank information in terms of quality, or differentiate shades of value, you may respond, "Ah . . . it was okay, I guess. Overall, I'm doing okay, but I have some things to work on." Notice how all of the information, including body language, was perceived to have the same level of importance. You didn't realize that the significant raise in pay outweighed the comments about following procedures and arriving to work on time.

Another way this review might be interpreted by your ADD brain is to hear and focus only on the positive or the negative. You may come away from the review and tell your coworker, "It went great. I have no problems. She's so happy with me that she gave me a raise." Or, "I'm really messing up. She's upset with me for not following procedures and getting to work late." In either case, you only see half the picture and so experience interactions differently.

As mentioned earlier, ADD is normal behavior that has been taken to the extreme. If the volume on your senses is turned up, you experience overload. Whether you are an auditory, visual, or kinesthetic type of perceiver, the excessive intake of stimuli can over-amp your senses and you begin to "melt down." Since meltdown is dangerous and unpleasant, human nature finds ways to relieve the feelings associated with it. Drugs, alcohol, food, and compulsive behaviors are commonly used by people with ADD to deal with sensory flooding and overload.

THE HIDDEN DISABILITY

ADD is disabling. Your parents and teachers would not have been as hard on you if they knew. If you were born with a deformed leg or suffered from polio as a child, nobody would expect you to run the track exactly like other kids. Your disability would be obvious. But ADD is a hidden disability. In our culture, if the cause of a problem isn't visible, the person with the problem may be blamed. While ADD is not an excuse for poor behavior, ADD is rooted in the brain and biology and contributes to social, financial, legal, career, and relationship problems.

Despite the many faces of ADD, ADD traits are consistent over time and don't change, regardless of context. Your ADD traits will not go away just because you take a vacation. Some situations will provoke your ADD traits more, while others will tend to mask them. However, there is no situation that will make your ADD go away.

ADD GOES ON VACATION

Not only does your ADD board the plane with you, it can make your vacation hectic, frustrating, and stressful. Many people say their ADD gets worse when traveling. Being out of your environment, your daily routines, and the structure that helps you adapt to your ADD can contribute to a chaotic trip. Do you know how much a rental car company charges to come out and replace lost keys? I do.

Let's take a quick trip with the Jones family and see

just how wild it can get for those with ADD. Virginia Jones has ADD, and so does her eight-year-old son, Todd. Husband Mike and five-year-old Marisa live in an ADD whirlwind. Virginia not only forgets her children's shoes, she often forgets to pick the kids up from school, from flute lessons, and from gymnastics. This has been extremely scary for the kids and painful for Virginia, who lives in a continual state of overload.

When the Jones family goes to Hawaii for two weeks, their ADD goes with them. They arrive in Honolulu only to realize they forgot which rental car company has reserved their car. Several hours later, they start out for their condo. Todd is rocking the car with his abundance of energy. Mike pulls over, thinking he has a flat tire, and Todd jumps out and runs in circles through the sugar cane.

They spend the next two weeks going, going, going. They hop from island to island, rarely stopping to breathe. They schedule several activities a day: hiking, bicycling, kayaking, snorkeling, all of which they pursue with a vengeance. Todd crashes his bicycle into a parked car and the family spends three hours in the emergency room while he gets stitches in his head.

They are already late for the plane home when they realize the plane tickets and Marisa's "Bear Bear" are missing. They frantically tear up the condo they've just cleaned, looking for tickets and teddy bears. All are found, and Virginia, Mike, Todd, and Marisa bicker as they break the sound barrier getting to the airport.

Sounds relaxing, doesn't it? If your vacations are continually like the Joneses', you might want to consider if ADD is vacationing with you.

CULTURALLY INDUCED ADD-LIKE SYMPTOMS

Contrast the above scenario with a family experiencing what I call culturally induced ADD.

Picture this: Margie is talking with her husband on her

car phone while half her daughter's soccer team sings in the back seat. Margie is asking her husband, Riley, who is stuck in traffic, to pick up their son, Keith, who is late for his drum lesson. Riley says okay and then rattles off a plethora of errands he must do that afternoon.

Margie, who didn't bring the grocery list, misses her turn because she suddenly remembers she needed to get a loaf of French bread for dinner. The soccer team is now chanting, "We're gonna be late! Were gonna be late!" Margie hits the gas as if she's suddenly involved in a movie chase scene.

Margie's van screeches into the parking lot of the soccer field and runs over a small shrub. All eyes in the bleachers turn to the van as a stream of brightly clad girls runs for the field. Driven by embarrassment and her need to get bread, Margie tears out of the parking lot and into the madness of her dwindling afternoon.

To the untrained observer, this insanity may look like ADD hyperactivity. Here's the difference: ADD is a pervasive way of being that begins at birth and continues throughout one's life. Although ADD traits can get worse in stressful situations, stress does not cause ADD. Some days may be a bit better or worse, but ADD is as consistent as the rising and setting of the sun.

Let's look at what happens to Margie, Riley, and kids when they go to Hawaii for two weeks. The kids have a great time swimming, snorkeling, and hiking with their parents. Margie and Riley slow down. They spend endless hours lying by the pool reading and calmly chatting with each other. There are no signs of any hyperactivity or ADD traits. Once they are taken out of their stressful lifestyle, they become calm and content.

Culturally induced ADD occurs when one's lifestyle cultivates ADD-like traits. People with culturally induced ADD do not have neurological differences in brain functioning. They may be constantly in high gear, bouncing from place to place or project to project, forgetting their briefcases or their children's lunches. They may not complete their sentences, may talk too quickly, and zoom from subject to subject. However, their ADD-like traits are a result of their lifestyle, not the workings of their brain.

THE MANY WHYS

There are a variety of reasons why your life has been difficult. You may suffer from depression, addictions, anxiety, eating disorders, grief over lost loved ones, problems with work and relationships. Life is even more difficult if you have untreated ADD.

There are many things you can learn and change about yourself to make life with ADD easier for you and those around you. The first and maybe most difficult thing is to get off your own back. Stop blaming yourself for things that are beyond your control and start taking responsibility for things you can control.

Regardless of what you may have done as a result of your ADD and addictions, you are a valuable person and you deserve a life of happiness, joy, and freedom. You've been persecuted long enough by others; you don't have to persecute yourself any longer. Please put away the whip and lighten up on yourself.

When ADD genetics are mixed with our culture's needs and values, we often get a strange brew indeed. You're probably wondering exactly how ADD is based in our biology and genetics. We'll talk about that next.

CHAPTER FOUR

IT'S NOT YOUR FAULT

Genetics and the Brain

It's not your fault. You haven't done anything wrong. You didn't choose to have ADD, and you've gotten this far in life in spite of it.

ADD is not a moral issue. Having ADD does not mean you are defective, stupid, uncaring, sick, or crazy. ADD is neurological. It is based in your brain functioning, not your character. Since you don't have conscious control over your biology, you can no more will away your ADD traits than you can make yourself taller or shorter. You can, however, get effective treatment for your ADD.

Addictions are also rooted in biology. You may be someone who is biologically predisposed to becoming an addict. ADD and the predisposition to addictions are genetically transmitted from generation to generation. There is no single cause for addictions; they are affected by genetics, biology, environment, and life circumstances. You may have a genetic predisposition for alcoholism, but if you don't drink you will not become an alcoholic. On the other hand, if you grow up in the turmoil and chaos of an alcoholic family, learn to cope with life's challenges by drinking, and then are bombarded with stressful circumstances, chances are greater that you will develop an addiction.

What Causes ADD?

As our wealth of information about genetics, brain functioning, and chemistry grows, we are learning that many problems thought to be rooted in poor parenting and family dysfunction are actually rooted in biology, in our genetic makeup, and in brain functioning—especially in chemicals called neurotransmitters. This is not to say that families don't contribute to the problems their members have. However, it's time to stop blaming parents for all their children's problems. We must look at how many of these problems are passed on through the generations by genetics as well as by learned behavior and environmental factors. Some of the answers are found in the brain.

This Is Your Brain

I want to simplify and synthesize hundreds of pages of scientific articles I've read on brain function and neurotransmitters into a few pages. For some of you this may be more information than you want to know; please feel free to read only what is interesting to you. Others may find this information to be oversimplified. I've listed articles and books that go into more detail about neurobiology and genetics in Appendix A.

Doctors and scientists have names for different parts of your brain. Different areas of your brain control or regulate your emotions, attention, activity level, memory, information processing, ability to move, speak, see, and talk. Here are some examples of just a few areas of the brain, which I have adapted from Dr. Daniel Amen's workbook, *Attention Deficit Disorder*.[1]

▶ *Prefrontal cortex*—a subdivision of the frontal lobe of the brain, sometimes referred to as the executive center, because it functions to help us sort out input, focus attention and conscious thought, make decisions, control impulses, and communicate with other areas of the brain.

▶ *Limbic System*—aids in regulating appetite, sleep, motivation, and sex drive; promotes emotional bonding and processes smells. This is where the emotional memories are believed to be stored.

▶ *The Basal Ganglia*—helps us regulate our activity level, integrate feelings and body movement, is a storehouse of learned behavior and programming from the past.

▶ *Cingulate System*—allows shifting of attention, helps our minds move from idea to idea; enables us to see options and think expansively.

Now let's look at how areas of the brain communicate with each other.

Brain Messengers

Your brain has more than fifty billion intricate cells, called neurons. Messages are carried from one neuron to another by chemicals called neurotransmitters. Each neuron depends on thousands of other neurons to carry messages about how we feel and what functions we perform through the brain. Sometimes people have too few, too many, or an imbalance in neurotransmitters.

Ronald Kotulak states in *Inside the Brain*, "A single neurotransmitter whose levels are only 5 to 10 percent off normal can affect the way other neurotransmitters work, setting in motion a chain reaction of chemical errors that result in a wide variety of mental problems."[2]

This may create physical and emotional problems, including an inability to regulate attention, control impulses, eating, sleeping, mood, and energy level. This in turn can lead to compulsive behaviors, addictions, depression, eating disorders, violent behavior, obsessive-compulsive disorders, and ADD, all of which can result in suicide, homicide, domestic violence, child abuse, lost opportunities, and incarcerations. This is not to say that all these behaviors are purely a result of neurotransmitter imbalance. Other factors play a role in our lives, such as the family we grew up in, how we learned to cope with life, and our ability to take responsibility for our behavior and get help when we need it.

Serotonin
Serotonin is a neurotransmitter that has gained great attention over the last two decades. Decreased levels of serotonin are linked to depression, sleep disturbances, eating disorders, activity level, increased awareness of pain, aggression, and violent behavior. Many of the newer antidepressants such as Prozac, Paxil, and Zoloft are referred to as Selective Serotonin Reuptake Inhibitors (SSRIs) because they stop the reabsorption of serotonin at the receptor site of the neuron, thus increasing serotonin levels and rebalancing the brain's chemistry.

Adequate levels of serotonin help alleviate depression, improve sleep, energy level and mood, and decrease impulsive behaviors such as binge eating and bulimia. Judith J. Wurtman, Ph.D., says, "Serotonin is the calming chemical. When the brain is using it, feelings of stress and tension are eased."[3]

Researchers have linked low levels of serotonin to aggression, violence, and completed suicides. In 1976 Marie Asberg documented the connection between violent suicides and low serotonin levels. "These involved people who killed themselves with guns, knives, ropes, or by jumping from high places. Asberg found that those with low serotonin levels have a tenfold greater risk of violent death than other equally depressed patients with higher serotonin."[4]

The antidepressant Prozac, which regulates serotonin, has become a household name. But did you know that disrupted serotonin levels also affect cravings for carbohydrates? Several researchers have connected serotonin imbalance with overeating, binge eating, and bulimia. This may be why Prozac and other medications that work on serotonin levels have been helpful in treating binge eating and bulimia. This also gives us some understanding as to why some people with ADD experience relief from symptoms such as impulsiveness, sleep disturbances, agitation, and irritability when prescribed these types of medications.

Dopamine

Dopamine is another important neurotransmitter that is related to ADD and a variety of emotional and behavioral problems. Disrupted dopamine levels in the brain are found in people with ADD; Tourette's Syndrome; impulsive, compulsive, and addictive behaviors; drug abuse; and posttraumatic stress disorder (PTSD).[5,6] Medications to treat ADD work on establishing the dopamine balance in the brain. Faulty receptor sites in the brain, which seem to be due to genetic defects, can impair the effectiveness of dopamine. Genetic research has uncovered several specific genetic defects related to dopamine levels that affect a large variety of human behavior.

As of this writing, researchers have located five dopamine receptor sites, or places, on the neuron that receives the neurotransmitter. They have also located defects on the gene that determine how the receptor sites operate. The first defect was found on what is called the D2 receptor gene. This defect interferes with proper reception of dopamine and contributes to ADD symptoms.

Doctors Hallowell and Ratey, in their book *Answers to Distraction,* write,

> The gene that codes for a specific type of dopamine receptor has been found to be abnormal 60 percent

of the time in ADD patients. It is a defect on one of the versions of the D2 receptor gene, and is also found to be abnormal about 60 percent of the time in alcoholics, cocaine addicts, those with posttraumatic stress disorder, and patients with Tourette disorders. This particular abnormality only appears in about 6 percent of the population overall.[7]

This suggests a strong genetic link between ADD and addictions.

Dopamine is also key in what Kenneth Blum, Ph.D. refers to as "reward deficiency syndrome" (RDS). RDS occurs when there is an imbalance of dopamine that causes someone to feel anxious or restless, to lose his or her sense of well-being and ability to concentrate and feel pleasure. Decreased dopamine levels set up cravings for more dopamine.

You may have already learned how to raise your dopamine levels. Alcohol, drugs, nicotine, high risk and compulsive behaviors, sugar and carbohydrates stimulate neurotransmitters in the brain that temporarily increase your sense of well-being.[8] Part of the reason you abuse substances, food, or behaviors is that you may be attempting to fix your brain chemistry. You may be more of a neurochemist than you thought.

GENETICS

Researchers are able to isolate specific areas of our genes and determine traits, characteristics, susceptibility for disease, and abnormalities such as Down's Syndrome, Sickle Cell Anemia, addictions, and certain forms of cancer. There has been an explosion of genetic research showing the genetic origins of ADD and how ADD is linked with a variety of other disorders.

Researchers such as David E. Comings, M.D., Dr. Kenneth Blum, Dr. Eric R. Braverman, Dr. Ernest Noble, and

Joseph Biderman, M.D., and their colleagues, are finding new and exciting genetic connections between variants or differences in areas of the gene responsible for dopamine regulation.

David E. Comings, M.D., and colleagues have taken genetic research beyond the D2 receptor site and explored the genetic relationship between the other dopamine receptor sites. When writing about addictions, Dr. Comings and colleagues state: "We believe that recognizing the role of dopamine and the D2 receptor in the manifestation of these addictions and disorders is the first step toward rational treatment for a devastating problem in our society."[9]

Genetic research has moved beyond the previously held belief that a gene was either dominant or recessive. Researchers are learning that genetics, similar to other contributing causes for human difference, do not have "either-or" answers. We now know that our genetic inheritance is based not only on which genes we get from our family pool, but the degree to which each gene expresses itself. In other words, we could say that the same gene can be brighter, louder, more colorful, and express its specific characteristics more in one person than it does in another.

Dr. Comings has documented what is known as polygenesis, or the inheritance of several different genes and their levels of expression, which predisposes people to a "spectrum" of emotional or mental conditions. This means that you inherited a combination of genes with varying levels of expression that can predispose you to a spectrum of characteristics.

Dr. Comings pioneered the concept of spectrum disorders, disorders in which there is genetic overlapping. ADD is on the spectrum along with other disorders such as Tourette's Syndrome; drug, alcohol, and nicotine addictions; eating and conduct disorders; depression; and compulsive, impulsive, and violent behaviors. All of these disorders can result from disruption of the dopamine pathway. Today we are clearly seeing that people who seek immediate gratification, have a low tolerance for frustration and discomfort, and use food, chemicals, and compulsive behaviors to feel better, are responding in part to inherited neurological differences in their brains.

Your genes, learned behaviors, and ways of coping are all passed on from one generation to the next. With new understanding of the genetic origin of behaviors and illnesses, we can let go of old myths such as: "If your parent was an alcoholic, you should have learned not to become one." The fact is, if you are genetically "loaded" for clusters of problems, you can't will that predisposition away. You can't change your genetic makeup, but you can take responsibility and get treatment for your problems. You can also let go of the moral judgments, criticisms, and shame that prevent you from getting the help you deserve.

SCANNING THE BRAIN

Over the past seven years there has been an explosion of research on adults with Attention Deficit Disorder, including the landmark Zametkin brain scan study (1990).[10] Dr. Zametkin and colleagues used PET (positron emission tomography) scans which measure how glucose with a radioactive tracer is metabolized in the brain. Brain activity can be observed by the rate at which glucose is absorbed in specific regions of the brain. The Zametkin study used adult subjects with histories of hyperactivity dating back to childhood who were also biological parents of a hyperactive child.

Adults with histories of hyperactivity were slower to absorb glucose than the "normal" adult control group. The specific areas of the brain that were slower to metabolize glucose were the premotor cortex and the superior prefrontal cortex (sometimes referred to as the frontal lobes).

The frontal lobes regulate attention, concentration, judgment, impulses, information processing, and the ability to think through consequences of behavior; they also interact with areas of the brain that regulate activity level. When the frontal lobes absorb less of the tracer, they are functioning more slowly. Less activity means less regulation of these functions.

The slower acting frontal lobes of the ADD brain do not provide the extra millisecond a non-ADD brain has to think through and decide to stop words or actions. For people with ADD, thoughts often become words and actions before they are consciously aware of what they were thinking. In other words, people with ADD often find out what they're thinking by what they have just done or said. The less active frontal lobes cannot control and maintain focus or concentration at will. The ADD mind wanders, races, falls asleep, shuts down, or gets stuck in a particular area.

ADD IS NOT A FAD

ADD is not a new condition. Unlike many conditions that are rooted in our biology, documentation of ADD began in the early 1900s. In 1902, George Still, a physician in Britain, began looking at highly active children who were disruptive and had behavioral problems. Still suggested that these children's problems were based in their brain function, rather than their character.

The words used to describe ADD have evolved, as has our understanding of this disorder. At first, doctors believed ADD was caused by viral encephalitis, or brain infection. Two journal articles, one by Hymen in 1922 and another by Strecker and Ebaugh in 1924, expounded this theory. In 1934, two psychiatrists, Kahn and Cohen, suggested that the syndrome, which was still believed to be caused by encephalitis, was also found in adults. They presented two case studies of adults with the disorder.[11]

These days, many fine doctors and therapists have limited knowledge about ADD in children and adults.

Education regarding the diagnosing and treating of children and adults with ADD is lacking in medical schools and graduate programs. Child psychiatrists and pediatricians seem to have the most training in ADD in children, and some psychiatrists and medical doctors have become specialists in treating ADD adults as well.

Since many health-care professionals have little knowledge of ADD, they are often unable to see it in the patient sitting across from them. Some of these patients actually tell their doctors they have ADD. Their doctors respond, "ADD is not as common as people think. I don't have anyone with ADD in my practice. ADD is just a passing fad. Your problems are caused by stress and anxiety and your unresolved feelings from your past."

Fortunately for people with ADD, information about it is spreading much faster than information about addictions did. Thanks to the Internet and the World Wide Web, information about ADD is racing electronically around the world. Characteristics of people with ADD, such as curiosity, talkativeness, and tenacity increase the pace at which information is spreading.

Even professionals who are aware of ADD in adults are not aware that many of their patients use alcohol, food, and drugs to soothe their ADD traits. Physicians who have made the connection between ADD and addiction are often afraid to prescribe medication for their ADD patients who have any history of addictions. This fear is based on a lack of knowledge about treating ADD in individuals who are in recovery from substance abuse. We will explore this in more detail in Chapter Eleven.

Other professionals think ADD is the hypoglycemia or Chronic Fatigue Syndrome of the nineties. So many people either have been diagnosed with these conditions, or simply identify themselves as having them, that the accurate medical criteria is lost. Hypoglycemia and Chronic Fatigue Syndrome are real medical conditions but have been reduced to popular fads in the minds of many. This narrow-minded view is dangerous for their patients who have ADD.

I am concerned that ADD might be seen as a fad, simply because so many identify with its symptoms. Danger exists when any diagnosis is diluted and generalized or popularized. If a condition such as ADD is seen as the cause of every symptom anyone could have, the diagnosis loses credibility. The unfortunate thing is that people who really do suffer are not taken seriously, and their medical conditions are seen as bogus.

I've told other professionals who believe that adult ADD is a fad, "If you think ADD is a fad, come spend the day with me. And if my ADD behavior doesn't convince you, I will guarantee that listening to the seven patients I see today will. You'll hear the anguish and despair of men and women who have suffered a life of untreated ADD. You'll witness the self-loathing of people who cannot stop self-medicating their ADD symptoms. You'll feel their uncontrollable restlessness. And if you really listen, you'll hear the pain and grief of lives with lost opportunities and potential.

"They will talk about the first time they tried to take their own life as a child and how many times they've tried to end their ADD suffering as adults. If you can stay emotionally present in the room, you will not be able to deny the existence of adult Attention Deficit Disorder."

If you have ADD, you understand how it permeates every area of your life. You know what it's like to space out in the middle of a conversation. You live with the embarrassment and shame of your disorganization or your compulsive attempts to appear organized. You live with the consequences of being controlled by your impulses. You experience the pain you cause others when you fly into spontaneous rages. You feel the shame of not being able to think and live like others.

This is your reality, and your reality is not a fad.

CHAPTER FIVE

HOW DO I KNOW IF I HAVE ADD?

Checklists for ADD Traits

With all the media hype about ADD, it's hard to sort out what's real and what isn't. How do you know if you really have ADD? In this chapter, you will have the opportunity to complete checklists to help you assess yourself for ADD. While the checklists will probably be enlightening, they are not meant as a tool for self-diagnosis. Getting an accurate diagnosis from a professional with expertise and experience working with ADD in adults is extremely important.

You and significant people in your life can answer the questions on the checklists. The questions provide you with opportunities to think back and remember ADD traits you had as a child and may still have as an adult. Since the lists begin with questions about infancy, you will want to contact relatives or close friends who can give you information you can't remember.

The checklists are meant to provide you with a skeleton of common ADD traits that may have affected you throughout your life. The human skeleton is the basic structure of our body. Most of us have identical skeletal structures, and yet our body size, type, and weight can differ greatly. The same is true of ADD. Although the core traits of ADD remain consistent over your life, they are expressed differently during each phase of your development.

One major problem since the inception of the ADD diagnosis is that until recently ADD has been viewed only in the context of childhood. Since professionals believed children outgrew ADD during puberty, adult ADD behavior and traits were given a wide variety of other inaccurate labels. It's important to view ADD in the context of your life-long development.

COMPLETING THE CHECKLISTS

Don't be concerned if you can't answer all the questions or are unsure of your answer. It's best to put down your first response and not ponder each question for too long. The questions are divided into periods of human development: infancy, toddlerhood, childhood, adolescence, and adulthood.

Rate each question with a 0 if it never applies to you, a 1 if it sometimes applies to you, a 2 if it frequently applies to you, and a 3 if it more than frequently or often applies to you.

Questions About Infancy

0=never   1=sometimes   2=frequently   3=often

_____ Were you described as a fussy baby?

_____ Were you diagnosed as having colic?

_____ Did you have irregular sleeping schedules, or sleep less than most infants?

_____ Were you sensitive to clothing and diapers, and happier when naked?

_____ Did you startle easily to sights, sounds, or touch?

68

_____ Were you described as a baby who didn't like to cuddle?

_____ Did you have food allergies?

_____ Did you have frequent ear infections?

_____ Did your mother use alcohol, marijuana, other drugs, or prescribed medication during pregnancy?

_____ Did your mother smoke cigarettes during pregnancy?

_____ Were you adopted?

_____ Did your mother have a long or difficult labor?

_____ Were you delivered by forceps or with the cord around your neck?

ADD in Infants

For most people, Attention Deficit Disorder begins at conception. However, ADD can also be caused by trauma to the brain at birth, drug or alcohol abuse by the mother during pregnancy, or head injury at any time during one's life. For the most part, though, ADD is inherited and passed on through families.

Some mothers are aware that they have an active child in utero. I've known of mothers who have had their ribs broken during pregnancy by their ADD babies. One mother's ADD child constantly battered her bladder for the last two months of her pregnancy. Just because a baby was an in utero gymnast, however, doesn't mean he or she will grow up to have ADD. Many mothers of babies with ADD also report "normally" active babies during their pregnancy.

Is It Colic or ADD?

Do you remember being told that you had colic as an infant? Have you heard stories of how your parents were up with you for months, took you for car rides in the middle of the night, and tried anything to help you stop crying? ADD babies can be fussier, more active, and, at times, cannot be consoled by physical touch. Frequently, these babies are misdiagnosed with colic. True colic is believed to be caused by an underdeveloped digestive tract. The infant has difficulties digesting milk and suffers from gas pains, bloating, and abdominal distress. Infants with colic look to be in physical distress. They scream and cry, sometimes for hours. The signs of colic are pretty consistent and usually disappear by about three months of age.

Colic seems to have become a generic diagnosis for infants who cry more than usual and appear to be in distress. When no medical condition can explain the infant's constant distress, colic is often the diagnosis of default. But infants cry for a variety of reasons. Not all babies who cry to express their discomfort and distress have colic.

After reviewing the history of many adults and children with ADD, I find that many were diagnosed with colic in infancy. What a coincidence. I'm sure that some people with ADD definitely had colic as infants, but I wonder if there wasn't more to it than that. I wonder if, like most things in life, there are a variety of conditions that are expressed with the same symptoms.

Could it be that some infants who are fussy are experiencing the neurologic sensitivity of ADD? They may be screaming because they can't filter out the lights and sounds and activity around them. Infants with ADD can also be extremely sensitive to touch. They might be trying to tell us that their diaper or sleeper feels like sandpaper on their skin. They may be screaming because they are totally helpless to do anything about their pain.

Some infants with ADD cannot be consoled by being held. As a matter of fact, holding and rocking them may actually make them feel worse. What is comforting for most infants can be overwhelming and overstimulating to infants with ADD. I am not in any way suggesting that infants who cry a lot should not be held; holding and rocking is comforting for most infants. However, we must treat children as individuals and be prepared to consider a variety of possible causes for their agitation.

I have heard mothers describe their powerlessness, frustration, and sense of failure because they couldn't comfort their ADD infant. If this is their first child, they are frequently extremely distressed about their baby's discomfort. They try everything their instincts tell them, as well as what they've read and are told by others. But their baby is not calmed by comforting; in fact, their baby cries even harder when suckled and rocked. Their baby may even stiffen when touched. It seems as if the harder the mother tries to calm her baby's crying, the more her baby cries. Mothers of ADD infants often feel anxious, angry, rejected, and ashamed of themselves for not being "good" mothers. These painful feelings can cause them to pull back from their infant, making the vital bonding process extremely difficult.

Meanwhile, these ADD babies are also feeling anxious, angry, and frustrated. Their needs are not being met. Because they are extraordinarily sensitive, they physically stiffen and pull away from both parents. These babies may exhibit difficulties with breast feeding due to the amount of physical body contact they must endure. They may wonder why their parents touch them so much when it's so uncomfortable. These infants cannot tolerate the contact and intimacy we typically think of as normal bonding.

Additional factors may impede bonding. For example, ADD "colic" doesn't necessarily pass at the magical age of three months. Some of these babies are in extreme discomfort for months. Also, babies with ADD can be more sensitive to clothing and temperature changes. They tend to startle more easily. They can be finicky about their food and tend to eat foods with similar texture, color, and taste. They also tend to be more active and restless. All of these factors contribute to an extremely tumultuous bonding process.

The bonding that takes place between parents and their new baby is essential. It creates the pattern for later bonding in childhood, adolescence, and adulthood. When this early bonding is disrupted, it can result in lifelong consequences. In some cases the disruption can lead to substance abuse, criminal behavior, violence, personality disorders, and incarceration. However, with education and understanding, parents of ADD infants can interrupt the downward spiral by finding alternative ways of bonding with their babies.

Questions About Toddlerhood

0=never   1=sometimes   2=frequently   3=often

_____ Were you a picky eater?

_____ Were you described as very active?

_____ Were you described as a daredevil or a fearless child?

_____ Were you involved in dangerous activities such as climbing up on the roof, running off in crowds, or eating cleaning agents?

_____ Were you frequently injured (falls, stitches, broken bones)?

_____ Have you ever had a head injury?

_____ Have you ever had a blow to your forehead?

_____ Were you ever knocked unconscious?

_____ Did you have difficulties transitioning from one place to another (leaving home, leaving day care, leaving a park or a friend's house)?

_____ Was it hard for you to entertain yourself?

_____ Did you demand attention from those around you?

_____ Did you have problems getting along with other children?

_____ Did you make contact by biting, kicking, or hitting other children?

_____ Were you quiet and withdrawn?

ADD in Toddlers

It can be difficult to diagnose ADD in children under three years. Some experts believe it's hard to differentiate between ADD behavior and the normal, active behavior of preschoolers prior to the age of five. Children are individuals and will develop at their own pace. No one wants to put an active toddler on medication, especially since research indicates that about a third of active toddlers calm down by age five. However, parents and family members can provide information about your behavior as a toddler that helps put the ADD diagnostic puzzle together.

ADD toddlers can be fearless little daredevils. These are the kids who run in front of cars and dash into crowds at shopping malls and parades. They are climbers and fallers who are so bruised and battered that their parents fear being reported to Child Protective Services on their frequent trips to the emergency room. Toddlers with ADD live in a state of constant motion and ceaseless activity. Their parents are frequently exhausted.

I've heard stories of toddlers with ADD who climbed out of their cribs at a year old; at age four they started their parents' car and backed it through the closed garage door. I've heard of others who, at eight months, moved chairs and climbed from counters to the top of the refrigerator to get cookies.

Infants and toddlers with ADD tend to have more ear infections than their peers. They can be finicky eaters who balk at new foods. Some will thrive on action, noise, and novel situations, while others are easily overwhelmed by any change in their routine.

Questions About Childhood

0=never   1=sometimes   2=frequently   3=often

_____ Did you have difficulty paying attention in school?

_____ Did your mind drift when the teacher was talking?

_____ Did you do poorly in classes when you weren't interested or didn't like the teacher?

_____ Were you easily bored?

_____ Were you forgetful, losing items such as books, homework, shoes, jackets, bikes . . . ?

_____ Were you able to focus intensely on subjects when you were interested?

_____ Did you daydream, fantasize, or act out during class?

_____ Did your grade in class depend on how much you liked your teacher?

_____ Do you think you got in trouble more than most kids?

_____ Were you the class clown?

_____ Were you quiet and unsure of yourself?

_____ Were you well-acquainted with the principal at your school?

_____ Was it hard for you to be part of a group, such as Scouts or sports teams?

_____ Did you take on a leadership role in group activities?

_____ Were you uncomfortable in groups?

_____ Did you feel awkward or less coordinated than your peers?

_____ Did you feel internally driven to move?

_____ Did riding your bike, skate boarding, ice skating, running, or swimming make you feel better?

_____ Did you spend hours in your own fantasy world?

_____ Was it more comfortable to fantasize and daydream than to play with others?

_____ Did you use reading as an escape?

ADD in Children

ADD traits become more noticeable and problematic during childhood. This is primarily due to the intellectual and social demands of elementary school. Children are now expected to stay seated, to listen and follow instructions, and to learn reading, writing, and arithmetic. It is in the classroom that many children with ADD cannot compensate for their attention, impulse, and activity level differences. Somewhere during preschool, kindergarten, first, or second grade these children quickly realize they are different, and for them, different is bad.

Children also have to learn to wait when they enter school. They have to master waiting for their turn, waiting to use the restroom, waiting for recess, waiting to eat, and waiting in lines. Do you remember waiting in lines in elementary school? Many adults with ADD still haven't mastered waiting in lines. You can see them flip out at the Department of Motor Vehicles, IRS office, or supermarket. If you were one of those children who never mastered basic line waiting, you know how hard school life was when you couldn't perform this "simple" requisite.

The self-esteem of young school-age children with ADD shrinks every school year they are not treated. These kids feel awful about themselves and powerless to change their behavior. They don't understand why they're not like other kids and blame themselves for being stupid, lazy, hyper, and disruptive. Unfortunately, too many teachers, therapists, doctors, neighbors, and family members blame these traits on poor parenting. Children with ADD are frequently viewed as misbehaving, undisciplined, stupid, or troublemakers who are victims of dysfunctional families. ADD *can* greatly contribute to family dysfunction, but dysfunctional families do not cause ADD.

School Daze

Kids with ADD can have an impossible time in kindergarten if they can't sit still, follow instructions, and restrain from distracting their classmates. Kids with moderate or severe ADD may be fortunate enough to be diagnosed and treated. However, others who aren't diagnosed will "fail" kindergarten or be passed on to the next teacher who may not have the knowledge or skills to help them.

Third grade seems to be another point where ADD kids encounter trouble. Memorizing multiplication tables, more extensive reading, and follow-through on homework are expected. Children with ADD may hit their wall when they have to turn in their first report, even if that report is only a page long. They lack the skills to organize their thoughts and information. Some ADD children who adapt well in the lower grades may begin experiencing difficulties in middle or high school.

Children with the less active type of ADD are less likely to be evaluated for ADD. They are not disorderly or disruptive. They usually daydream their way through school unnoticed. If you were one of these kids, you know what it's like to feel invisible. You may have studied two to three times longer and harder than your siblings or the other kids. You made up for what you couldn't learn by being quiet and good. You were your teachers' idea of the perfect student; they had no idea how hard you struggled and how much you suffered.

Questions About Adolescence

0=never   1=sometimes   2=frequently   3=often

_____ Did it seem harder for you to do things that appeared easy for others?

_____ Did you daydream or fantasize?

_____ Did you "zone out" when watching TV?

_____ Were you a risk taker or thrill seeker (driving fast, diving from high places)?

_____ Were you cited or arrested?

_____ Did you get traffic violations?

_____ Did you steal for the thrill of it?

_____ Did you drink alcohol?

_____ Did you take other drugs such as marijuana, LSD, cocaine, speed, or heroin?

_____ Did your drinking or drug use get you into trouble?

_____ Did you ever think about killing yourself?

_____ Did you use reading as an escape?

_____ Were you clumsy?

_____ Did you feel uncoordinated?

_____ Was it hard for you to think through the consequences of your actions?

_____ Were you physically, emotionally, or sexually abused?

_____ Were you the "class clown"?

ADD in Teens

For most of us, adolescence is the developmental stage in which we change the most. Adolescence is the long hallway between childhood and adulthood; the door to childhood is still open behind us as we walk or run to the open door of adulthood which looms ahead. For several years we vacillate between wanting to be adults and our desire to remain children. As a result, we tend to rush indecisively up and down that long hallway, not tightly connected to either stage of development.

Adolescence is a time of huge hormonal, physical, emotional, moral, and spiritual changes. Teenagers are bombarded by intense hormonal surges that change their bodies into replicas of adults. While they now have many of the physical characteristics of adults, they remain emotionally and psychologically immature. Adolescence is a critical and pivotal time in life where many begin self-medicating their untreated ADD.

Understanding how ADD and addictions affected you as an adolescent will help you today as an adult. Like most people with addictions, your emotional development may not have progressed much after you started self-medicating your pain, depression, shyness, anxiety, or ADD.

Questions About Adulthood

I've broken down the adult portion of this questionnaire into several categories. Each concentrates on a specific area of adult behavior. You will have the opportunity to answer questions about your attention, sensitivity, activity level, and impulsiveness. We'll start with two areas of attention: expansive/distractible, and highly focused, or zoom lens, attention.

Expansive/Distractible Attention

0=never   1=sometimes   2=frequently   3=often

_____ Are you easily distracted?

_____ Do you go on autopilot when doing a routine task such as paying the bills?

_____ Do you use TV, computer games, or the Internet as an escape?

_____ Do you frequently find yourself in a particular room and wonder why?

_____ Do you find yourself gazing into the refrigerator until you get cold?

_____ Do you ever feel you may have early onset Alzheimer's?

_____ Does your mind hippity hop from thought to thought like bunnies in a hurry?

_____ Can you do several things at the same time?

_____ Do you misplace your car in parking lots, your car keys, sunglasses, credit cards . . . ?

_____ Are you an expansive thinker?

_____ Do you get bored, irritated, or tired when filling out questionnaires like this one? (feel free to take a break)

Zoom Lens Attention

_____ Do you lose track of time when your attention is captured?

_____ Do misspelled words and typographical errors distract you when reading?

_____ Is it hard for you to be interrupted?

_____ Do you get so involved in an activity that you lose track of time?

_____ Are you compelled to do everything perfectly?

_____ Is it hard for you to do more than one thing at a time?

_____ Do you have thoughts that repeat over and over in your mind?

_____ Is it hard for you to see a variety of solutions to your problems?

_____ Do you have difficulty switching from one project to another?

_____ Do you work well with details?

_____ Do you feel uncomfortable around clutter?

_____ Are you a frequent worrier?

_____ Do you have negative or fatalistic thoughts?

_____ Are you judgmental of yourself and others?

_____ Do you feel that something bad is going to happen?

_____ Do you hold on to grudges and resentments?

_____ Do you debate and argue over details with others?

Sensitivity

_____ Are you sensitive to bright or fluorescent lights?

_____ Are you distracted by noises that others don't seem to notice?

_____ Have you ever felt like leaving your items in the cart and fleeing a crowded store?

_____ Do you cut the tags out of your clothing?

_____ Are there materials you can't stand to wear? (polyester, wool, nylon)

_____ Do the seams in your socks irritate you?

_____ Do you feel overwhelmed in crowded places?

_____ Do you avoid loud or crowded places?

_____ Do you find yourself wanting to turn down the volume of the TV or radio?

_____ Are your feelings easily hurt?

_____ Do you misinterpret what people say as being critical of you?

_____ Do you tend to feel your feelings and the feelings of others intensely?

_____ Do you frequently feel the need to explain or defend yourself?

Activity Level

_____ Do you have an abundance of energy?

_____ Is it hard for you to relax and do nothing?

_____ Do you feel driven to be active?

_____ Are you a fast talker?

_____ Do you shop as though you're on a supermarket sweepstakes?

_____ Is it hard for you to get up in the morning?

_____ Do you sleep through your alarm(s)?

_____ Does it take you several cups of a caffeinated drink to get moving?

_____ Is it hard for you to find your focus for the day?

_____ Do you feel the need to nap during the day?

_____ Do you doze in meetings, movies, when reading, or during conversations?

_____ Do you feel as if you move in slow motion compared to others?

Impulsiveness

_____ Do you say things you later regret?

_____ Do you interrupt others?

_____ Do you blurt out answers before others finish their questions?

_____ Do you lose control of your temper?

_____ Are you impatient?

_____ Have you abruptly changed relationships, jobs, or residences?

_____ Do you read the directions only as a last resort?

_____ Have you told lies before you realized it?

_____ Have you shoplifted, gambled, or spent money without thinking through the consequences?

_____ Do you receive traffic violations?

_____ Have you physically hurt people or property when angry?

_____ Have you flown into a rage and not known why?

Now that you've finished this lengthy questionnaire, give yourself some time to review your answers. Be especially aware of the questions you answered with a 2 or 3 (often or frequently). These are the places where your answers will give you information about how ADD may be affecting your life. The more 2 and 3 answers you have, the more likely it is that you should be evaluated for ADD. Again, this questionnaire is not a diagnostic tool; the questions are designed to help you think about specific ADD traits that may be affecting your life.

THE DIFFERENCES IN ADD BETWEEN THE SEXES

John Grey captured some of the differences between women and men in his best-selling book, *Men Are From Mars, Women Are From Venus.* Recent research cites differences in brain functioning that may contribute to some of the many emotional, cognitive, and perceptual differences between the sexes.

Before having children, I strongly believed that most differences between boys and girls were due to upbringing and socialization. I read numerous studies concluding that gender differences were based on how children were treated and believed that gender roles are affected by the expectations of our society. I downplayed the role of genetics until our daughter and son were born. We created two children: same parents, similar upbringing, acute awareness of gender biases, yet with huge differences in how they experience the world. The more children I spend time with, in and out of my office, the more I'm convinced that girls and boys, men and women, are biologically wired very differently. These biological differences, as well as the norms of our culture, contribute to our wonderful yet sometimes problematic, differences.

Men and women not only experience the world differently, they have different experiences with ADD. For years, it was erroneously believed that boys had ADD ten times more than girls. Even the 1994 Diagnostic and Statistical Manual of Mental Disorders, fourth edition, (or DSM-IV) states, "The disorder is much more frequent in males than in females, with male-to-female ratios ranging from 4:1 to 9:1, depending on the setting (i.e., general population or clinics)."[1] However, I agree with many experts in the field who report an almost even distribution of ADD in males and females.

Girls and women are under-diagnosed due to how they experience and express ADD traits. For example, men and boys exhibit hyperactive behavior more often than girls or women, yet only recently have experts understood that you don't have to be hyperactive to have ADD. As a result, many women and girls with ADD were not diagnosed because they didn't demonstrate this behavior.

ADD in Women

Stephanie is fifty-eight years old. She has been married for thirty-five years and has three grown children. As far back as Stephanie remembers, she has felt slow, stupid, less than, inadequate. She grew up in a family whose values were based on achievements. Stephanie's siblings ran circles around her. She couldn't keep up, let alone compete with the actions and accomplishments of her brothers and sister. Stephanie's mother was always on the go. She worked for a large newspaper and received numerous awards in journalism. Stephanie's father was a real estate broker who made a small fortune buying and selling properties.

Stephanie did okay in school. She remembers that her

teachers would comment on what a sweet girl she was and how easy it was to have her in their classes. Stephanie was not only an easy student, she was an invisible one. She didn't ask questions, disrupt the class, or in any way let on how lost and alone she felt.

High school was even more difficult for Stephanie. She spent hours and hours trying to memorize names, dates, and places in history. The harder she tried, the more difficult it was for her to retrieve information during tests. Stephanie spent so many hours studying during high school that she had no social life. She missed out on critical activities of adolescence, such as having close girlfriends, attending parties, and dating.

Stephanie's relief at her high school graduation was overshadowed by her abject fear of attending college. College became the reality she had feared—reading she couldn't keep up with and an avalanche of facts that buried her. She graduated from college after six years of intense and relentless struggle, feeling like an impostor when she received her degree. Stephanie looks back on her college years as having a profound negative effect on her already fragile self-esteem.

Stephanie did what most women did in the fifties: she married a man she felt would take care of her. The traditional unspoken deal they struck was similar to most families of that generation. He worked and provided a good income, and Stephanie did the rest. Like many women of her generation, she accepted her responsibilities of providing emotional, educational, spiritual, cultural, and moral guidance for their three children. She fed her family well, washed and pressed as much laundry as the local wash and dry, and kept the house as clean and orderly as she could.

Stephanie constantly compared herself to the other mothers in her neighborhood who appeared to handle everything with grace and style. No matter how fast she moved, she couldn't keep up with her family, let alone appear calm, cool, and collected. Stephanie was so over-loaded by her family's demands that she would some-times get so frustrated with the laundry and bounce the Tide box off the wall. Sometimes she would feel so explo-sive, she would have to leave the house with her hand over her mouth to keep from saying something hurtful to her family.

She lived her life in a constant state of stress and feel-ing overwhelmed. She felt devastated when she would for-get to send a birthday card to one of her husband's relatives, or be late taking her children to school or any of the after-school activities they were involved in. Stephanie's core beliefs that she was stupid, slow, explosive, and incompetent were reinforced by her husband, children, and parents, who constantly complained about what she didn't do and then put her down for being stressed.

Stephanie's self-confidence had a slow leak like a car radiator's, but she didn't notice until she was so severely overheated that she couldn't go on. The year her last child went off to college and her husband retired early after an accident that left him partially disabled, Stephanie real-ized how awful she felt. She was so depressed she could hardly get out of bed in the morning.

It wasn't until she could not shake her suicidal thoughts that she sought treatment for her depression. Serendipitously, Stephanie made an appointment to see a psychiatrist who had knowledge of ADD. Stephanie knew nothing about ADD, and was perplexed and resistant to her doctor's diagnosis. She was unable to focus on the information and books her doctor suggested. Since her doctor understood this as a symptom of ADD, they spent several sessions discussing ADD in women. Stephanie related to almost all of the ADD traits they discussed.

Through an adult ADD coaching group, therapy, and medication, Stephanie has become better able to accept herself. After two months, her depression lifted. Recently, she realized that her mother suffers from ADD. She now sees the impact that untreated ADD has had on her mother and their relationship.

The Times They Are A-Changin'

Slowly, men's and women's roles in the family and the workplace are changing. Although many families are creating ways to share parenting, household responsibilities, and work, many families still operate out of traditional gender roles. Father is the head of the house and financially responsible for the family. Mother is responsible for caring for the children, cooking, doing laundry, cleaning, organizing all family appointments, paying bills, social engagements, birthday and holiday celebrations, and shopping for food and clothing. And, of course, Mom also has a job away from home.

The basic job description for women these days is staggering. With duties like these, who would apply? Top all this off with the required need for multi-tasking (doing several things at once), intricate information processing capacity, focused and expansive attention, beyond average organizational skills, and ability to contain one's impulses and frustration, and you have what Sari Solden refers to in *Women With Attention Deficit Disorder* as the Job Description From Hell.[2]

Women without disabilities have a hard enough job in families. No wonder more women than men suffer from depression and anxiety. Women tend to self-medicate their feelings of pain, sadness, shame, guilt, and overload with food, compulsive behaviors, alcohol, and street and prescription drugs. When we add the handicapping aspect of ADD to all of this, it can be like having a brain in a wheelchair. Getting around and functioning effectively becomes extremely difficult. If you're a woman with ADD, chances are that "normal" female duties take extreme effort for you, even if you have an abundance of energy. If you have the less active form of ADD, being a mom and wife can set you up to "fail" again and again and again, until you get your ADD treated.

Feeling like a poor parent, wife, or employee creates tremendous shame. Untreated ADD contributes to feeling less than others because you can't do what other women do. You, more than the average woman, cannot pull off the Myth of the Super woman. You find it impossible to create the perfect dinner party and remember to send your child to school with lunch money. Your house is constantly trashed and you don't have the ability to keep it the way you would like. You feel frustrated because you can't keep up with the relentless demands. Somewhere, you've gotten lost among the ten piles of dirty laundry, the soccer games and dance recitals, and, of course, the forty-hour-a-week job you're late for because the kids' lunches haven't been made yet. While life might be easier if you have a participating partner, you may still feel overwhelmed most of the time.

Not only is all of this exhausting, it's also brutal on a woman's self-esteem. Many women with ADD whom I treat experience a level of fatigue that sleep alone will not restore. Many are chronically depressed, anxious, and obsessed with doing things "right." For these women, restoration comes from ADD treatment and from making life changes that are compatible with their capabilities, dreams, and desires.

The first life change you can start with is putting *your* needs on top of your daily To Do list.

ADD IN MEN

ADD men and women, boys and girls, all have problems in the three major areas we have discussed: attention, activity level, and impulse control. But because males and females are biologically different and have different cultural expectations put on them, they experience ADD differently. Some of these differences are subtle, and some are not so subtle. Acknowledging the differences in how men and women experience ADD is important, not to cause gender separation, but to help the genders understand each other, learn to get along better, and support their common goal of ADD recovery.

More men than women have the highly active type of ADD. Without trying to promote stereotypes, males in general engage the world with their bodies more than women. They are more likely to use their bodies in work and play. Many adults with high energy ADD learn to channel their need to be active. Men who are so inclined are able to expend energy, have contact with others, have fun, and release frustration while playing sports. Some men find that working out at the gym, running, swimming, surfing, and playing tennis or racquetball are valuable ways of expending energy.

In our increasingly technological world, too many people find themselves sitting behind desks or in front of computers. Human beings weren't meant to spend their days thinking and working in this sedentary way. This is especially frustrating for men with ADD who need to move their bodies to think and to release energy. Some men with high activity ADD are fortunate enough to work outside in construction, land survey, sales, agriculture, tree trimming, law enforcement, fire fighting, gardening, the military, and a host of professions where they can move their bodies, work under novel and changing circumstances, and think on their feet.

More and more, however, occupations that are compatible with the ADD style are becoming unavailable to people with ADD. There are more rigorous academic standards for people wanting to become fire fighters or enter law enforcement. Many people with ADD cannot follow through with the months of paperwork and interviews necessary to obtain a position they are well suited for. Not only that, but the military will not consider anyone who is taking stimulant medication to treat their ADD.

The times are changing for men as well as women. As more women enter the work force and contribute financially, men are being asked to help with the responsibilities of raising a family. The days of Ward Cleaver reading the paper in his cardigan sweater while June cooks dinner in high heels are disappearing. Children want more from their fathers than a snippet of advice now and again. Fathers are rising to the challenge of working full-time and carving out time to be with their families. Not only are women expecting men to be more involved with their children and the household, more men really want that quality time with their families.

For the man with ADD, however, these new demands and challenges add more balls to the juggling act when he already feels he's juggling as many as he can. This can be exceptionally difficult for the man who feels he uses all of his physical and emotional energy trying to keep up at work. He may already be bringing work home at night and on weekends in order to catch up on what he can't do at the office.

Many men also have the job description from hell. They are expected to be financial providers. This can be extremely difficult for the man with ADD who can't hold down a job for more than a few months at a time. As a result, he suffers from tremendous feelings of inadequacy when he fears that he can't provide for his family.

Emotional and Relationship Problems
For many men in our society, expressing feelings is difficult. For men with ADD, the process of identifying and articulating feelings is an even greater challenge. Some men with ADD are great storytellers and are able to talk quite a bit about trivia, sports, computers, and the like. But when it comes to talking about intimate subjects such as feelings, sex, vulnerability, and fears, they can't find the words. Men who have a hard time identifying emotions find it hard to express them in healthy ways.

Many men with ADD are accused of not caring enough to listen, or of being so self-centered that they interrupt others. Sometimes this is true, but the man with ADD may actually want very much to hear what his partner has to say. Unfortunately, he gets distracted. He may not mean to interrupt, but his impulsiveness makes it hard for him to wait until his partner is finished talking.

Rage

Men with ADD usually have an even harder time than other men expressing their anger effectively. Some men with ADD are volatile and can become violent before they even understand what has happened. This is true for women with ADD as well, but men tend to get themselves into more trouble when they can't control their anger. Some men do not realize how terrifying they are to others when they fly into a rage. The tragic thing is that so many men with anger control issues feel tremendous remorse and shame about their behavior. Unless their ADD is treated, they tend to repeat violent behavior, no matter how hard they try not to.

THE OUTSIDER

Do you ever feel as if you're on the outside looking in? Do you ever wonder why others seem to take life events in stride while you take things so seriously? Both men and women with ADD report suffering from feeling like outsiders.

In 1956, a twenty-one-year-old high school dropout named Colin Wilson published his first book, *The Outsider*. Wilson, who went on to become a prolific British author, tried to define the characteristics of a certain type of person. This person, an outsider, sees the world in a radically different way from most. Wilson refers to French novelist Henri Barbusse's discussions about the outsider. Barbusse, Wilson thought, had shown that the outsider was a person who couldn't live in the comfortable, insulated world of modern society. The outsider couldn't accept the conventional reality others saw. Wilson quotes Barbusse, "He sees too deep and too much," and then Wilson writes, "and what he sees is essentially chaos."

Wilson continues, "For the Outsider, the world is not rational, not orderly."[3]

Wilson's book is not about ADD; however, my experience working with people with ADD has shown me that many experience the world around them the way Wilson described. Wilson wrote about artists, philosophers, and writers, such as Camus, Sartre, Van Gogh, Hemingway, and Dostoevsky. These "outsiders" were people who saw and felt deeply and with great intensity. The expressions of the depths they saw are still with us, long after they have gone. People who see and feel deeply cannot avoid the pain of human existence, or what poet John Keats called "the strife of human hearts." Their gifts to the world were born out of their willingness to feel their pain, search for meaning in the chaos, and share what they found with us.

When you have ADD, it's easy to live on the fringe of life, never feeling a part of, always feeling apart from. The intensity of seeing too much too deeply is isolating. You may wonder, "Why don't other people see this? Why is everyone so superficial?" It may be impossible for you to chitchat or be social when your mind is immersed in the depths of a different reality.

Many people with ADD are intense. By intense I mean that whatever they do, they do with extreme effort and commitment. You see them in business, working out, playing racquetball, shopping, or driving. These are the people who live life with a vengeance. They don't go grocery shopping; they go on a mission to procure food. Their agendas follow them to the neighborhood barbecue. There's no time to talk about how anyone is doing when there is meat to be cooked. They become myopic and intently focused on their goal and have a hard time differentiating between what is important and what is trivial. They maintain the same level of intensity in everything they do.

If you have ADD and relate to this style, you may be trying hard to keep yourself on track. In order to avoid being distracted, you move through your agenda as if no one else is present. People with ADD frequently don't notice how their intense behavior and style affect others. Intense people can come across as arrogant and rude. They are misunderstood by others who view them as self-centered and egotistical. To make matters worse, they are sensitive to criticism and feel hurt when shunned by others. So many people with ADD remain outsiders, feeling alienated, estranged, not knowing how to connect. After years of disconnection, outsiders often stop trying to be a part of the world around them.

When two outsiders meet, an intense bond is usually created. At last they know they aren't crazy. Someone else also sees far below the surface. If you're an outsider, you're in luck, because the ADD world is filled with people like you. You will find many outsiders on the Internet, in online chat rooms, and at ADD conferences. Check it out.

The Funny Side of ADD

While ADD is a biological condition that can complicate every aspect of daily life, people with ADD have qualities that I see and experience as gifts: a sharp wit and keen sense of humor being just two. You may relate to some of the funny side of ADD.
You know you have ADD when:

- ▶ The cab driver lets out a sigh of relief when your feet hit the curb and says, "Been nice listening to you, Ma'am."
- ▶ You find yourself in the restroom of a restaurant cutting the tag out of your new shirt or blouse with your steak knife because the tag is irritating you.
- ▶ You get your dinner out of the microwave and realize it's last night's enchiladas.
- ▶ You forget your own name.
- ▶ Your dog is so used to your hyperactivity that she barks at people who sit still.

▶ Getting extensions on everything becomes a way
of life.

▶ You spontaneously do animal impressions in staff
meetings.

▶ It's second nature for people in your life to
remind you that your fly is open or your blouse is
inside out.

▶ You fall asleep with your eyes open so no one
notices.

You know your mate has ADD when:

▶ It takes him at least three trips back into the
house to get his shoes, keys, kids, coat, and list
before he can leave.

▶ She'd rather have a root canal than wait in lines.

▶ He talks to himself so loudly he even distracts
people without ADD.

▶ She can't pull herself away from the commercial
on TV to listen to what you're saying.

▶ He walks out to get the newspaper in his boxer
shorts because he forgot to put his pants on.

▶ She blames everyone who has been in the house
for the past week for taking her appointment book.

You know your coworker has ADD when:

▶ She goes on vacation to New Zealand and takes
the office keys with her.

▶ He goes to the restroom and takes two hours to
find his way back.

▶ She talks faster than the speed of light.

▶ He constantly breaks into song as if he were in a
musical.

▶ She accidentally shows up at work on Saturday
or holidays.

▶ You feel distracted after being near him for more
than five minutes.

- ▶ She reports an Elvis sighting during an important meeting.
- ▶ He says, "You talking to me?" at least five times per conversation.
- ▶ You agree to do her work for her if only she will go home.

A good sense of humor is not the only positive trait many people with ADD have. While ADD is a serious disability that has a huge negative impact on people's lives, most people with ADD have very positive, adaptive, enriching, and creative traits. We'll look at these in the next chapter.

◈◈◈

CHAPTER SIX

THE ATTRIBUTES OF ADD

Appreciating Your Assets

It can be a tricky balancing act to acknowledge the serious impairments of ADD without getting lost in the pathology of the condition. You are far more than your disability.

Have you noticed how some people with physical, intellectual, or mental disabilities have a tremendous capacity to adapt to life? Would they have the same level of courage and inner strength without the disability? We don't know for sure. People don't want to be disabled. However, many respond to the trauma of disability in admirable ways. They accept their disabilities as opportunities to grow and adapt, believing that the painful experience of being disabled allows them to develop a deeper sense of gratitude, meaning, and purpose.

Many people in Twelve Step programs talk about being "grateful" alcoholics or addicts. Who in their right mind would be grateful for suffering from the ravages of addiction? Most people are not grateful for the disabling, life-thrashing humiliation that heroin or alcohol brings into their lives. However, they are grateful that these addictions have led them into recovery and a renewal of their spiritual lives.

Not everyone in early recovery is grateful to be clean and sober, but as they continue to recover, many feel the gratitude of not taking a drink or a drug. They are grateful to be released from bondage. They are grateful for the gifts that recovery provides. They are grateful for the joy, healing, adventure, self-exploration, spiritual awakening, and growth of recovery.

The same is true for ADD. No one expects you to jump up and down and say how grateful you are to have ADD. But with treatment, with time to heal and to practice new skills, you will be able to accept the "by-products" or traits of ADD. And you'll begin to recognize and appreciate the assets you have that are common among people with ADD.

I frequently observe some great characteristics in people with ADD. These traits have not yet been clinically documented as having anything specifically to do with ADD, but I've witnessed them in hundreds of children and adults with amazing regularity. What you are about to read is not listed in the DSM-IV as symptomatic of ADD; the DSM-IV lists only the problematic behaviors or what is known as the pathology of each diagnosis. Yet more and more experts in the field are talking and beginning to write about the common abilities and gifts of people with ADD.

Adaptability

Adaptability is a key to living with a disability. One's capacity to adapt to a disability can create abilities others may not have. Our bodies adapt to loss and new challenges without conscious effort. For example, people without eyesight naturally depend to a greater extent on their ability to hear, smell, and touch. They also have the ability to feel the presence of people around them and have a keen sense of the placement of objects, such as doorways, curbs, steps, and furniture. These senses are more developed because of the body's need to compensate for the loss of sight. With practice and dedication, many visually impaired people learn to read Braille and graduate from college; they have families and lead fulfilling lives.

People with ADD spend their lives adapting to a disability they may not know they have. Since ADD is a hidden disability, those with ADD do not get the support they would get if they were hearing-impaired, missing a limb, or in a wheelchair. To make matters worse, their disability is viewed by others, and sometimes by themselves, as a lack of discipline, laziness, disregard for others, or stupidity. Despite these obstacles, people with ADD are creative adapters.

Some people with mild ADD get by quite well by adapting, especially when they learn which adaptations work best for them. Roberta, for example, quit high school to live in Costa Rica. She quickly learned Spanish and apprenticed with a successful silversmith. When she returned to the United States, Roberta married Blake, an exceptional businessman. Today they own a very successful jewelry import business that allows Roberta the freedom to travel and be creative.

With help and guidance, people like Roberta not only function in ways that maximize their gifts, they also let go of the disabling shame inherent in ADD. Others have more serious ADD and are unable to adapt beyond a basic survival level, no matter how hard they try. These people need their brains treated with medication. They are similar to someone with serious diabetes. If you have mild diabetes you can regulate your blood sugar with diet and exercise; but if your pancreas is no longer producing insulin, you must give yourself insulin or you will die.

Many other physical conditions, such as high blood pressure, under or overactive thyroid, depression, allergic reactions, and bacterial infections can be life-threatening without medical treatment. I am an advocate of teaching people how to improve their medical conditions without medical intervention when appropriate. However, I am also quick to recommend evaluation for medication if the situation warrants it.

Intuition

A highly developed ability to intuit is frequently one of the helpful byproducts of ADD accommodation. The sense of intuition is similar to the senses of seeing, hearing, smelling, tasting, and feeling. Intuition is your gut feeling. Since many people with ADD miss large portions of information and sensory input, they develop the ability to perceive the large picture from what bits and pieces of the puzzle their brain latches on to. Many people with ADD have great instinct. They can predict the next real estate boom, know how to market products that have not yet been invented, and anticipate others' behavior. These abilities can lead to some very creative and sometimes lucrative careers.

Western culture does not value intuition in the way many other cultures do. Western culture tends to be predominantly linear in its pattern of thinking and reasoning, and bases "truth" on facts. Our culture prizes the ability to replicate the process by which we decide something is true. We want documentation, verification, and statistics. Other cultures accept truth as individuals and groups define it. They work more from what Carl Jung called the "collective unconscious," the common themes of human beings of all cultures, whether they are Native American, Hawaiian, Greek, Chinese, Japanese, Peruvian, or African.

Many people with ADD solve problems by using a combination of knowledge, divergent thinking, and intuition. The ADD brain works something like the World Wide Web. You can enter the Web and access information from a multitude of sources in a multitude of ways. Many people with ADD have brains that scan for information like a search engine scans the Web. They assimilate information from all aspects of their environment. They learn by doing—by trying new things, taking risks, experimenting, and asking questions.

Sometimes we know things just because we know them. If you have ADD, you may possess ideas, information, and truths you can't explain. But having the correct answer is not always enough; your teacher, spouse, or employer may be more interested in the steps you took to get there. It is often quite difficult for people with ADD to explain their conclusions, because they may not understand the process that got them there. Their brains work quickly and from all directions at once. This makes the linear backtracking necessary for a scientific explanation or proof next to impossible. When your boss asks how you came to a decision, the answer "I don't know" or "It just felt right" doesn't cut it.

I can remember getting an F on a sixth-grade math test, even though all the answers were correct. When I asked the teacher why I failed the test, she replied, "You didn't show your work, so I must assume you cheated." She was not impressed by the fact that I did the problems in my head; however, she allowed me to retake the exam, showing my work. I was even more shocked and confused to get the second exam back with an F. "But I showed my work," I pleaded. Her response: "You showed your work, but you did not do the problems the way you were taught in class."

It was agonizing for me to know the answer and then go back and try to remember how I was supposed to have arrived at it. By eighth grade I had given up on math. I look back and see that my divergent thinking was getting me in trouble in a linear environment.

When we rely solely on intuition, miss key information, or deny reality, we can get ourselves into trouble. If life is too expansive, it can become chaotic. The ability to think and live in a linear fashion is important. We need linear paths to follow in order to function in our world. Yet, linear thinking is the opposite of creative thinking. Many of our divergent, creative thinkers are lost and undervalued as children in an educational system that teaches them as if they were all the same.

Uncensored Honesty

Over the years, I've met many people with ADD who are honest to the core. They tell you the truth about everything, partially because they don't have the option to censor.

Whatever they think, they say. This type of honesty can be valuable and endearing. There are some people with ADD who are loyal and incredibly trustworthy. They have a level of honesty that goes beyond answering questions truthfully. They will openly share their innermost feelings and thoughts. They tend to tell people personal information that is often helpful to others and creates rich bonds. Their honesty is refreshing and people are attracted to them. They have the ability to forge great friendships.

The flip side of uncensored honesty is brutal truthfulness. Just because something is true doesn't mean you always have to be the messenger. I wonder if the child who blurted, "The emperor has no clothes," was blessed with the uncensored honesty of childhood or if his honest statement was a result of his ADD. After all, none of the other children at the emperor's parade told the truth about what they really saw; yet this child couldn't help telling the truth.

People with uncensored honesty often reveal intimate details about their lives in situations that are not to their advantage. By doing so, they expose themselves to the negative scrutiny of others. Learning to assess a situation and counter impulses to tell the truth, the whole truth, and nothing but the truth, are highly valuable skills.

Divergent and Expansive Thinking

Divergent thinking is unique, uncharacteristic, and different. The ADD brain often detours, digresses, pinballs, and rockets into new dimensions of thinking. As mentioned earlier, this type of thinking can be distracting and chaotic, making it difficult for the person with ADD to stay focused and track information.

However, divergent thinking is also expansive, elastic, extensive, sweeping, and comprehensive. Divergent thinkers will answer a question or solve a problem by accessing a plethora of information and possibilities. They are able to sift through the multitude of information and find what they need. This style of thinking can be overwhelming and overloading for some people with ADD. All they want to access is the name of the museum they visited in Boston, yet they are bombarded with memories of Boston Commons, the conversation with the woman sitting next to them on the plane, the Orsay Museum in Paris, and suddenly find themselves singing out loud, "Orsay can you see by the dawn's early light . . . Now what was I trying to remember?" they mumble, as their brain goes into meltdown. Uncontrollable, elastic, bouncy thinking can be frustrating, confusing, and, at times, immobilizing.

As with many things in life, one person's problem can be another's solution. When you have ADD, divergent and expansive thinking can be invaluable one moment and disabling the next. Some people, however, find careers where their thinking style is essential to the work environment and greatly appreciated. Some of the best advertising and marketing campaigns are created by people with ADD. Their minds are able to expand in all directions and return with bits and pieces of seemingly unrelated ideas and information. Then they integrate these thoughts resurrected from "thought junkyards," adding fresh twists and slants to create images and ideas that are universally appreciated.

Some experts speculate that Walt Disney, Thomas Edison, the Wright Brothers, Albert Einstein, and Henry Ford had ADD. Many innovative computer start-up companies that grow into household names are staffed with divergent, expansive ADD visionaries. With good secretarial and clerical support, these men and women are exceptional in their careers. However, many of them experience problems with substance abuse, relationships, and self-esteem, in spite of their business success.

Some people with ADD describe themselves as being octagons trying to fit into square holes. If that sounds familiar, finding a compatible work environment that makes use of your thinking style can make a huge difference in your life. It's also helpful and enjoyable to find others like yourself. Pinballing—following and bouncing off each others' tangents—is great fun. Being with others who think like you is incredibly validating.

Talking and Thinking on Your Feet

ADD is so paradoxical. Some people have tremendous difficulty accessing information and presenting it quickly, while others process information so rapidly they answer questions as if playing "Name That Tune." Instead of saying, "I can name that tune in three notes," they might say, "I can answer that question hearing only the first three words." Unfortunately for them, responding after hearing only part of the question may mean they're answering the wrong question. Their impulsive eagerness to respond before hearing what is being asked leads to misunderstanding. They are sometimes viewed by others as rude and impatient "know-it-alls."

For some people, however, the ability to think and respond quickly is essential to their jobs. Some people with ADD have fine-tuned the ability to talk spontaneously and eloquently on the spur of the moment. They have either trained themselves to contain their impulsive nature or they have a type of ADD without impulsiveness. These people are excellent emergency medical professionals, police officers, negotiators, firefighters, private investigators, FBI agents, and military personnel. Their decisiveness and rapid responses save thousands of lives. They thrive on the highly stimulating excitement and danger inherent in their jobs. When they're working, they're extremely engaged and focused.

Many people who have ADD live the "thinking on one's feet" concept very literally. I've heard countless stories from clients who think best when pacing, walking, jogging, swimming, bouncing their legs, tapping their fingers, and fidgeting with pens, pencils, or whatever. Some examples of careers that can turn thinking on one's feet into an advantage are teaching, trial law, politics, public speaking, acting, preaching, and athletics.

Creativity

Creativity is an experience and expression of energy. It is the ability to cause something to exist, yet it is more than the end product of a poem, photograph, garden, music, or dance. Creativity is the internal energy we are born with that enables us to express our unconscious and conscious thoughts, feelings, and experiences in our own unique way.

Many people with ADD are highly creative. Some play music, paint, sculpt, write, dance, and sing. Others are photographers, videographers, visionaries, inventors, church youth group leaders, architects, seamstresses, mechanics, and parents. It is not a coincidence that so many people with ADD are creative. ADD characteristics that can be liabilities can also be assets, especially in situations where they are valued and encouraged.

Physicist Albert Einstein said, "Imagination is more important than knowledge." I believe that many people with ADD have heightened creativity because they can best express themselves in divergent and expansive ways. The gift of creativity gives people ways to express themselves in nonacademic, less linear and traditional ways.

The Blessing and the Curse

We are all born with creative energy that demands expression. But some children learn early in life that coloring outside the lines is wrong, that trees are not red, and sky is not green. In time, many learn that doing it like everyone else gets the best reactions from the people they want to please. What happens to creative energy? Does it just go away? No, it needs an outlet, just as does physical, emotional, sexual, spiritual, and intellectual energy.

Without expression, creative energy implodes, or blows up inside of us. Imploded energy of any type can lead to depression, physical and emotional illness, discontent, and restlessness. As American poet William Carlos Williams said, "The imagination will not down. . . . If it is not a dance, a song, it becomes an outcry, a protest. If it is not flamboyance, it becomes deformity; if it is not art, it becomes crime."[1]

The blessing of highly developed creativity is often accompanied by the curse of *having* to express it. Creative people need to create, just as physical people need to run, climb, hit, catch, or kick a ball. If the child with ADD continues to draw red trees no matter what others think, she may be able to salvage and express that creative part of herself. But if she can't find ways to express her imagination, she becomes even more frustrated, because now she's stuck. Children like her are described as having "too much" energy, imagination, and impulsivity, and not enough logic, attention, seriousness, and socialization.

The person with ADD may deal with her "stuckness" by drowning it with alcohol, numbing it with drugs, or stuffing it with food. We know this doesn't work, so what does?

I find that many of the adults I work with suffer from what I call "creative implosion." This is true of adults without ADD, but it seems to be even more prevalent for those who have ADD. If you are wired for creative expression, it's important to honor that about yourself. Support your need to create whatever your heart desires. The *process* of creating, not the outcome, is the important thing.

For some people, creating is right up there with other basic needs such as sleeping, eating, loving, and working. And some of those people are fortunate to make a living from their creative endeavors. Most of us are not so fortunate. Most of us do not get paid for exercising, yet we swim or run because it's good for us or we like doing it. The same is true with creative expression; it's good for you. You don't have to make a career out of expressing your creativity, just do it. You and the people in your life will feel better for the effort.

In the next chapter, you will have an opportunity to take an honest look at your relationship with substances and how they affect your life and the lives of those around you.

CHAPTER SEVEN

USE, ABUSE, OR ADDICTION?

Evaluating Your Relationship with Drugs and Alcohol

Picture an alcoholic. What do you see? Many people picture an old man, a skid row bum. Did you know that only a very small percentage of alcoholics are skid row drunks? So what do the vast majority look like? You and me. Many alcoholics have professional careers. They are parents, Girl Scout leaders, soccer coaches, grandparents, bank tellers, executives, ministers, police officers, therapists, brick layers . . . Alcoholics come in all sizes, ages, and genders. There is no "classic alcoholic."

Now picture a drug addict. What do you see? A grungy guy shooting heroin in an inner city slum? How about your doctor or dentist; your church pastor, rabbi, or priest; your child's teacher; the teenager who mows your lawn; the pot-smoking granny who lives next door?

Did you picture yourself? Do you think of yourself as a social drinker or recreational drug user? Could you be dependent on alcohol or other drugs? Could you be addicted to one or a combination?

Your family, friends, and professionals may have their opinions about your relationship with drugs and alcohol, but in the end you are the only one who can honestly answer the question, "Am I using, abusing, or addicted?" In this chapter, you will learn the difference between experimental use, social or recreational use, abuse, and addiction. You will hear stories from people who have been there.

I struggled with these questions for longer than I care to admit. I'd like to spare you that struggle and help you get an accurate perspective on your involvement with substances. The purpose of this chapter is not to label you or make you feel bad about yourself. You've already experienced that. You deserve to feel better and live your life to the fullest. If drugs and alcohol are affecting how you live and how you feel, you may want to take a closer look at your relationship with these substances. If you are already in recovery from substance abuse, you may wish just to skim this chapter or move on to the next chapter on how people self-medicate their ADD.

Addictions are not issues of character and morality. Like ADD, addictions are rooted in your genetics, biology, and family history. They are activated by trauma, stress, life circumstances, and learned behaviors. Both ADD and addictions are characterized by loss of control.

This chapter gives you the opportunity to answer questions regarding your involvement with substances and how they affect your life and the people around you. The following questions are not standardized research tools to give you a precise clinical evaluation as to the effects of your use of substances; they are meant to help you evaluate your relationship with drugs and alcohol in general. I have divided the questions into six areas that substance use can affect: work or school, relationships, health, finances, the law, and self-esteem. Answer the questions as honestly as you can; no one is grading you.

Is Your Substance Use Causing You Problems?
Please answer yes or no to the following questions:

At Work or School

_____ Is your work or school performance suffering as a result of your substance use?

_____ Are you avoiding work or school because of your substance use?

_____ Have you received feedback from employers or teachers who are concerned that you may have a drug or alcohol problem?

_____ Do you feel that if you weren't using substances you could perform better at work or school?

_____ Do you feel that using substances helps you perform better at work or at school?

_____ Do you live in fear of others finding out how much you drink or use drugs?

_____ Does your effectiveness decrease because you are hung over?

_____ Do you drink or use drugs before or during work or school?

_____ Have you dropped out of school or are you presently unemployed as a result of your substance use?

_____ Do you drink or use drugs during your lunch time?

_____ Have you had an on-the-job injury while you were under the influence of substances?

_____ Have you been fired or asked to resign as a result of your substance use?

_____ Does your substance use affect your duties at home?

You may be someone whose substance use has not yet affected your work or school, or you may be painfully aware of how your career and education have suffered. Many people with addictions are able to hold themselves together during working hours and continue educational pursuits for a period of time. However, since addictions are progressive, it may be only a matter of time before your work is affected.

In retrospect, many recovering alcoholics and addicts realize they have stayed in jobs below their abilities because they were often under the influence or hung over. Others feel they were passed over for promotions, lived in fear of losing their jobs, and were in denial about how their addictions affected their work.

Many young people experience substance related problems as early as elementary school. In these cases it's difficult to separate the role ADD plays when looking at substance related problems, but drug and alcohol use eventually make ADD worse for children, adolescents, and adults who are trying to learn.

Substance abuse and addictions contribute greatly to the soaring high school and college dropout rates. I've worked with many bright, talented individuals who didn't finish their education as a direct result of addictions. Recovery offers some a second chance to pursue their education, as well as careers and families; others, however, feel only the grief of their missed opportunities.

Your Relationships with Family, Friends, Coworkers

0=never   1=sometimes   2=frequently   3=often

_____ Does your drinking or drug use negatively affect your relationships?

_____ Do you avoid relationships in order to drink and use drugs as you please?

_____ Do people in your life express their concern or anger about your use of substances?

_____ Is it hard for you to be present in relationships with others?

_____ Do you put drugs and alcohol before your relationships?

_____ Do you regret things you say and do to the people in your life when under the influence of drugs or alcohol?

_____ Do you sometimes forget conversations or actions?

_____ Do you put yourself at risk by engaging in risky sexual behaviors while under the influence?

_____ Have you lost or left a significant relationship because of your drinking or drug use?

_____ Has your substance abuse cost you relationships?

_____ Do you argue and fight more when under the influence or when hung over?

_____ Is your parenting affected by your substance use?

When people become addicted to a substance, they develop a relationship with that substance. Their relationship with alcohol, pot, cocaine, nicotine, amphetamines, or narcotics becomes more important than their relationships with people. No one starts drinking or using drugs with the intention of becoming so addicted that alcohol or drugs are more important than a spouse, children, parents, and friends. Addictions, however, are so powerful that addicts frequently end up alone, feeling that their only friend is the substance that is actually killing them. The addictive substance can become more important than life itself.

Addicts may be physically present but emotionally absent. They may be obsessed with thoughts about getting loaded or they may be engaged in behaviors necessary to get loaded; they may be under the influence or feeling the physical and emotional pain that results from hangovers and withdrawals. This doesn't leave much time to have relationships with people.

What's Happening to Your Health?

Please answer yes or no to the following questions:

_____ Do you experience hangovers?

_____ Do you suffer from stomach problems, chronic headaches, shakiness, obesity, high blood pressure, lung infections, or liver problems?

_____ Have medical professionals expressed concerns about your use of substances?

_____ Do you minimize or exclude information about the amount and frequency of your drug and alcohol use when talking with your doctor?

_____ Have you been putting off a physical exam for fear of learning the damage your use of drugs or alcohol has caused?

_____ Do you use drugs and alcohol to relieve anxiety, stress, help you sleep, or decrease emotional or physical pain?

_____ Have you injured yourself while high or hung over?

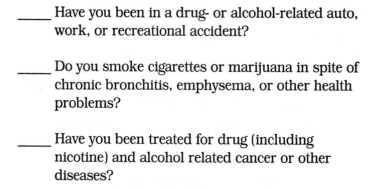

_____ Have you been in a drug- or alcohol-related auto, work, or recreational accident?

_____ Do you smoke cigarettes or marijuana in spite of chronic bronchitis, emphysema, or other health problems?

_____ Have you been treated for drug (including nicotine) and alcohol related cancer or other diseases?

Drug and alcohol addictions take a tremendous toll on your body. If you're young, you may not have yet experienced the damaging physical effects of addictions. Addictions affect your body by causing and contributing to diseases such as high blood pressure, heart disease, and cancer, which may not show up for several years.

Substance abuse and addictions cause damage to vital organs such as the liver, lungs, pancreas, heart, brain, and kidneys. Ronald Kotulak, in his book *Inside the Brain,* wrote: "One out of four hospital patients has an illness brought on by drinking. Alcohol accounts for one out of every twenty deaths in this country."[1] Drugs and alcohol also contribute to accidents that result in anything from a few stitches to broken bones, paralysis, or death. Addictions can also cause you to feel sluggish in mind and body, which in turn decreases your desire and ability to exercise.

Alcoholics and addicts commonly suffer from malnutrition and depletion of essential vitamins and minerals. Drugs and alcohol often take the place of nutritious food. Proper nutrition and good self-care often take a back seat to using substances. Many addicts are either in denial or unaware of the damage their addictions are causing until it's too late.

Money Troubles

Please answer yes or no to the following questions:

_____ Has your drinking or drug use cost you money in the form of fines, DUI classes, attorney fees, medical treatment, divorce, or business losses?

_____ Do you spend more of your income than you would like on drugs or alcohol?

_____ Have you borrowed money to buy drugs or alcohol?

_____ Have you compromised yourself or your values to obtain alcohol or drugs?

_____ Do you overspend or lose money when you are under the influence?

_____ Would you be in better financial shape if you didn't drink or use drugs?

Financial trouble can go hand in hand with addictions, although not everyone must navigate these troubled waters. Some addicts and alcoholics are able to stay afloat and can even be financially successful. However, many who suffer from addictions experience financial ruin, which not only affects them but their families as well. Maintaining cocaine, heroin, amphetamine, narcotic, marijuana, and even alcohol and nicotine addictions are costly. Some people create huge debt that costs them their homes and possessions.

The financial loss of addictions goes even deeper than supporting a habit. Some pay huge sums to defend themselves or family members against legal charges related to drug possession or sales. Others spend everything they have in attempts to stay out of prison for crimes like driving under the influence, vehicular manslaughter, domestic violence, child abuse, and robbery. Still others make poor investments or lose businesses because of their addictions.

Legal Problems

Please answer yes or no to the following questions:

_____ Have you ever been arrested for driving under the influence?

_____ Have you ever been arrested for any alcohol or drug violation?

_____ Have you committed a crime while under the influence?

_____ Have you committed crimes to pay for drugs or alcohol?

_____ Have you had legal problems because of poor judgment due to drinking and drug use?

_____ Do you put yourself at physical or legal risk in order to obtain drugs or alcohol?

_____ Are you doing anything in your life now that is illegal?

We've touched on the financial impact of legal problems related to substance abuse, but let's go into more detail about what can happen when you're addicted or abusing substances. You may be the kind of alcoholic or addict who hasn't yet encountered the law. If you are, please don't use your "good luck" to deny that drugs and alcohol are creating problems in your life.

More common is the person who has been arrested for driving under the influence (DUI). As this occurrence has become more unacceptable, the penalties have become more expensive and more severe. Gone are the days of a warning and citation. You can go to jail for a DUI, even if there was no accident and no injuries. Juries are less tolerant of offenders and are imposing tougher prison sentences for repeat DUI offenders.

Ronald Kotulak quotes psychopharmacologist Klaus Miczek of Tufts University as saying that "one of the overwhelming statistics that should impress everybody is the fact that about 60 percent of all violent acts, whether murders, child abuse, family abuse, assault, or felonies are associated with the consumption of alcohol."[2] The mixture of cocaine and alcohol is particularly dangerous to families. When people get drunk, their thinking and judgment is impaired and they can become irrational, paranoid, and violent. If they continue to drink, they are eventually rendered helpless and pass out. But if they're also using cocaine or amphetamines, they have the drug-induced energy to perpetrate drunken violence on themselves and others. An extremely high percentage of prison inmates readily admits that if not for their alcohol and drug use, they would not be incarcerated.

You don't need to be selling drugs to be arrested; just being in a place where drugs are used can land you in jail. Some addicts resort to robberies, burglaries, car thefts, or snatching purses. Others support their habit with white collar crimes such as embezzlement (a fancy word for stealing money) and large-scale drug import and sales businesses. The even greater crime is drug use and sales on school grounds. Kids and teenagers become addicted before they even know what hit them, which leads to a fresh crop of addicts. And so it goes.

Self-Esteem: How Do You Feel About Yourself?

Please answer yes or no to the following questions:

_____ Do you feel bad about your drug and alcohol use?

_____ Do you try to keep your use of substances a secret?

_____ Is it hard for you to forgive yourself for the ways you have treated others?

_____ Do you feel ashamed of yourself?

_____ Do you suffer from periods of self-loathing?

_____ Have you tried to stop drinking or using drugs, only to relapse?

_____ Have you ever felt demoralized or humiliated by your behavior?

_____ Do you suffer from remorse or regret as a result of your use of substances?

_____ Have you ever attempted suicide while under the influence?

_____ Have you felt so bad about your substance use that suicide felt like an option?

_____ Do you feel guilty if you lie about your drinking and drug use?

_____ Is your use of substances contributing to feelings of low self-worth?

_____ Do you feel powerless to stop using drugs and alcohol?

It's hard to feel good about yourself when you're help-less and out of control. We would rather feel shame, anger, guilt, self-loathing, or anything other than our powerless-ness to stop our addictions. Every day that you swear to yourself or to God that you won't drink or use drugs, and then you do, causes you to feel worse about yourself. The vicious cycle of abstinence and relapse creates tremendous feelings of shame, depression, despair, and hopelessness. These powerful feelings have led many alcoholics and addicts to take their own lives.

Over the years I've witnessed the loss of too many alcoholics and addicts who committed suicide because they couldn't maintain their sobriety. I've also felt the loss of those who killed themselves while in recovery because they weren't able to forgive themselves for things they had done, or couldn't deal with their feelings of guilt, shame, and self-hatred. Many had been in recovery for years but were suffering from untreated depression and sometimes ADD. The tragedy is that with proper treatment they could still be with us as clean and sober, productive members of our families and communities.

LOOK AT YOURSELF

Now that you've finished answering the questions, sit back and look at your yes answers. The more yes answers you have, the greater the chance that you have an addiction.

If you continue to use substances in spite of problems at work or school, in your relationships, with finances, the law, your health, and your self-esteem, you are addicted. If numerous attempts to control and modify your substance use haven't worked over the long haul, you are addicted. Addiction is a powerful physical and emotional disease that willpower alone cannot conquer.

If you're not sure if you have an addiction, it's a good idea to talk with a professional who can help you look at your use in more detail. Some people need to keep abusing substances until it gets so bad they can no longer deny their problem.

William Blake, the eighteenth-century English poet, said, "If the fool would persist in his folly, he would become wise." In other words, if you keep participating in damaging behavior, you may eventually realize your "folly" and seek help. However, you don't have to lose your relationships or job, hurt or kill someone while driving intoxicated, or humiliate yourself or your family in order to "become wise" enough to get help. You also don't have to live with the degradation and humiliation of your addictions. You can get help now.

If you can't stop drinking or using drugs, you need help. You don't deserve to live the way you are living. You deserve recovery. Understanding more about the disease of addiction may help you understand why willpower alone will not keep you clean and sober.

DISEASE OR WEAKNESS?

For hundreds of years, alcoholics and drug addicts were thrown into dungeons or jails, locked up in mental institutions, or executed. Unfortunately, even today too many alcoholics and addicts are treated only as criminals and not for the disease that contributes to their criminal behavior.

In the early 1930s, William D. Silkworth, M.D., wrote that "the action of alcohol on these chronic alcoholics is a manifestation of an allergy; that the phenomenon of craving is limited to this class and never occurs in the average temperate drinker."[3] In 1960, Dr. E. M. Jellinek wrote the book that would help change our understanding of alcoholism. In *The Disease Concept of Alcoholism*, Dr. Jellinek stated that alcoholism was caused by a biological sensitivity to alcohol, which could be inborn. He also spoke of the psychological influences that contribute to alcoholism. Dr. Jellinek's work was a springboard for more scientific research into the roots of addictions.

Today, researchers have located several biological origins of addictions, such as deficiencies in neurotransmitters and the genes that cause these imbalances. Even with all this understanding there is still stigma, shame, and misunderstanding about the diseases of alcoholism and other addictions. The rest of this chapter will give you insight into addiction and help you determine if you need to seek treatment.

LOSS OF CONTROL

When you have ADD, you don't always have control over your attention, impulses, or activity level. The same is true with substance abuse and dependency. You lose the ability not only to control your intake, but to control your behavior.

No one starts out the day thinking, "Maybe I'll go out and get arrested for driving under the influence tonight." Nobody thinks, "I'm going to get so stoned at lunch that I'll spend a half hour talking to the vegetables at the grocery store."

What happens is that some people start out drinking or using drugs to have a good time, relax, feel more social, or alter their feelings. In time, they lose control. They not only lose control over how much they drink or use, they lose control over their impulses, behavior, and judgment. Once the chemical is in their bodies, they can't stop. The same is true for those with behavioral addictions like gambling or compulsive spending.

Untreated ADD and addictive behavior can become a vicious cycle. Loss of control breeds shame. The desire to avoid feeling shame can create a craving for more drugs or addictive behaviors, which in turn leads to more loss of control.

How much and how often you drink alcohol, smoke pot, snort cocaine, shoot heroin, take amphetamines, eat sugar, drink coffee, or smoke cigarettes is not as important as what happens when you put these substances in your body. Do you lose control? Do you drink or use more than you intend? Is it hard or impossible for you to stop drinking or using drugs in spite of the pain they are causing you and the people you love?

Have you ever quit smoking and later turned to a cigarette for consolation during a time of crisis, then not been able to stop? This is loss of control. Once you lose control over a substance, you will never regain it. For you, the first puff, drink, donut, pill, or line of cocaine will awaken the addictive dragon that sleeps restlessly in your brain. Abstinence keeps the dragon slumbering, but when the addictive substance enters your system, the beast raises its ugly head and roars, "More!" This doesn't always happen the moment you take a drink or a drug. You may get away with it for a while, but eventually you will lose control and become consumed by your addiction.

Why Doesn't Everyone Become Addicted?

There are a variety of reasons why one person becomes addicted and another doesn't. No single cause for addiction exists; rather, a combination of factors is usually involved. Genetic predisposition, neurochemistry, family history, trauma, life stress, and other physical and emotional problems contribute. Part of what determines who becomes addicted and who doesn't is the combination and timing of these factors. You may have a genetic predisposition for alcohol, but if you choose not to drink you will not become an alcoholic. The same is true for drug addictions. If you never smoke pot, snort cocaine, shoot or smoke heroin, you will never become a pot, coke, or heroin addict.

Unfortunately, potentially addictive behaviors such as eating, spending, working, and sex can't realistically be avoided. Food addictions are by far the hardest addictions to heal, because you have to learn to moderate and eliminate certain foods. Since you have to eat several times a day to stay healthy, this can be very difficult.

"Just Say No" may sound simple, but if it were, we wouldn't have millions of children, adolescents, and adults using drugs every day. For some their biological and emotional attraction to drugs is so powerful that they don't think much about the risks. This is especially true for the person with ADD who may have an affinity for risky, stimulating experiences. This also applies to the person with

ADD who is physically and emotionally suffering from untreated ADD restlessness, impulsiveness, low energy, shame, attention and organization problems, and a wide range of social pain.

THE POWER OF GENETIC INHERITANCE

Scientists have noted differences in the brains of alcoholics and nonalcoholics. In the late 1970s, the P3 factor study brought to light genetic implications for alcoholism through the comparison of brain waves. In one group were seven- to thirteen-year-old boys who had never drunk alcohol or taken drugs, even though their fathers were alcoholics. These boys were compared to boys whose fathers were not alcoholics. A brain wave known as P300 was smaller in the boys of alcoholic fathers than in their peers whose fathers were not alcoholic.[4] The evidence drawn from this study was that brain differences were inherited, and that these differences were present before the child ever took a drink.

Since then, genetic markers indicating differences in the D2 receptor sites have added to the evidence that addictions are inherited (see Chapter Four for more detail on genetic transmission of ADD and addictions). Even if we were to choose to disregard scientific findings, it's hard to deny that addictions run in families. All you have to do is take a family history of someone with a chemical or behavioral addiction to see addictions growing like a choker vine down the family tree.

We Repeat What We Learn

If you grew up in a family where drugs, alcohol, or food were used to soothe, numb, or forget problems, you learned that this was how adults handled the challenges of life. Alcohol and drug use may have been such an important part of your family life that you just assumed all families were like yours. You accepted crazy, addictive, or dysfunctional behavior as normal. This process of normalizing the abnormal contributes to the repetition of addictions and other behaviors from one generation to the next.

I remember a client telling me she spent as much time as possible with her best friend's family when she was in high school because she couldn't stand the alcoholic chaos at her home. "I was so surprised when I started staying at Mindy's house," she said, "because no one drank. My parents and their friends were always drinking. Mindy's family would play Scrabble and Monopoly after dinner, and her father helped us with our homework. I just assumed that all families were like mine—drinking, fighting, and sitting in front of the TV."

If you grew up in a family with heavy drinking and drug use, you will be more likely to adopt these practices yourself. The genetic component is so strong that if your grandparents had addiction problems and you grew up in a family without substance abuse, you are still at risk of becoming addicted.

PUSHED OVER THE EDGE

People without genetic predisposition toward addictions can also become addicted. No one knows exactly how much use of a particular substance will push a person over the line from social or recreational use to addiction. The amount differs for each of us.

Trauma is one factor that can cause us to abuse substances and become addicted to drugs, alcohol, and food. We've observed this over the years with veterans of the Vietnam and Gulf wars. Many were severely traumatized by their experiences. They also lived under constant stress. Many of these men and women came home with addictions and a disorder known as posttraumatic stress disorder (PTSD). PTSD is caused by being subjected to stress beyond the realm of normal human experience.

You don't have to go to war to experience the symptoms of PTSD—nightmares, intrusive recollections of trauma, anxiety, jumpiness, and severely impaired concentration. Survivors of child abuse, sexual assault, serious accidents, and natural disasters also suffer from PTSD.

PTSD differs from ADD in that the symptoms are related to trauma, whereas ADD is a pervasive part of a person's entire life. It's understandable why some people try to self-medicate their PTSD symptoms with alcohol and drugs.

You don't have to suffer from PTSD to seek relief from stress. Stress is inherent in everyday life. Some people decrease stress by changing their lifestyle. I have a friend who was a very successful tax accountant in a large metropolitan city. After suffering a heart attack at age forty-six, he moved to Maui and set up a small accounting practice that supports his more economical lifestyle.

Not everyone can live in paradise, and people with ADD can be stressed out whether they live in L.A. or the Caribbean. For the person with ADD, it takes a phenomenal amount of energy to get out the door in the morning. The ADD person may be disorganized, chronically rushed, and overly dependent on external deadlines and time crunches to stay on track. Life just seems to be harder for him or her.

Many of us are so used to living with "off the scale" stress that we can hardly function without it. When life calms down, we create stress just to feel normal. Many people with ADD are stress addicts; a part of them enjoys the stimulation of being in stressful situations. Some even make a career out of their addiction to stress by becoming emergency medical personnel, firefighters, police officers, and schoolteachers. Many find themselves desperately self-medicating their stress with addictive substances and behaviors.

CHASING THE MAGIC

As human beings we can abuse anything from ice cream to nicotine, but for now, when I say drugs, I mean alcohol, marijuana, cocaine, amphetamines, heroin, psychedelic drugs, nicotine, and caffeine. I am also referring to pre-scription narcotics such as Vicodin, Percocet, Talwin, codeine, Fiorinal, Demerol, and morphine, as well as tran-quilizers like Valium, Xanax, and Ativan, and sleeping pills such as Dalmane and Restoril. For the addict, these drugs seem to scratch an itch the nonaddicted person doesn't even feel. A drug's ability to relieve emotional pain and cre-ate feelings of well-being becomes so powerful that the addict will risk everything to get it.

For some, that first encounter with alcohol and drugs was magic, even if they threw up all over themselves and their date. Something very "special" happens to the alco-holic-in-the-making that doesn't happen to those who grow up to be social drinkers. Have you ever wondered why some kids you knew got drunk, got sick, and didn't drink again for many years, while you—regard-less of the many deals you made with God or how much trouble you got into—couldn't wait until the next time you could get drunk? Alcohol did something for you that made it worth the pain you suffered just so you could drink again and again and again. Eventually, your body not only got used to the toxins that initially made you sick, it craved them.

I frequently hear stories from adults in recovery who describe in graphic detail the first time they drank alcohol or took drugs. Many were small children who were sick, and their parents gave them a bit of whiskey with sugar to stop a cough, relieve a toothache, or help them sleep. This is not a recommended practice today, but many small chil-dren took their first drink from a parent or relative. Some remember the first time they took cough medicine that contained codeine and alcohol.

I'm amazed at how vivid are the memories of a first encounter with alcohol and drugs for many people, even if the incident occurred forty years ago. They say things like:

"For the first time in my life I felt calm."

"I had never felt so good before. I wanted more."

125

"I fell in love with how alcohol made me feel and spent the rest of my life trying to capture that feeling again."

"Cough syrup tasted awful, but it made me feel so wonderful that I tried to catch coughs from my brothers and sisters."

"My mind stopped chattering. It became quiet and so did I. It was magic."

The problem is that addicts and alcoholics can spend the rest of their lives desperately searching for that "magic." They hunt for it in a bottle, a joint, pills, or a syringe. The feelings are never as good as the first few times they used. In time, using drugs and alcohol makes them feel worse. Yet some alcoholics and addicts chase the elusive magic up to and through the "gates of insanity or death."

Not all alcoholics and addicts lie about how much they drink or use drugs. Sometimes they aren't aware of just how much they are actually consuming. While working in a DUI program, I noticed that almost everyone who was arrested for a DUI had consumed only three drinks. *What a coincidence!* I thought.

I soon realized I needed to ask more specific questions about the size of the container, what type of alcohol they were drinking, how often, and what happened when they drank. Were we talking about a seven-ounce wine glass or a sixteen-ounce tumbler? Did they use a shot glass or the "pour to the top of the tumbler" method? Did they buy their alcohol by the pint, quart, case, or shopping cart?

Martin's story is similar to many I heard when I questioned first offender DUI clients. The answer to the first question was almost always the same. From there, we would follow a sort of script, much like this conversation with Martin.

"How much do you drink?" I asked.

"Not much," Martin responded.

"Do you drink every day?"

"Not really."

"What do you drink?"

"Just beer."

"How many beers do you drink in a day?"

"Three."

"Do you ever drink more than three beers in a day?"

"No, I don't have a drinking problem."

"Do you drink eight ounces, sixteen ounces, or quarts?"

"I drink talls."

"Sixteen ounce?"

"I guess."

"How do you buy your beer?"

"I pick it up after work."

"Do you buy it by the case?"

"No, I only buy a six-pack."

"Do you stop at the liquor store every night?"

"Yes, just about."

"Let me make sure I have this straight. Every night after work you buy a six-pack of sixteen-ounce tall beers."

"Yes," he said.

"And every night you go home and drink three beers?"

"Right."

"Is there anyone else who drinks the beers with you?"

"No. I live alone."

"So, if every night you buy six beers and every night you drink only three, you must have a refrigerator filled with beer."

Martin looked at me with sincere confusion. He honestly had no idea that he was drinking a six-pack, or ninety-six ounces of beer, every night. Martin is what is known as a maintenance alcoholic.

Maintenance Addicts

There are people who have smoked pot almost daily for years. Others, like Martin, drink almost daily. They need the drug in their system to function and to avoid the pain of withdrawal. Many do not realize this until they try to stop. When they do stop, they may experience physical and emotional withdrawal symptoms. They may experience powerful cravings. Their minds and bodies scream for relief. They are plagued by obsessions. They can't stop thinking about getting loaded. Without help, physical and emotional cravings lead people back to their addictions. That's why many people live on the treadmill of stopping and starting.

We can find clever ways to rationalize or minimize our behavior, especially self-destructive and addictive behavior. The voice of the addict inside tells us things like, "You can handle it. You haven't smoked for a week. What's the big deal? You don't really drink that much. You can snort just one line of coke. You'll quit tomorrow." Before you know it, that one glass of wine has turned into a gallon; the line has become a gram; the one hit has burnt up a lid.

The Periodic User
The periodic alcoholic and addict usually has a difficult time maintaining abstinence. Periodic users may not drink or use drugs for weeks, months, or even years. But when they do, they lose control. They may lose control with a one-time bout with substances, or they may binge. A binge is when you drink or use drugs and can't stop. Binges are usually interrupted by external forces, such as the police, family members, or medical professionals. Binge addicts may snort cocaine until they are too physically ill to get more. Binge eaters will eat until they are too ill to eat another bite or, in some cases, they will purge themselves by vomiting, as in the case of bulimia.

Many periodic addicts suffer from the illusion that they can control their use because they can attain periods of abstinence. They're proud of the fact that they don't drink every day. In their minds, only people who drink or use drugs daily are addicted. Therefore, they believe they do not have a problem. And that is a serious problem.

I Drank Three Times in Twenty Years

Samuel is a good example of how dangerous alcohol can
be for the periodic alcoholic. Samuel will tell you his story.

I quit drinking when I was twenty-five years old. My
life was a mess, and I knew it was because of my
drinking. It wasn't that hard to quit drinking. I
didn't need any help. I just quit. It was no big deal.

Six years later I was feeling great. My wife and I
had two kids and my career was on the rise. One
day I was having a business lunch with a new client.
He encouraged me to have a glass of French wine he
had ordered. *Why not?* I thought. *I haven't had a
drinking problem for years.*

I had forgotten just how much I enjoyed a good
glass of wine, so I ordered another bottle. I drank
most of that bottle by myself as my potential client
ate his lunch. I was feeling pretty good by now and
suggested we have a drink or two in the bar. I
ordered a double scotch on the rocks while Mr.
Social Drinker had a soda. By late afternoon my
not-so-potential client had left for his office.

The next thing I remember was the sound of the
saw they used to cut me out of my car. I somehow
survived, even though the car engine was in my lap.
I didn't drink again for ten years.

The next time I drank was on New Year's Eve.
This time I quickly got drunk and became convinced that our family friend was making a pass at
my wife. I woke up in jail, having been arrested for
assault and battery. I had ruined the party, broken
my hand, and my friend's arm. My wife told me she
would leave me if I ever drank again.

The last time I drank was three years later. My
wife left me as promised. This time I got help. I
have been sober for twelve years now. The difference this time is that I have no illusion that I can

ever drink again. I spend time with a group of people who remind me of that. Thank God, my wife is back in my life. She too reminds me that I am an alcoholic. Today I know that no matter how long I go without a drink, one drink will be too many.

CONTINUUM OF SUBSTANCE USE

I like to look at people's involvement with drugs and alcohol on a continuum of use like the one below. Starting with abstinence, I will discuss each stage briefly, moving through experimental use, social use, abuse, and addictions.

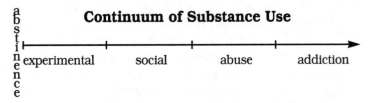

Abstinence
Abstinence means that you abstain, or do not use a substance. You may abstain from coffee, tobacco, cigarettes, sugar, alcohol, heroin, or other substances for short periods of time or for the rest of your life. Abstinence is a choice; even if you're locked up in prison you can get drugs if you want them.

Some people abstain for religious, cultural, or medical reasons. Others may have learned from the pain of loving someone who is addicted and have decided not to risk ending up on that path themselves. For some, abstinence is the only answer if they want to live. More and more, people are choosing to abstain from nicotine, alcohol, and drugs because they want to be more healthy.

Experimentation
Experimental use is experimenting with alcohol or other drugs once or twice. Experimenting with marijuana means smoking it one or two times, whether you inhale or not.

Taking LSD, peyote, psychedelic mushrooms, or snorting cocaine once or twice is experimenting to see how these drugs affect you.

Frequently, parents are convinced that their adolescent son or daughter is experimenting with drugs. When these parents describe several occasions when their child was under the influence or got himself into trouble at school, home, or with the law, what they are describing is drug abuse or possibly addiction, not experimentation.

There can be consequences to experimental use. Young people are especially vulnerable to losing control and getting hurt or getting in trouble the first time they experiment with a drug. This is especially true for adolescents and adults with ADD. The thrill-seeking behavior and impulsiveness of ADD combined with an inexperienced drug user can be a deadly combination.

For the most part, experimental use usually does not lead to serious consequences. The young person experiments, feels what it's like, and doesn't need or choose to repeat the experience.

Social and Recreational

Social drinkers and recreational users drink or use drugs at social occasions with other people. They do not drink or use drugs to get loaded; they drink to celebrate at a wedding, graduation, or birthday party. They rarely lose control and do not undergo major personality changes. Social drinkers are the kind of people who may leave half a glass of beer or wine at the table when they leave. They don't feel the need to finish it, because they're drinking alcohol as a beverage, not a drug.

A recreational drug user may take a hit or two off a marijuana joint every once in a while. This kind of person may smoke a cigarette now and again at a party and not feel any compulsion to smoke again. Some of these recreational users may use psychedelic drugs as part of a ritual or celebration on rare occasions. Their drug use is more about connecting with others and with themselves than disconnecting from themselves and others.

Social drinkers and recreational users don't experience blackout, become violent, obnoxious, or try to seduce the bride or groom at the wedding. If a social drinker experiences a problem as a result of drinking too much, he or she will be cautious not to drink that much again. Social drinkers not only learn from their mistakes with alcohol, they are able to control themselves and not get into difficulties again.

Cynthia, who is a social broccoli eater, is a good model for social use. Cynthia likes broccoli and enjoys eating it. She doesn't spend time thinking about broccoli, nor does she seek out people who are likely to have broccoli. If she is invited to dinner, she doesn't call the host to make sure that broccoli will be served, already deciding that if it isn't, she won't go. She doesn't have to restrict her broccoli eating to weekends only.

When Cynthia is at a social occasion where broccoli is served, she doesn't eat so much broccoli that she embarrasses herself. Cynthia doesn't shop at different grocery stores to conceal how much broccoli she eats. And she doesn't hide the bags and little ties that come with broccoli at the bottom of the garbage can. If Cynthia found out she was allergic to broccoli and could never eat it again, she would not plunge into panic and deep despair. Why? Because Cynthia is a social broccoli eater.

Abuse

Drug and alcohol abuse means trouble. You are not drinking or taking a puff to celebrate at an event or social occasion. You are using to alter your thinking or feelings. You may be drinking and using drugs to numb your feelings, help you to forget your pain, or make yourself feel better or at least different. People with untreated ADD are at high risk to want to do all of the above and may not have the impulse control necessary to regulate their intake and behavior.

With abuses come consequences. Consequences can involve legal or financial problems, relationship difficulties, problems at work or school, low self-esteem, and health problems. Some people can abuse substances temporarily as a result of a life event or stressor. With minimal help they are able to abstain and even go back to true social drinking once they've worked through the situation that caused their pain, depression, or stress. Once they deal honestly with the underlying problems, they're able to stop medicating themselves with substances.

Many people like to think they've only abused drugs or alcohol and are not addicted. They hope to learn to control their substance use and become social or recreational users. This will be impossible if they have never really been social or recreational users. Some people simply lack the ability to drink or use drugs socially. Their bodies are predisposed to addiction.

Addiction
Addiction and dependency are the same thing. Some prefer the phrase chemical dependency; others prefer alcoholism or drug addiction. What you call it is not as important as what you do about it. With addiction comes loss of control. You may be a daily or maintenance alcoholic or addict, or you may not drink or use drugs regularly. If you lose control over your use and cannot stop using in spite of the consequences in your life, you are addicted.

THE UNIQUE CHARACTERISTICS OF ADDICTION

Addiction differs from abuse in three ways. With addiction comes increases or decreases in tolerance; emotional or physical withdrawal; and obsessive thoughts and compulsive behaviors.

Tolerance

Drugs, including alcohol and nicotine, are substances that our bodies initially want to reject. In other words, they are substances for which we have no tolerance. For the most part, straight alcohol doesn't taste good and our bodies won't tolerate it. This is why many people combine gin and tequila with sweet mixes. Makers of sweet fruit wines and wine coolers use a similar strategy with their products, which can be especially attractive to children and teenagers.

Many people report feeling nauseated and dizzy the first time they smoke a cigarette. In all these cases, the body's natural response to the toxin is to reject it. Yet the effects of alcohol, nicotine, and other drugs are so powerful and so attractive that many people will override the body's desire to rid itself of toxic substances.

People don't consciously tell themselves that when they grow up they want to be an addict. Even with strong family histories of addiction, many deny that they can become addicted. And so most people begin by using substances to have a good time, to be like their peers, and to forget their problems.

Eventually, the user finds that it takes more drinks, pills, puffs, or lines to get high. When it takes more and more of the substance to obtain the desired effect, we say the person has developed a tolerance to the chemical. As substance abuse moves into addiction, people who have developed a tolerance must use more alcohol or drugs just to feel normal, and they no longer receive as much pleasure from the substance. Eventually, addicts experience withdrawal symptoms if they are not under the influence. At this point, they are compulsively using the substance to keep from experiencing withdrawal.

I've observed over the years that some people who are predisposed to addictions start out with a greater than average tolerance. These are the teenagers who outdrink their peers and end up driving their sick and passed out friends home. Their tolerance for drugs and alcohol will continue to increase over the years. At some point, depending on the health of their bodies, their tolerance may decrease. In the latter stages of addiction, people may snort very little cocaine, drink small amounts of alcohol, smoke less pot, and yet get very intoxicated, because their bodies can no longer process the toxin.

Withdrawal

When the addict's substance or chemical is taken away, he or she will go into withdrawal. Withdrawal symptoms are physically and emotionally painful. They vary, depending on the specific drug, the amount of the drug the addict has been using, and the duration of use. It seems to be much harder for someone who has smoked two packs of cigarettes with a high nicotine content each day for thirty years to give up the addiction than for someone who has smoked less than half a pack of "light" cigarettes per day for a few years.

The physical withdrawal symptoms of most drugs pass within a few days to a week. Drugs such as marijuana, which are stored in the fat cells of the body, take longer to leave the system, causing a longer duration of withdrawal symptoms. Other drugs, such as Valium, also stay in the system for a long time, thus increasing the period of withdrawal. Emotional and psychological craving can last long after the physical effects of withdrawal have passed.

Obsessive Thoughts and Compulsive Actions

Addictions are progressive; they get worse over time. Addictions progress even if you have been abstinent for months or years. I listen carefully to people who have relapsed after many years of recovery. Many of them report that their addiction was much worse when they went back to it.

With addictions come obsessions and compulsions. You find yourself constantly thinking about using drugs or alcohol. You can't stop thinking about it, no matter how hard you try. The obsession takes on a life of its own and becomes the set-up for the compulsion.

There's a saying frequently heard at Twelve Step meetings: "Insanity is doing the same thing over and over and expecting different results." A compulsion occurs when you repeat the same behavior over and over. For the addict, the compulsion is fed by taking the first sip, cooking the first spoon of heroin, snorting the first line of coke, taking the first pill, or inhaling the first puff.

Now, take a moment, if you like, and go back to the Continuum of Substance Use on page 130. Mark with a pencil or pen or put your finger on the spot where you fall on the continuum. You are the only one who can honestly place yourself. You are the only one who can accept where you are today.

DENIAL

We tend to think of denial as a bad thing—the blinding force that prevents people from seeing the obvious. Denial, however, can be good. It keeps us from being constantly aware of the fragility of our lives. Denial provides us with the emotional buffer necessary to survive traumas. Without denial, we might suffer from disabling anxiety as a result of living in a world with nuclear weapons. Denial helps us deal only with what we are able to handle when we are able to handle it. Denial would not be a part of our consciousness if it did not serve an essential function.

Too much of anything, no matter how essential for survival, can become destructive. Excess denial kills people every day by preventing them from getting the help they need. How many times have you heard someone say, "It's not that bad" or "Other people are worse off than I am" or "I'll get help later; I really don't have time now"? People die because they deny the seriousness of a medical condition, the danger of drinking and driving, their high blood pressure, or the fact that they are seriously overweight. Yes, excess denial kills and causes tremendous human suffering.

If you are in recovery from addictions, you know how powerful denial can be. The same denial that made it hard for you to accept your addictions may make it hard for you to accept your ADD and the need to have it treated.

If you are not in recovery from addictions, you may have read this chapter and still be in denial about the seriousness of your addictions. If this is the case, please read on, for you may see yourself in some of the stories in this book.

Other people in your life who may be suffering from addictions may not only be in denial of their problems but will deny that you have a problem. These "friends" and family members may tell you, "Don't be crazy. You don't have a problem. Look at me. I smoke pot more than you do, and I don't have a problem." These well-meaning people can't have a clear vantage point from which to view your life if their minds are clouded by their addictions. Unconsciously, they may also not want to lose you as a drinking and using partner, because if you get clean and sober, you won't be hanging out with them and getting loaded. Even more important, if you honestly look at your addictions, they'll have to look at theirs.

FACTS ABOUT ADDICTION

As with ADD, our understanding of addiction is plagued by myth and misinformation. Over the last three decades, with increased research and education, many commonly held but inaccurate beliefs about addiction have been dispelled. However, some people still hold on to old ideas. Here are some facts about addictions.

▶ It isn't how often you drink, but what happens when you drink that makes you an alcoholic.
▶ For years, the incidence of addiction in women was under reported, but women are as likely as men to become addicted.

- Alcohol is alcohol, whether you drink beer, wine, liquor, or mouthwash. So, if you "just drink beer," you could still be an alcoholic.
- Addictions are characterized by loss of control and are medical disorders, not moral diseases related to a lack of willpower.
- People can become physically and emotionally addicted to certain foods, especially sugar and highly refined carbohydrates.
- Even medicines prescribed by doctors can be addicting, so check with your doctor to see if your medication has the potential for abuse.
- Many drug addicts are white and considered to be middle and upper class.
- Marijuana can cause permanent damage to vital organs such as the brain, lungs, and reproductive system.
- Addictions to behaviors constitute a serious problem in our country. Recent research estimates that there are almost a half million compulsive gamblers;[5] this does not include the thousands of compulsive spenders, workaholics, or sex addicts.

You may still not be sure if you have a drug and alcohol problem, or you may still be wondering if someone you love is addicted. Sometimes information needs to settle in for a while. You will have many opportunities while reading this book to develop a greater understanding about your relationship with alcohol, drugs, food, and behaviors. The next chapter will illuminate the reasons why and, specifically, how you or someone you love may be self-medicating ADD.

CHAPTER EIGHT

∽∾

PUTTING OUT FIRES WITH GASOLINE
Self-Medicating ADD with Alcohol, Drugs, and Food

As human beings we find very creative ways to avoid or alleviate our pain. Whether we suffer from physical pain, emotional pain, or spiritual pain, our natural response is to avoid it. When we self-medicate, we are trying to avoid suffering. But what does it mean to "self-medicate"?

We self-medicate when we use substances, including food or behaviors, to alter how we feel and how we function. There are three primary reasons why people self-medicate. First, we want to numb painful feelings. We use substances or behaviors much like we might use Vicodin, a narcotic painkiller, to alleviate tooth pain from a root canal. Root canal pain is relatively short-term and the Vicodin reduces our physical pain. However, since Vicodin also produces feelings of well-being and pleasure that go beyond the dental pain, some people want to keep taking it after they've healed. When someone takes Vicodin to alleviate the pain of living, or to alter how they feel, we would say that person is self-medicating. The feelings she or he is trying to anesthetize with Vicodin, or with other substances or behaviors, are often rooted in deep wounds, in life's everyday difficulties, and in his or her brain chemistry.

A second reason for self-medicating has to do with our belief that we function better when we're under the influence of substances. For example, we might use cocaine to help us concentrate and have the energy to complete a task. Or we might smoke pot, feeling it enhances our ability to write a song, sculpt a human figure, or paint a landscape. On the other hand, we might smoke that same joint to help us get through a day of tedious and repetitive work.

The third reason we self-medicate is for the intoxication. We do it because it feels good. This is connected to a desire to obliterate pain; however, in this case we also love the euphoric sensations the drug or behaviors give. Many alcoholics and addicts chase this initial euphoria for years, never quite able to attain it again.

There are two ways we medicate ourselves. One is with substances: alcohol, marijuana, cocaine, tranquilizers, amphetamines, food, narcotics, nicotine, and caffeine. The other is with compulsive behaviors such as gambling, spending, working, and sex and love addictions. These I referred to as "addictions of doing."

Using substances and behaviors, we self-medicate depression, low self-esteem, anxiety, manic depressive illness, or pain and trauma from our pasts. As you have probably anticipated, ADD is one of the many things that people try to self-medicate. Unfortunately, self-medicating ADD is, as we shall see, like putting out fires with gasoline.

FANNING THE FLAMES OF ADDICTION

There is a burning pain inside you. It hurts so bad that all you can think of is putting it out. Drown it, smother it; you'll do anything to stop the burning. And yet, what you use to douse the flames, the substance or behavior you choose to throw on the intolerable fire, is "gasoline." When you pour it on the flames, they rage out of control until, eventually, they explode. Too late, you discover you've made the wrong choice. You can kill yourself in your attempts to save yourself.

Realistically, everyone self-medicates at one time or another. You may drink a cup of coffee to stay alert or have a glass of wine after a stressful day. Others find occasional retail therapy (shopping) a way to temporarily feel better. You may have times in your life when you bury yourself in your work until you are ready to deal with situations in your life. Self-medicating on an occasional basis is not terribly destructive, especially if it's a temporary way to deal with a situation or feelings and you soon find other options. However, self-medicating becomes a problem when you use it as a way to avoid your feelings and not accept life on life's terms.

Not everyone who self-medicates will become addicted. Who becomes addicted and self-destructive is determined by a variety of factors. One factor is a genetic predisposition toward addiction. Those people who do not have this predisposition may be able to self-medicate for short periods of time with minimal or no consequences. But even the nonaddictive person will experience negative consequences if he or she self-medicates long enough. No one knows exactly how much heat, fuel, and wind it takes to turn a burning cigarette into a forest fire.

Later in this chapter we will examine more closely the substances people use to medicate their ADD. Before we do that, let me introduce you to Matt, who was not treated for his ADD and addictions until he was facing a potentially long sentence in a state prison.

From Law School to Law Breaking

Matt, a Phi Beta Kappa college graduate, graduated from a prestigious law school at age twenty-seven. Not only was he brilliant, he was genuinely charming, funny, and good-looking. To the outside world Matt had it all. What most people didn't know was that Matt was addicted to prescription amphetamines and the narcotic Vicodin.

Matt's parents took him to an addiction specialist after he told them at age sixteen that he was using alcohol, smoking pot, and snorting cocaine. Matt had been able to hide these addictions, partly because cocaine had actually helped him to study and do well in school. Oddly, the cocaine did not make him hyper or speedy. Instead, he felt calm and omnipotent. He could focus his mind. Matt snorted cocaine not only to party but to study.

In college his distractibility, procrastination, and impulsiveness became increasingly difficult to manage. He frequently pulled all-nighters to get his work done. He sometimes swam laps in the pool at 1:00 or 2:00 A.M. because he couldn't sleep or slow down his active mind. As a result, Matt began drinking alcohol and smoking pot daily. Eventually, he returned to cocaine use on a weekly basis. After he graduated from law school, Matt used up to $400 of coke a day, a habit that cost him nearly $80,000 in a few months. He needed more and more cocaine to keep from getting sick.

Out of desperation, Matt went into a thirty-day treatment program. While in the treatment program, Matt befriended a man, Frederick, who was a prescription amphetamine and narcotic addict. Frederick told Matt how he would go to doctors and psychiatrists and pretend he had ADD. He researched the doctors who would treat ADD with amphetamines and had received prescriptions from several different ones. He would also scam doctors from nearby cities for prescriptions of Vicodin.

After thirty days in the country club-like treatment program, Matt felt great. He was convinced he would never use drugs again. In the months after his discharge, Matt became bored with Twelve Step meetings. He couldn't sit still and his attention bounced off the walls of the meeting rooms. He felt desperate for relief from his racing body and mind.

Matt had no idea that he had ADD but was able to present himself to doctors as having ADD symptoms. He went to several doctors to get prescriptions for Didrex, a mild stimulant, and Dexedrine. Soon, Matt was taking one hundred 10 mg. tablets of Didrex, or thirty to forty 15 mg. long acting Dexedrine capsules a day. When he couldn't get stimulants, he would feign back pain to get Vicodin prescriptions and was taking as many as forty a day. He wasn't taking these massive amounts of narcotics and amphetamines to get high. He was taking them to feel normal. Eventually he was taking them to keep from going into withdrawals.

When he became too sick and exhausted to go to doctors, he stole prescription pads and wrote his own prescription. He was able to pull off this scam about ninety times in a nine-month period before he was arrested the first time. The second time he was arrested was the day he received his certificate for completing the drug diversion program he was sentenced to the first time he was arrested. The day he got out of jail, Matt returned to writing his own prescriptions. Three weeks later he was back in jail, where he went through horrible withdrawals. Every cell in his body ached, and all of his bones felt as if they'd been shattered.

Meanwhile, Matt's mother began reading information about adult ADD. All the traits of ADD fit Matt, even though he did well in school and had never before been in trouble. The pieces began to fit together. Could it be that her son was self-medicating ADD? She and Matt's father took their son to have his brain scanned. Matt's SPECT scan showed that the frontal lobes of his brain had probably been traumatized and confirmed that he had severe ADD. With this new information his parents were willing to help him get the treatment he needed for his ADD as well as his addictions.

Matt was charged with two felonies and was facing up to four years in a state prison. His ADD in no way excused him from breaking the law. However, his attorney presented expert witnesses who showed how his untreated ADD contributed to his addictions. Matt was one of the first people to be given an alternative sentence for having untreated ADD. He did not have to go to prison. Instead, one felony count was dropped and he received a year of a very tight and rigorous probation. If he did not comply in any way, he would go directly to prison. If he was able to adhere to the many explicit demands of his probation, his felony would be expunged and he would be able to take the bar exam. Since Matt's ADD was being treated, he was responsible for his behavior. There would be no leeway for him.

Matt has been clean and sober for over a year as of this writing. His recovery has been precarious. Even with high doses of medication, he still suffers from ADD symptoms that make daily living difficult. However, Matt is working and adjusting well to his recovery program.

When the Solution Becomes the Problem

Human beings are creative at finding substances and behaviors that make them feel better. The substances and activities we choose are not as important as how and why we use them. When we self-medicate, substances perform a different function than they do for the person who drinks or smokes pot at a party or social gathering. If we use substances as a primary way of dealing with life's ups and downs, we are abusing them. Likewise, anyone can have a bad day and plug into the television, get lost on the World Wide Web, or do a bit of retail therapy. Each of these behaviors in itself is not the problem. However, when we abuse these behaviors, become compulsive about them, and lose control over them, we create new problems that are greater than the ones we're trying to avoid.

Relying on substances and behaviors for relief never works for long. We start out gambling now and then, smoking an occasional joint, eating candy bars several times a week, or playing computer games. We discover that these substances or behaviors make us feel better, or not feel at all. Perhaps we're distracted from the sorrow or frustration or anger in our lives. We feel we've discovered a way of soothing life's wounds. We're thrilled, because it works. Excited about our discovery, we step up the pace of self-medicating. When we do this, we lose our ability to control our behavior. We can't stop spending, gambling, working, having sex, in spite of the negative consequences we experience. Eventually, what we thought was the solution to life's problems has become a new and dangerous problem in its own right.

Some people are fortunate enough to find recovery from their substance and behavior addictions. However, if their other problems, such as depression, anxiety, emotional illness, ADD, or learning disabilities are not treated, they are at greater risk to relapse or have a miserable life in recovery. We deserve to have all of our problems treated. But medicating ourselves with substances and behaviors is not the answer. It may appear to work in the short run, but it can turn our life into a dismal mess in the long run.

WHY DO PEOPLE SELF-MEDICATE PAIN?

If we live long enough we will experience pain—emotional, physical, and spiritual. There is no way to avoid experiencing the pain that is inherent in being human. Not even alcohol, drugs, or compulsive behaviors can keep us from experiencing the pain and the suffering of life. In fact, the harder we try to avoid our pain, the more painful our life becomes. The only way out of pain is to go through it. While this may not sound appealing, what are our options? We either continue to self-medicate our pain, or we get both our ADD and addictions treated and commit to walking through the pain. Walking through it means feeling our pain rather than medicating it. Once we feel the pain, it can heal.

This does not mean you need to suffer physical or emotional pain. It does mean that you are not the one to medicate that pain. If you need medication, let the experts prescribe and provide it. Take medication for the prescribed reasons, and take it only as prescribed. Most of us are not physicians or pharmacists. However, if you happen to be one, let another professional prescribe your medication for you.

Keep in mind that in spite of the millions of dollars spent by drug companies each year to advertise medications, all human pain does not need to be medicated. Sometimes it just hurts to be alive.

SELF-MEDICATING ADD

I understand the desire to avoid or alleviate the pain and humiliation of having ADD. Living a life with untreated ADD can cause you to feel frustrated, depressed, hopeless, chronically overwhelmed, isolated, ashamed, and full of rage. You may have lived with these powerful feelings and had no idea that ADD was a contributing factor. If your attempts to alleviate your ADD have in turn caused you more problems or become new addictions, your self-esteem may have fallen lower than you ever thought possible. Abusing substances and having ADD can create tremendous feelings of shame and humiliation. Over a period of time, you may have accepted unconsciously that this shame was *you*. Eventually, shame may have become the foundation of your life.

If you have untreated ADD, you are at risk for self-medicating. Not everyone with ADD self-medicates, but somewhere between 25–50 percent of people with drug and alcohol addictions also have ADD. And this does not include people who use food and compulsive behaviors to soothe their ADD traits.

An article in *American Scientist* tells us that "in the United States alone there are 18 million alcoholics, 28 million children of alcoholics, 6 million cocaine addicts, 14.9 million who abuse other substances, 25 million people addicted to nicotine. . . ."[1] That's 63.5 million Americans addicted to substances! If we conservatively say that each of the 63.5 million people affects only four others, we are now looking at a number close to the population of our country who are directly affected by someone else's addictions.

No one is immune to the effects of addictions. At some point you will be touched by someone else's addiction, if not your own. We can't put a price on this human suffering, but we do know that alcoholism alone "costs the nation more than $100 billion annually in medical costs and lost work."[2] This doesn't even include the hidden costs generated by our "54 million citizens who are at least 20 pounds overweight, our 3.5 million school-aged children with Attention Deficit Disorder or Tourette's syndrome, and about 448,000 compulsive gamblers."[3]

There is no one drug or type of behavior that people with ADD abuse. People, whether they have ADD or not, use a variety of approaches. Those with ADD will use a combination of different substances in their attempts to activate or slow down their brains. In the rest of this chapter we'll explore how you or someone you love may be using food, alcohol, illegal and legal drugs, caffeine, or nicotine to treat ADD. In the next chapter we'll discuss common addictions of doing: compulsive gambling, high-risk activities, addictions to electronics, compulsive spending, sex addictions, and workaholism. Let's begin by talking about food.

FOOD

Although we don't think of food as a drug, it can be used as one. We have to eat, but eating too much or too little of certain types of food has consequences. Because there is no way to totally abstain from food, food addictions and eating disorders are extremely hard to recover from. You may have to abstain from certain foods, perhaps those containing sugar, because they trigger a compulsion for more, but everywhere you look you see these foods.

Food is legal. It is a culturally acceptable way to comfort ourselves. Paradoxically, our culture is obsessed with thinness. "Food is okay, but don't gain weight." No wonder so many adolescent boys and girls, as well as women and men, become imprisoned in binge-purge cycles, chronic dieting, and anorexia nervosa.

For the purpose of examining self-medicating with food more carefully, we will divide this problem into several areas: compulsive overeating, binge eating, bulimia, anorexia, and sugar cravings and addictions.

Compulsive Overeating

Many of us overeat at times. We may eat for sheer enjoyment, even if we're not hungry, or we may eat more than we intend at a dinner party or celebration. But for some, overeating becomes a compulsion they cannot stop. Compulsive overeaters lose control of their ability to stop eating. They use food to alter their feelings rather than to satisfy hunger. Compulsive overeaters tend to crave foods high in carbohydrates, sugars, and salt.

Remember in chapter four where we talked about the neurotransmitter serotonin? Serotonin helps regulate mood, sleep, appetite, and activity level. Sugars and highly refined carbohydrates such as cakes and cookies increase the serotonin level in your brain. I've never yet met a person who chooses meat and vegetables as binge foods.

Eating can temporarily calm ADD physical and mental restlessness. Eating can ground some people with ADD, helping them focus better while reading, studying, or watching television or movies. If your brain is not quick to contain your impulses, you will eat without thinking. Some compulsive overeaters are shocked to realize they have finished a carton of ice cream or a king-sized tub of theater popcorn. They weren't consciously aware of how much they were eating. It's as though they had gone into a trance.

Binge Eating

Binge eating differs from compulsive overeating. The binge eater enjoys the rush and stimulation of planning the binge. Buying the food and finding the time and place to binge in secret creates a level of risk and excitement that the ADD brain craves. The binge usually includes foods high in sugars and highly refined carbohydrates such as cookies, ice cream, pasta, and breads. Large amounts of these types of foods are rapidly consumed in a short period of time. The binge itself may only last fifteen to twenty minutes.

It's no accident that binge food is usually high in sugars and carbohydrates, especially when you take into consideration how the ADD brain is slow to absorb glucose. One of the Zametkin PET scan study's results indicated that "global cerebral glucose metabolism was 8.1 percent lower in the adults with hyperactivity than in the normal controls. . . ."[4] Other research has also noted slower glucose metabolism in ADD adults with and without hyperactivity. This suggests that the binge eater may be using these foods to change his or her neurochemistry. In Chapter 4 we also talked about the relationship between the neurotransmitters serotonin and dopamine and impulse control problems such as binge eating.

Bulimia

Bulimia is binge eating accompanied by purging. Purging is the process of eliminating food by self-induced vomiting and/or using laxatives or enemas.The bulimic experiences the rush of planning the binge, which can be very stimulating for the person with ADD. In addition, the bulimic may be stimulated by the satiation bingeing provides. Then, he or she adds an additional dimension to the process: the relief of purging. Many bulimics report entering an altered state of consciousness, experiencing feelings of calmness and euphoria after they vomit. This cleansing provides short-lived relief, and so the bulimic is soon bingeing again.

Untreated ADD can contribute to the vicious cycle of

bulimia. Since bulimics perform their rituals in secret, they tend to become more and more isolated. In addition, the ritual itself induces shame. The shame and isolation are compounded by a person's ADD. Many people with eating disorders are not able to completely recover until they get their ADD treated.

Anorexia

Anorexia Nervosa can be deadly. Anorectics have lost control of their ability to eat or to monitor their eating in a healthy way. They are obsessed with thoughts of food, body image, and diet. Most doctors, psychiatrists, and therapists see anorexia as being rooted in the family one grew up in, enmeshment with a parent, perfectionism, and a high need for control. This can all be true, but self-starvation is a loss of control. I have never met an anorectic who can control his or her repetitive thoughts about food, calories, and body image. Anorectics can also use laxatives, diuretics, enemas, and compulsive exercise to maintain their distorted body image of being fat when they are in fact thin.

As we learn more about ADD, we discover that people manifest ADD traits differently. Professionals in the field of ADD have developed subtypes to describe these differences. These subtypes help explain how many people with anorexia and ADD use their obsessions with food to self-medicate. Obsessing on food, exercise, and thinness gives the anorectic a way to focus his or her sometimes chaotic ADD brain.

Dr. Lynn Weiss refers to "Highly Structured ADD" in her book, *ADD on the Job: Making Your ADD Work for You*. People with this type of ADD get stuck on thoughts and behaviors, are geared toward perfectionism, get preoccupied with details, and tend to be judgmental of themselves and others. Several years ago I heard Dr. Weiss talk about this subtype of ADD, which provided me with the piece I had been looking for to understand my clients who were anorectic. They also had ADD, but their ADD was expressed in a unique way.[5]

Another reason why anorectic behaviors are attractive to some people with ADD is that it is hard to be hyperactive when your body is starving. Frequently, these people will only become aware of their high level of activity, distractibility, and impulsiveness after they have been in recovery from anorexia.

Being distracted and spaced out are characteristics of both anorexia and bulimia, whether or not they are accompanied by ADD. In each case the inability to concentrate or focus results because the brain is not being properly nourished. For people with ADD, however, there is a history of attention difficulties that predates the eating disorder. Their concentration, impulse problems, and activity level may not improve when their eating disorder is treated. As a matter of fact, their ADD traits can get worse once they are no longer self-medicating with food or organizing their lives around food and exercise. If you are someone who has struggled with eating disorders, and you suspect you may have ADD, it's important to get an evaluation. Both your eating disorder and your ADD must be treated.

Sugar Cravings and Hyperactivity

Researchers have searched for the connection between sugar and hyperactivity. Some studies have reported that sugar causes hyperactivity in children. When these studies have been duplicated, however, the results have been contradicted. The idea that sugar causes hyperactivity is relatively new in our culture and has not been passed on from previous generations. This is why grandparents are often miffed when they're told not to give their grandchild any sugar.

A 1994 article by Scott D. Lindgren, Ph.D., which appeared in *ADHD Report*, comprehensively reviewed research involving the controversial debate regarding the cause-and-effect relationship between sugar and hyperactivity.[6] The conclusions were that sugar and the artificial sweetener Aspartame do not cause hyperactivity in children. There are other factors that contribute to high energy behaviors followed by low energy crashes, such as the excitement of the party or event and caffeine contained in chocolate and soda. Some children, however, have allergic reactions to sugar and artificial sweeteners and coloring. These children will benefit from an evaluation by an allergist.

What if we have been looking at the question backwards? What if ADD hyperactivity actually causes people to crave sweets? If the ADD brain is slower to absorb glucose, it would make sense that the body would find a way to increase the supply of glucose to the brain as quickly as possible.

I've worked with many ADD adults who are addicted to sugar, especially chocolate, which also contains caffeine. They find that eating sugar helps them stay alert, calm, and focused. Prior to ADD treatment many report drinking six to twelve sugar sodas, several cups of coffee with sugar, and constantly nibbling on candy and sweets throughout the day. It is impossible to sort out what is pure sugar craving when it's mixed with the desirable effects of caffeine.

It is not uncommon for recovering alcoholics to find their source of sugar in sweets once they stop drinking alcohol. Since beverage alcohol contains large amounts of sugar, I am convinced that the body's craving for sugar is also a part of the alcoholic's craving for alcohol. This is in no way to say that alcoholism is caused solely by one's desire to get glucose to the brain; it's not that simple. Alcoholism is caused by a variety of biological, genetic, and environmental factors, but sugar may contribute to this complex picture.

Over the years, I have heard many stories from parents of ADD children like Rachel regarding addiction to sugar.

Trick or Treat
Rachel was a lanky, thin, pasty-looking teenager when her parents brought her in for an ADD assessment. Rachel had already been diagnosed by two other professionals as having ADD. Rachel's father, however, was sure Rachel did

not have ADD. He was convinced that Rachel would be okay if she stopped eating sugar.

After assessing Rachel, I told her parents she had ADD. The father blasted me as well as all medical and psychological professionals. He was talking so fast that his words were like the blur of a motorcycle passing at ninety miles an hour. My attempts to redirect him or get a word in edgewise were fruitless. Then he turned on Rachel and began a disjointed tirade about Rachel's failures. A few times over the past twenty years of working with couples and families, I've resorted to using my fingers as a whistle to stop someone who was verbally abusive; this was one of those times. Rachel's father was shocked. Rachel was relieved. We then had a more civil talk about ADD and how it was affecting the entire family. I was surprised when they made an appointment to return the next week.

Part of me hoped they would never return. I wanted to help Rachel, but the thought of having to take on her father again was not pleasant. Then it struck me that what I didn't want to deal with for an hour was Rachel's everyday reality. I placed a call to confirm and remind them of their next appointment.

Rachel's father began the next session by pouring the contents of a grocery bag onto my office floor. "See," he said, "there are 156 candy bar wrappers." My floor looked like the aftermath of a feeding frenzy by a dozen trick-or-treaters.

"I found all of these wrappers in Rachel's room," the father growled. "I told you sugar, not ADD, is this girl's problem." While he was making Rachel pick up the candy wrappers, I gave the mother the name of a psychiatrist who specialized in treating adolescents with ADD. She sheepishly took the name while Papa Bear obsessed about exactly how Rachel was cleaning up the candy wrappers. Once the mess was picked up, they all vanished. I felt bad for Rachel, whom I feared was not going to get the help she deserved.

Six months later, Rachel's mother called to thank me for my help. I listened, puzzled, as she related the events of the past half year. She said that Rachel had only been off sugar for five days when they were called in for an emergency parent-teacher conference. Rachel's teachers were concerned with her abrupt increase in activity, disruptiveness, and inability to pay attention. Two weeks later, Rachel was expelled for getting into a fight and breaking another student's nose.

Rachel had unknowingly been medicating her ADD with sugar. Once she was taken off sugar, her ADD behavior got worse. Rachel's mother somehow found the strength to stand up to her husband. Together, they took Rachel to a psychiatrist, who put her on Dexedrine. Within a month, Rachel was a new kid. Not only was she focusing better in school, she was more cooperative and beginning to feel better about herself. And guess what? Rachel had no craving for sugar. She enjoyed eating the occasional Snickers bar, but she was not obsessed with sugar the way she used to be.

Medicating Rachel's ADD was not the whole answer to the family's problems. Although Rachel was the identified patient in this family system, ADD runs in families, and other members could benefit from ADD assessments. In addition, Rachel's family could benefit from some good family therapy. There were problems in her parents' relationship that went beyond their concerns for their daughter. As in many families, Rachel's ADD had been used to pull the attention away from her parents' marital problems, as well as the possibility that they too might have suffered from ADD.

ALCOHOL

Do you think of alcohol as a drug? Alcohol is, in fact, a very powerful drug that is made from the fermenting of fruits and grains and can dissolve in water and fat molecules.

Since alcohol is such a "natural" product, it affects the brain in a wide variety of ways. Alcohol in itself is not bad. Many people enjoy a drink now and then, a beer or two at a party, or wine with dinner. They experience very few, if any, negative consequences. However, alcohol can be addicting, both physically and psychologically.

Alcohol can cause physical deterioration of the body. Excessive use damages vital organs such as the liver, kidneys, pancreas, stomach, heart, and brain. Alcohol use has also been linked to cancer, in particular cancer of the mouth, stomach, pancreas, esophagus, and liver.

Chronic alcohol abuse and addiction can cause damage to the brain. When this damage becomes permanent, it is referred to as organic brain syndrome (OBS). People with OBS can barely think or express their thoughts. Their memories are so damaged that they become a danger to themselves and others if they smoke cigarettes or try to cook. Many end up institutionalized.

Alcohol abuse and addiction cost us billions of dollars in medical bills, loss of production, criminal behaviors, incarcerations, and drinking-related automobile accidents. There is no way to estimate the cost of human suffering that results from alcohol abuse and dependency. You don't even have to be the one drinking to experience extreme pain and suffering from alcoholism. The damage of alcoholism lives on, even if the alcoholic does not.

For people with ADD, alcohol can be an attractive solution to their symptoms. Alcohol will calm the physical, emotional, and intellectual restlessness of ADD. One woman put it like this: "When I get drunk, my brain disengages, my feelings numb, noises are not as loud. I can be still. My body doesn't have to move. Finally, I get some peace."

While alcohol can initially appear to be a solution, the problems that come with using it to medicate ADD are many. Alcohol decreases the brain's frontal lobe activity. Instead of activating the brain, alcohol anesthetizes it. This "putting to sleep" affects the already sleepy ADD frontal lobes, and impairs concentration, memory function, judgment, and impulse control.

Alcohol relaxes the inhibitions of people who don't have ADD. Have you ever watched people get drunk at an office holiday party? The more people drink the less inhibited they become. Drinkers may not be aware that the volume of their voices are increasing exponentially. By the end of the evening they may sound like they are talking through megaphones. The normally quiet and shy bookkeeper may not be able to stop laughing. Meanwhile, the serious and sullen production manager from down the hall is doing Whoopi Goldberg and Robin Williams impersonations. By the end of the night, you may have a near stranger blubbering at you about how they hate the holidays.

All these extraordinary behaviors are triggered by alcohol in non-ADD brains. What happens when you disinhibit an already disinhibited brain? Put another way, what happens to the bookkeeper or production manager if they also have ADD? Now the risk increases and the consequences can be irreversible. The drunk with ADD at this party may impulsively tell the president of the company that he or she has the personality of a stop sign. Or he may be sexual with that person from the sales division he suddenly finds so attractive, then later suffer from severe remorse and regret. Due to ADD impulsivity and difficulty thinking situations through, a person with ADD who drinks may be more likely to drive while under the influence.

Marijuana

Marijuana can be referred to as pot, smoke, weed, joint, dope, reefer, and whatever else creative drug users think up. Over the years marijuana has been referred to as a "soft" drug, an herb, a love drug, or Mother Nature's way of saying "high." Marijuana has enjoyed a reputation as being nonaddictive, natural, and harmless, in spite of research and literature that clearly states otherwise.

Pot smokers frequently dispute the idea that smoking marijuana may lead to using harder drugs. However, smoking marijuana doesn't have to lead to harder drugs, because marijuana in itself can cause serious problems. Many longtime pot smokers cling to their beliefs about the effects of marijuana and deny that regular pot smoking can contribute to their problems.

Over the past twenty years, I have witnessed people kick heroin; withdraw from alcohol, cocaine, tranquilizers, amphetamines, and nicotine; yet they continue to smoke pot. Sometimes people in alcohol and drug treatment or Twelve Step programs continue smoking marijuana while in recovery. For many, pot is the last drug they give up, if in fact they do give it up.

The effects of pot are not as overt as being under the influence of other drugs. Also, the damage caused by marijuana smoking is usually more subtle but no less real. Marijuana contains over four hundred chemicals, many of which we know little about. Years of research have documented the problems caused by THC, one of the activating ingredients in pot. Marijuana can impair our neurotransmitters, diminish concentration, cloud our thinking, diminish motivation, disturb sleep cycles, damage motor coordination, alter depth perception, and cause physical, psychological, and spiritual ailments. To top it off, pot today is "25 to 30 times stronger than the pot people smoked 20 years ago."[7] This increased potency seriously changes and intensifies the effects of the drug, causing marijuana to be much more damaging than once believed.

AMPHETAMINES

Speed, crystal, crystal meth, ice, bennies, whites, black beauties. These are names used to describe amphetamines. Amphetamines are stimulant drugs. When people take them in high doses, they feel euphoric and energized. To get higher with smaller amounts, some people turn to injecting, snorting, or smoking amphetamines. A potent form of methamphetamine, called "ice," is prepared in a form that is smokable. Smoking ice gives the user an immediate and powerful high. Ice is the "crack" of amphetamines.

Amphetamine use has been on the rise over the past few years. Makeshift labs in abandoned shacks, garages, mobile homes, and hotel rooms are set up to make methamphetamines. The necessary chemicals are relatively easy to buy and the recipes are apparently easy to follow. These recipes are passed or sold from one "manufacturer" to another. However, if there is a spelling error or transposed number in the recipe, the lab can blow up. Also, amphetamine "cookers" sometimes die from the toxic fumes released by their preparations.

When high doses of amphetamine are used, especially when smoked, the abuser can experience extreme agitation, paranoid thoughts, and hallucinations. He or she can also become aggressive and violent. Many amphetamine abusers will drink alcohol to take the edge off the speedy effects of the drug. At that point, they become speedy drunks, a condition which can create some bizarre and dangerous behaviors. Unlike the conventional drunk who would eventually pass out, speedy drunks can become aggressive, getting into fights or battering a loved one. They might go for a joy ride, driving too quickly and erratically.

Since there has been little research on addictions and ADD, there are no precise statistics on the percentage of people with ADD who have abused amphetamines. However, my clinical observations and those of some of my colleagues suggest that amphetamines are a drug of choice for many with ADD. They accidentally found a street drug that helped their ADD symptoms. Some of these patients were able to put the drug down when their "solution" turned into a new and ravenous problem; others could not and became addicted.

I have also worked with people who have used prescribed amphetamine or an amphetamine type of diet pill to lose weight. Often I hear that while the appetite suppressant did not suppress their appetite, they sure got a lot done. Some people with eating disorders look back fondly on their time on amphetamines or drugs that acted in a similar way. One woman said, "I didn't lose weight, but I was able to think clearly, focus on what was in front of me, and finish what I started. The weird thing is that I felt calm. I wasn't blowing up at my family. My life became more manageable. My doctor took me off them because they weren't helping me lose weight. But I haven't felt right since." The amphetamines were working, not for her obesity, but for her hidden ADD.

Amphetamines have been prescribed over the years to effectively treat obesity, narcolepsy, and ADD, with infrequent side effects. The amount of amphetamine or stimulant medication used to treat ADD is only a tiny portion compared to what is used on the streets to get high. Also, with street amphetamines, you're never sure of the dosage or the contents of what you take. With street amphetamine abuse comes the dangers of using needles, overdosing, and incarceration.

When properly and closely monitored by a professional with expertise in ADD and addictions, amphetamine treatment for ADD can be highly effective. We will talk more about prescribed medication to treat ADD in chapter eleven.

COCAINE

Coke, snow, blow, snort, and crack are words used to describe cocaine. Cocaine has been used for centuries by the indigenous people of central and South America. However, the effects of chewing leaves from the coca plant can hardly be compared to the potency of "crack" cocaine that is smoked in the United States.

Initially, cocaine was believed to be only psychologically addicting. However, over the years professionals have witnessed the physically and emotionally addictive properties of the drug. This is especially true of "free base" and "crack" cocaine, where the drug is prepared so that it can be smoked. Smoking cocaine gets more of the drug into the bloodstream immediately. Flammable and volatile chemicals are used to turn cocaine into free base. Free base became popular in the seventies but eventually fell out of favor because it tended to ignite and set the user on fire. By the early eighties, "crack" had hit the streets of America, and a new epidemic of cocaine abuse and addiction spread among young people and adults.

Cocaine has the same appeal for the person with ADD as amphetamines do, even though there are differences between the two. Cocaine provides most users with a greater sense of euphoria and well-being. However, the effects of cocaine do not last as long as the effects of amphetamines; therefore, the user must use cocaine more frequently to maintain the desired effect. Cocaine is also more expensive than amphetamines. Cocaine addicts can quickly find themselves in trouble trying to pay for a habit that no longer feels good. The desire for cocaine can be so powerful that addicts will give anything, including their lives, for it.

Many people with ADD who have had experience with cocaine report that it initially felt like a wonder drug. It not only helped them concentrate better, it made them feel calm and dissipated their feelings of shame and self-hatred. However, over time they found themselves in situations similar to Matt's. Their solution to their problem stopped working. Before they realized it they were experiencing such serious cocaine-related problems that their ADD took a back seat.

NARCOTICS

I learned about heroin (dope, smack, junk, H, China white,) in the mid-seventies when I worked in a methadone detox program in a large city. I watched addicts in their twenties and thirties age in front of my eyes. Some detoxed over and over. Many overdosed and never returned. All of them had a sense of fear and desperation that permeated my office.

Looking back on the addicts at the clinic, I remember that many of them had other addictions that were usually not treated. A commonly held belief in the seventies was that addicts could drink alcohol in moderation. This practice had disastrous consequences for many. Some addicts who had never liked or even used alcohol became addicted to it once they kicked heroin. For others, alcohol use became the route they took back to heroin or earlier addictions.

Some clients at the methadone clinic had been sexually abused as children and adults. Many suffered from depression, anxiety, personality disorders, and lifestyles that most people would want to seek relief from. I now know that some also suffered from ADD.

For people with ADD, narcotics provide a calming effect that some say no other drug could ever match. Narcotic drugs can decrease ADD restlessness of the body and brain. They can also turn irritable, agitated, and aggressive people into passive, "nodding out" loaded people who could care less about what's going on around them. This "high," which is actually a low, can be very inviting for the person with ADD. Narcotics can also soothe feelings of rage, which are common to people with ADD. If you have ever been under the influence of narcotics intentionally, or have used them to treat pain after surgery or dental work, you may remember being quite docile, feeling like everything was okay, and not really caring if things were not.

Severe consequences, such as addiction, withdrawals, incarceration, overdoses, and disease accompany heroin use. For decades heroin has had a reputation as an addictive drug with nasty withdrawals. And yet people continue to become addicted.

Heroin addiction is becoming more prevalent among children and adolescents who smoke the drug. Many adolescents feel immortal, grandiose, and immune to the dangers of drug abuse. But look around. You may have noticed that there are very few practicing heroin addicts who die of old age. Heroin overdose is just one reason for this. One of the problems of self-medicating with street drugs is that you never know how pure and potent the drug you are using really is. Also, the person with ADD may be more apt to test the limits of what his or her body can tolerate. As a result, ADD addicts are even more likely than others to die from overdosing and combining drugs such as heroin and cocaine.

Addicts are also being infected by the HIV virus, even when they are careful about sharing needles. I had one young woman client who thought that rinsing her "outfit" or syringe with bleach would kill the HIV virus. She and her boyfriend shared needles, believing they were taking the necessary precautions. Although she has been clean and sober for two years, she recently tested positive for HIV.

CAFFEINE

Oh, the joys of that morning cup of coffee or tea. Author Richard Brautigan said, "Sometimes life is merely a matter of coffee and whatever intimacy a cup of coffee affords." Caffeine is caffeine, whether we get it from chocolate, cola, iced tea, or a double espresso. Research has bounced back and forth for decades trying to prove the hazards of caffeine, especially in the form of coffee. The controversy rages, and meanwhile Americans continue to consume coffee, tea, and caffeinated sodas.

Today most experts agree that moderate amounts of caffeine are not harmful, especially if you're not pregnant or nursing a baby; yet even that research has contradicted itself over the years. Despite the presumed safety of caffeine when used in moderation, it is an addictive drug with the potential to cause withdrawal symptoms when a person abruptly stops drinking it.

Drinking coffee is one of many rituals that is a part of our culture and cultures throughout the world. Most people do not abuse or overuse caffeine. Many of us are sensitive to the stimulating effects of too much caffeine. How much caffeine is too much differs from one individual to another. Some people have a higher tolerance than others. I know people who can enjoy a double cappuccino at 10:00 p.m. and still sleep like a baby an hour or two later.

People with ADD frequently medicate their sleepy frontal lobes with caffeine. I have a friend who was drinking thirty-six cups of coffee a day. Now that his ADD is being treated with medication, his caffeine use has plummeted.

Caffeine consumption is a frequent topic in the ADD coaching and support groups I facilitate. Members often deal with cutting down their daily caffeine intake. This is especially true if they are on stimulant medication to treat their ADD. Caffeine can cause a synergistic reaction with the medication that results in anxiety, tremors, and agitations.

I remember one group meeting in which participants talked about their past and present relationship with caffeine. One man stated emphatically that he did not use caffeine in any form. He said that he didn't like coffee, didn't drink tea or cola, and rarely ate chocolate. An hour into the group, when we were talking about another subject, this same man said, "But you know, I used to buy a box of No Doz whenever I had a project to complete. I would chew up the box of tablets and work for hours. It was amazing how I could finish my project." This man had just had a revelation. He realized that he'd been self-medicating with caffeine by using over-the-counter medication meant to be taken in small doses to keep people alert.

His experience is not unique. Some people with ADD also use over-the-counter diet pills and appetite suppressants; others abuse cold medications that contain ephedrine, which can have a stimulating effect on some people.

NICOTINE

According to the U.S. Public Health Service, nicotine addiction is "the most widespread example of drug dependence in our country." Here are some facts about smoking from a recent pamphlet printed by the American Cancer Society.[8]

- ▶ Smoking has been implicated as a risk factor in cancers of the mouth, pharynx, larynx, esophagus, pancreas, uterine cervix, kidney, and bladder.
- ▶ Smoking is related to almost half a million premature deaths each year.
- ▶ Smoking is the single most preventable cause of death in our society.
- ▶ Smokers have twice the risk of dying of heart attacks.
- ▶ Smoking has made lung cancer the number one cancer killer of American women.
- ▶ Smoking increases the risk of miscarriage, lowers the birth weight, and increases the likelihood of health problems during infancy.
- ▶ More than 80 percent of current smokers started smoking before age twenty-one.

The good news, as of the printing of this 1994 pamphlet, is that "44 million Americans have quit smoking."

Many recovering alcoholics and addicts are able to kick all drugs except nicotine. Nicotine addiction is powerful and insidious. With the knowledge we have today about the health hazards associated with smoking cigarettes, cigars, pipes, and chewing tobacco, it's surprising that young people are starting nicotine habits, but they are. There seems to be a correlation between early onset of nicotine addiction and difficulty quitting.

Smoking is glamorized. In magazine advertisements and films young people are depicted enjoying this life-threatening drug. Some tobacco companies use cartoon characters to advertise their product and then deny that they are targeting the youth market. However, nicotine is usually the first of a series of drugs children use to self-medicate their ADD; it is usually preceded only by the use of food in an attempt to treat their ADD discomfort.

What is it about nicotine that is so enticing for people with ADD? First of all, nicotine stimulates the brain, an effect that is especially desirable to people with ADD. Second, smoking gives many with ADD ways to express their restlessness. When they have a cigarette, they have an object they can hold and fiddle with. They also have an object—whether it's a cigarette, pipe, cigar, or chewing tobacco—to put in their mouths.

I have one client who is addicted to gum that contains nicotine. The packages she buys cost about $55 for 108 pieces and are meant to help smokers withdraw from nicotine. Unfortunately, for the last year she's been using approximately three packages a month. For this client, nicotine gum has become a very expensive nicotine maintenance program, one she cannot shake.

I hear people without ADD express their frustration about their inability to stop smoking and stay stopped. But throwing the smoking monkey off their backs seems to be especially difficult for people with ADD. Their impulsiveness, compulsiveness, and craving to stimulate their brains only makes matters worse. However, some of the clients I've worked with have been able to stop smoking with support, once their ADD was properly treated.

PRESCRIPTION DRUGS

There is a difference between using medication properly for the prescribed condition and abusing that same medication. Sometimes, people will feign illness or injuries to get the prescription medications they abuse. They may be taking painkillers to deaden feelings rather than physical pain. They may be using tranquilizers and sleeping pills to slow down their bodies and brains. Self-medicating with prescribed medications can lead to addictions and all the consequences that come with being an addict.

You or someone you know may be operating as a kind of lay pharmacist, creatively combining drugs to help yourself feel better, to become numb to pain, or to enhance your functioning. This is especially true of people with untreated ADD. Sometimes this process can lead to painful and horrifying consequences, as we will see in Martha's story.

She Drank Her Child's Cough Medicine

Martha is a thirty-two-year-old single parent of three children. Five years ago, the children's father left Martha and their kids, who were all under the age of six. He neither pays support for his children nor is involved in their lives. Martha works full-time and is always just scraping by. After her husband left, she became very anxious and suffered from two full-blown panic attacks. The pressures of working full-time and bringing up three small children overwhelmed her.

Martha's doctor prescribed Valium for six months after her husband left. Neither Martha nor her doctor paid attention to how much she was taking, but Martha was aware that her prescription wasn't lasting as long as it used to. Finally, her doctor refused to renew her prescription unless she would come in and talk about how she was taking the Valium and consider a referral to counseling. Martha, however, felt she had neither the time nor the money for therapy.

Martha found a new doctor who was willing to pre-scribe Xanax, another anti-anxiety drug. Martha went through these prescriptions even faster. Soon she was see-ing three different doctors in two different towns who were each prescribing tranquilizers for her. Martha would take so many pills to sleep at night that her kids could hardly wake her in the morning. She was on probation at her job for tardiness and decreased productivity. Martha had also become a recluse, rarely leaving her home. Even worse, she constantly felt guilty for taking pills; however, she couldn't face her inability to meet her children's needs.

Martha hit bottom when she ran out of prescriptions. She felt like she was going to explode. To top it off, her six-year-old daughter, who had a bad cough, had kept her up for two nights. Martha had a moment of disturbing clarity as she drank her daughter's codeine cough medicine. She held the empty bottle and listened to her coughing child. In that moment, Martha knew she had become an addict. Fortu-nately, that moment was the beginning of Martha's recovery.

Most people use prescribed medication appropriately. They are clear as to why they are taking the medication. They take it as prescribed and are not trying to alter their feelings. When the condition they are being treated for goes away, they stop taking the medication and have no craving for more. These people do not feel compelled to finish a prescription of pain medication simply because they have it. They may throw out the unused portion of a codeine or Vicodin or Valium prescription. This would be unthink-able for an addict.

ACCEPTANCE IS THE BEGINNING OF RECOVERY

It is impossible to get help if you don't think you have a problem. For many, their denial is their biggest problem. People in your life may be telling you that you have an alco-hol, drug, spending, or gambling problem. They may also be telling you that your forgetfulness, impulsive actions, and inability to stay focused for more than a millisecond are painful to be around. If you've read this far, my guess is you're aware that something in your life isn't working.

It's easy to accept good things; it's much harder to accept tragedy, missed opportunities, and illness. Acceptance of our difficulties is a process. We don't just automatically accept the death of a loved one, the diagnosis of ADD, or our addictions. The process of acceptance usually begins with denial, then anger. We progress through bargaining, depression, and finally, acceptance. It's common to bounce in and out of these stages and not experience them in sequence. If you do not interrupt this process by self-medicating it, you will eventually move through all of the stages.

You don't have to like what happens to you in your life, but the ability to accept what you cannot change is essential. Acceptance is liberating. Acceptance can provide you with the freedom to get the help you need and deserve.

We'll talk about that help at length in chapter ten and chapter eleven, but first let's explore addictive behaviors—those things you just can't stop doing, no matter what they cost you.

∽∾

CHAPTER NINE

ADDICTIONS OF DOING
Self-Medicating with Addictive Behaviors

Misusing and abusing substances are not the only ways to put out the fires of ADD. Some people use a combination of substances and behaviors in their attempts to activate or slow down their brains.

Because many with ADD also have difficulties controlling impulses, you can see how easy it might be to become a compulsive spender, gambler, worker, or sex and love addict. We can become addicted to any behavior, even behaviors such as exercising, studying, or working, which are normally good for us. If we lose our ability to control our behavior, in spite of negative consequences, we are addicted.

Do you find yourself repeatedly doing things you know are not good for you? Do you promise your family you will work less, then stay late at the office or bring work home? Do you spend money to make yourself feel better? Do you take risks that border on crazy? Do you continue to exercise even when you're hurting your body? Again, it is not the behavior but how you use it and your inability to control it that cause the problems. Let's look at some common behaviors that can become addictions.

GAMBLING

Some people enjoy a trip to Las Vegas once in a while. Others enjoy the thrill of gambling at the race track or playing the lottery. Their gambling is not frequent and doesn't create negative consequences. If they lose money, they won't gamble again in desperate attempts to win it back.

Compulsive gamblers, on the other hand, live to gamble. They're hooked on the rush they get from gambling. The excitement and stimulation gambling gives them are even more important than any money they may win. They fantasize about gambling, about winning big, and ways to get money to gamble. They'll gamble on just about anything.

If compulsive gamblers are not gambling, they are thinking about gambling. Relationships with people become secondary to the thrill of gambling. This is why compulsive gamblers will spend rent and food money at the race track or on lottery tickets. In spite of how they hurt others and how guilty they feel, they can't stop. For some, gambling becomes more important than life itself.

People with ADD are frequently drawn toward gambling because the thrill activates their brains. They not only feel good when they gamble, they become focused, energized, and alert. A recovering compulsive gambler once described gambling as the biggest rush he had ever felt from any drug. "There's nothing like having a thousand dollars on the table and shaking those dice. It's a real thumper. My heart is pounding and I feel powerfully alive."

For those with ADD, combining the high they receive from gambling with the impulsiveness of ADD can result in a very serious addiction.

According to the DSM-IV, approximately one-third of compulsive gamblers are women.[1] As with alcoholism and ADD, women do not usually gamble in the high profile ways that men do and are less likely to be treated for this devastating addiction. Consider Emma's story.

Bottoming Out on Bingo

Emma hit her gambling bottom when she was caught stealing money from the cash register where she worked. She felt relieved to get caught, because it put an end to her secret life.

Emma loved her children and would never intentionally jeopardize their well-being. However, when she lost control of her gambling addiction, Emma began to leave her children alone while she played bingo. Her craving for gambling became more important than anything or anyone in her life and progressed from bingo to lottery cards and poker. What started out as fun became a life-altering addiction. She nearly lost custody of her kids when her six-year-old got scared and dialed 911; Emma had left her three children, ages six, four, and eleven months, home alone to go out to gamble.

SPENDING

Spending money and buying things for ourselves and others is part of life. But what if you can't control your spending? What if you buy things you don't need with money you don't have? Now your spending is a problem. Compulsive spenders buy because it feels good at the time and because the process is so absorbing that they can't think about anything else. The thrill of spending is short-lived, and the compulsive spender is left feeling shame and remorse. Similar to overeating, the buying is not out of legitimate need but to soothe emotional needs.

People with ADD are vulnerable to compulsive spending problems, especially because the impulsive quality of ADD makes it hard to think through the purchase. You see it. You want it. You buy it. That fast. Compulsive spending, like other addictions, leads to a variety of other problems, such as debt, poor credit, lying, guilt, and shame.

When Spending Becomes Brutal

Chris remembers having problems with spending most of her life. "My father used to say that if he gave me my

171

allowance in front of the hardware store I would spend it all on nuts and bolts." Chris's spending began to cause debt when she was seven years sober, making a good living, and she discovered credit.

She would go on a spending binge about every three months. Chris's compulsive spending triggered painful dynamics between her and her husband. It's common for spouses of compulsive spenders to attempt to manage their fear by controlling the money. This usually results in the spender creating even more debt and being deceptive about it. Huge arguments and power struggles went on between Chris and her husband for years. At one point they refinanced their home to pay off her debt, only to have thousands of dollars of new debt quickly incurred. "It was brutal," Chris said, "and nearly tore my family apart."

Chris has been working the Debtors Anonymous (DA) program for the past four years and now feels relieved of the compulsion to overspend. Like many people with behavioral addictions, she is regularly confronted with situations in which she used to lose control. Staying sober for nineteen years has not been as much of a struggle for her as dealing with her compulsive spending.

ADRENALINE JUNKIES

Another way to stimulate your ADD brain is by engaging in activities that increase adrenaline levels. Increased adrenaline activates the brain. Anyone can become addicted to adrenaline rushes from highly stimulating, or "high stim," activities. High stim activities such as bungee jumping, skydiving, and motorcycle racing can be glamorous. Some people make a career out of them. Some people die in pursuit of the rush these activities provide. Other high stim behaviors, like taking huge financial risks and traveling to remote parts of the world, are more subtle but can be equally dangerous.

High stim activities are especially attractive to certain

people with ADD and provide novelty and excitement that their ADD brains crave. When an impulsive person seeks out high stim activities, the consequences can be devastating. This is especially true when you add alcohol and drugs to the mix.

Kissing the Red Light

Rob was walking home with friends from a night of drinking when he spotted a crane on top of a twenty-story hotel under construction. The hotel was high enough that a red light had been mounted on the crane so planes landing at the nearby San Diego airport wouldn't hit it.

Rob impulsively said to his friends, "I'll race you to the top. First one to kiss the red light wins." One of his friends (who probably also had ADD) accepted the challenge and took off at a trot. Impulsiveness, thrill seeking, and alcohol could have killed them. Instead, they climbed up the crane, kissed the red light, and raced back down, uninjured.

No bets were made. Rob did it for the excitement and adrenaline rush. He risked his life to stimulate his brain. Alcohol increased his impulsiveness and decreased his judgment. It is by the grace of God and sheer luck that Rob is alive today.

PLUGGING IN

There's a huge difference between watching television, playing video games, "surfing" the Internet, and getting lost in these devices. Nothing is inherently wrong with any of this electronic technology; it can provide entertainment, relaxation, information, and never-ending global conversations. However, the way we use electronics, or the extent to which we use them, can cause problems.

When you "plug in," you don't feel or think about much beyond what's right in front of you. Your brain waves actually change by increasing theta waves, which are common in states of daydreaming and ADD. Adults and children with ADD are especially prone to hyperfocusing on television, computers, and video games to the point of getting stuck or addicted to being plugged in. Hours pass. They feel nothing. Never once do they think about how disorganized and out of balance their lives are.

The latest wave of electronic addictions involves the Internet. It makes sense that people with ADD would be attracted to the World Wide Web, because cruising the Web is similar to how the ADD mind thinks. The Web is expansive and nonlinear, with connections the user intuitively moves through. There is no wrong way to cruise the Web. How perfect for the ADD brain! Many people with ADD report feeling at home when they enter the Web.

Through the Internet, you can chat with people from all over the world. This can be heaven for the person with ADD who loves to talk with interesting and diverse people. Major on-line services provide electronic "rooms" listed by topic and interest where you can communicate with people with similar interests or problems. Some rooms are even dedicated to ADD. In these rooms, people with ADD, friends, spouses, relatives, and parents of ADD kids share experiences and information. The dialogue in the ADD chat rooms can be fast, hilariously funny, painful, and touching.

When people with ADD lose control over how often or how long they stay on-line they have become addicted. The next story illustrates what can happen when surfing the Net becomes a destructive obsession.

Tony Crashes on the Information Highway

What started out as an interesting, relaxing way to spend his free time turned into an addiction that cost Tony life as he knew it. At first Tony was only losing sleep. As he chatted with new friends he had met on the Internet, Tony began spending almost all of his free time at the computer. He virtually forgot about his wife, Melissa, and daughter, Cari.

Initially, Melissa was only a little concerned about the

hours Tony spent online. Her concern, however, turned into hurt and, eventually, resentment. She couldn't get Tony's attention. The distance between him and Melissa increased in proportion to her complaints, while he denied that his relationship with the Internet was affecting her or their daughter. Tony rebuffed Melissa's pleas that they go to counseling. After a year of almost no emotional contact with Tony, Melissa and Cari moved in with Melissa's parents.

Tony hardly minded when they moved out. Now he had even more time to spend on his computer. But after a few months Tony began to experience the void of real human contact. His consulting business was failing because of the lack of attention he gave it. One day an online friend told Tony that he needed professional help, so Tony eventually began seeing a therapist. He had to learn how to create intimate relationships with real people who were actually available to him, and not be dependent on computers to meet his needs.

Tony's therapist referred him to a psychiatrist who diagnosed him with ADD. Tony took medication that gave him the ability to shift his ADD brain from one activity to another. He learned how to monitor his tendency to get so captivated that he would get lost in whatever behavior he was engaged in . . . except for the Internet. Like most addicts, Tony couldn't moderate his Internet addiction. He found himself getting lost on the information highway, but before he crashed he canceled all online access. For now, Tony has decided to remain abstinent from the behavior he cannot control.

SEX AND LOVE ADDICTIONS

What turns sex and love into addictions is the same thing that turns spending into an addiction: loss of control. Sigmund Freud, who contributed to the psychiatric field in both positive and negative ways, defined mental health as "the ability to work and to love." Working and loving are basic components of emotional health unless we work or love to extremes. Let's talk about love addictions and then we'll turn to sexual addictions.

Love Addictions

The ability to give and receive love is a joyous gift. Love truly is the answer to many of life's questions and dilemmas, but what if your feelings of love become obsessive? Is it possible to become addicted to a feeling such as love? Absolutely.

Healthy love is the ability to love and nurture yourself as well as others. Love addiction occurs when you become dependent on, or addicted to, the love of another in order to feel a sense of self-worth or to be able to function in your daily life. Love addicts develop unrealistic or distorted perceptions of what love is and, like a heroin junkie, are willing to sacrifice themselves in order to obtain what they mistakenly perceive as love.

Love addiction is characterized by obsessive thoughts about another person and compulsive behaviors such as driving by your love object's house. When you are addicted to love, you feel intense and relentless possessiveness, anger, fear of abandonment, jealousy, and other emotions. Not only do you feel these emotions deeply, you lose your ability to control your behavior and may act on these feelings. You disregard your own needs in your attempts to get an unrealistic type of love from another. People with ADD are susceptible to becoming love addicts for several reasons:

▶ They may not have received the early bonding during infancy and childhood necessary to ensure a sense of security in adult relationships.
▶ Some people with ADD tend to feel less worthwhile than others as a result of their disabilities. They spend their lives desperately seeking love and approval from others because they have such difficulty loving and approving of themselves.

176

▶ Children with ADD are at risk for physical, verbal, and sexual abuse. This abuse contributes to their willingness to sacrifice themselves for love and attention.

Although Sasha's story is an extreme one, it will illuminate the dangers that may confront the love addict.

Loved to "Death"

Sasha grew up with untreated ADD and learning disabilities. Even though she was bright, she had always felt stupid and unworthy of love. Sasha's life changed when she met Troy. Troy was good-looking and charming. And to Sasha's amazement, he adored her. When they were together, he gave her his constant and undivided attention; he seemed to want her to be with him exclusively.

Sasha felt that his lavish attentions compensated for the fact that, while she worked full-time, Troy hung out all day, drinking and snorting cocaine with his friends. That wasn't so bad, she reasoned; he was home every evening, totally devoting his time and energy to her. Sasha was in a state of love she had never thought possible. She couldn't believe that a man like Troy could be so in love with her.

As the relationship progressed, so did Troy's addictions to drugs and to Sasha. At times he became jealous and paranoid, accusing her of seeing other men. Sasha assured Troy that he was her only love. Besides, she pointed out logically, she was either working or with him.

One night, Troy's possessiveness escalated to anger. He blackened Sasha's eyes and broke her nose. Sasha was shocked and terrified, but Troy was so remorseful, promising that he would never touch her again. Sasha had become so dependent on Troy's love and the tenuous sense of self-worth it had nourished in her that she told her friends and coworkers she had been involved in an auto accident.

Troy was so fearful of losing Sasha that he disconnected

their telephone, took her to and from work, and demanded that she not leave the house without him. Sasha accepted his demands as an expression of how deeply Troy loved her, until the night Troy became convinced that Sasha was secretly seeing another man. When Sasha denied his accusations, he flew into a rage and beat her into a state of unconsciousness, sending her to the hospital with a fractured skull.

Troy went to prison for assault and battery, even though Sasha would not press charges. Sasha went on to receive treatment for her love addiction and ADD. At times she still finds herself obsessed with Troy. Troy remains in a men's correctional facility where he is not getting help for his violent behavior or his love and chemical addictions.

Addicted to Sex

Love and sex addictions frequently accompany each other, but they can also be separate problems. Our ability to be sexual and procreate is part of our humanness, but if we are unable to control our sexual impulses and desires, the consequences can be serious.

When it comes to sexuality, a person with ADD can have a low, average, or high sex drive. Some people with ADD constantly feel the need to express themselves sexually. Add poor impulse control to this need and you can see how sexual addiction might occur. This is not to say that everyone with a sexual addiction has ADD, only that some people with ADD are more vulnerable to sexual addictions than others.

Sex becomes an addiction when

- ▶ we lose our ability to control our sexual behavior;
- ▶ we violate our moral, cultural, or religious values;
- ▶ we put ourselves at risk to be physically and emotionally harmed;
- ▶ we risk exposure to sexually transmitted diseases and risk exposing others;

178

▶ we lie and are deceitful about our sexual behavior.

Sex becomes an addiction when, in spite of the consequences, you can't control your behavior. Mario's experiences speak directly to the conflict between his sexual addiction and his values.

Please Forgive Me

When Mario was a child he wanted to be a minister like his father, but he couldn't sit still in church or Sunday school. His mind and body wandered even when he wanted to pay attention. Mario grew up in a family that taught him Christian values, and he knew the difference between right and wrong. Yet his impulsive actions frequently got him into trouble and put him in conflict with his deeply held beliefs.

Puberty hit Mario hard. His undiagnosed ADD got worse. He found himself obsessed with sexual fantasies. It was important to Mario that he remain a virgin until he married and so he felt horrible when he broke his commitment at age sixteen. He felt even worse a week later when he had sex with a different girl. For the next three years Mario was either thinking about sex, looking at pornographic magazines, or being sexually active with anyone he could. No matter how hard he tried, Mario couldn't stop his addictive sexual behavior. He felt so ashamed and hopeless that he contemplated suicide. He prayed to God for help. His prayers were answered in a way he didn't expect.

At a friend's wedding Mario met a woman named Allie to whom he was very attracted. After some friendly conversation, Mario put his hand on Allie's leg. She politely asked him to remove his hand, and said, "I'm a recovering sex and love addict. If you are interested in a friendship, I might be available, but if you are looking for sex, look elsewhere." Mario asked her to tell him more about sex and love addiction. He couldn't believe how much he related to Allie's story. Mario confided to her about his addiction to sex, and she shared with him the recovery she had experienced with the help of a group called Sex and Love Addicts Anonymous (SLAA).

The next night, Allie took Mario to a SLAA meeting and he began his recovery. Through his involvement with SLAA, Mario has been able to make peace with himself and with God.

WORK ADDICTION

Work is good. It can provide us with a purpose, help others, and enable us to express our talents and be financially responsible for ourselves and our families. But, as we are learning, too much of a good thing can be harmful. Yes, people do become addicted to work. The high energy and highly focused characteristics some people with ADD exhibit can predispose them to using work as a way to medicate their ADD restlessness, relationship difficulties, and need for constant stimulation. Let's look at William's story, because it provides an example of someone who used work to cope with ADD.

Work Until You Drop

William, who has ADD, is forty-six, married, and the father of two children. He is overweight, rarely exercises, smokes two packs of cigarettes a day, and works sixty to seventy hours a week at a company he owns. He also holds a seat on the city council.

When William is not working, he's thinking about work. As a result, William provides more income than his family needs. What they want from him is more time, but they've given up on asking for it. William is rarely physically and emotionally present for his wife or children. When he takes his family on exotic vacations to the Cayman Islands or Hawaii, he brings his laptop computer and a suitcase full of files. His wife, Tori, and their children have accepted his lack of participation in their family. William has no close friendships, and his superficial social life revolves around his employees and colleagues.

William has tried to work less. During these brief times, he felt restless and uncomfortable because he wasn't doing something "productive." He always quickly returned to the security he finds in the ceaseless challenges of work activities.

William was working alone at the office late one night when he felt a crushing pain in his chest. He was so overwhelmed with pain and fear that he could barely call 911. William had suffered a moderate heart attack. Initially he felt that his life had crashed in around him and was panicked by the lifestyle changes his doctor insisted he make.

It was the look of pain and fear in his children's eyes that convinced him to change. William went through a month of serious work withdrawals; he was obsessed with thoughts about work, which made him irritable and restless. With urging and support from Tori, they attended therapy together. Gradually, William began to accept that his compulsive working was an addiction that was hurting him and his family.

EXERCISING TO EXHAUSTION

We know that exercise is good for us. It keeps our bodies healthy and improves our mental health. Exercise is especially important for those who have high energy ADD, because it offers a healthy, constructive outlet for that energy. However, even something as valuable as exercise can become an addiction. You know exercise is an addiction when

> ► you have difficulty functioning if you miss a day of exercise;
> ► you can't stop exercising, in spite of injuries;
> ► the amount and type of exercise you participate in harms your body;
> ► the amount of time spent exercising causes

problems in other areas of your life, such as
work, relationships, and physical health;
▶ exercise is part of a compulsion to lose weight, as
in the case of anorexia.

Vera is a good example of someone who couldn't stop exercising. As far back as she can remember, Vera's favorite parts of school were recess, physical education, and after-school sports. Even though she didn't know she had ADD, she did know that when she didn't exercise she couldn't control her abundance of energy. Vera's athletic abilities, rather than her academic abilities, got her through high school. She received an athletic scholarship to a university in another state.

The combination of her untreated ADD, being away from her structure at home, and the academic demands of college changed Vera's relationship with exercise. At first the shift was subtle. Vera was preparing for a triathlon, which called for long and arduous hours of physical activity. Gradually she began spending most of each day running, cycling, and swimming herself into a state of exhaustion. One day her roommate brought to her attention the fact that she hadn't attended classes for weeks and might be failing.

Vera desperately wanted to stay in school because she was the captain of the volleyball team. She made a commitment to herself to reduce her workouts and attend her classes. However, as she sat in class she was obsessed with the need to exercise. No matter how hard she tried, Vera could not stop herself from either thinking about or doing compulsive exercise. In spite of the consequences of failing at the university, Vera could not stop her exercise addiction.

When she returned home for a holiday break, her family became aware of the severity of Vera's problems. They took her to a therapist who diagnosed Vera's ADD. Vera is now making progress in her treatment. She has decided not to return to college until she has learned to control her exercise addiction.

WHAT DO I DO NEXT?

If you realize that you're suffering from a behavioral addiction, now is the time to get help. You may want to contact a Twelve Step program such as Gamblers Anonymous, Debtors Anonymous, Workaholics Anonymous, or Sex and Love Addicts Anonymous. Now might also be a good time to talk with a therapist about your behavioral addictions. Both your ADD and your behavioral addictions must be treated in order for you to fully enjoy life.

In the next two chapters we'll look at specific solutions to ADD and addictive behaviors.

CHAPTER TEN

BEHAVIORAL SOLUTIONS FOR ADD

Practical Tools to Help You Cope

By now you have an understanding of the biological and genetic causes of ADD and the link between ADD and addictions. You also probably have a good idea about whether or not you should seek treatment for ADD and addictions.

This chapter will begin by discussing the diagnosis of ADD. Is it as overdiagnosed as some people believe? We will talk specifically about how to go about getting an evaluation for ADD and the specific questions to ask before you even enter the doctor's or therapist's office. Then we'll highlight some of the ways ADD can make your life miserable and give you specific suggestions for coping more effectively with each problem.

The purpose of this chapter is to provide you with tools to help you cope with your ADD, whether or not you take medication. These tools are not meant to be a substitute for medication. It's hard to build a house with building material, hammer, and nails if there's no foundation to build upon. For some of you, medication will provide the foundation on which to build a different life. I do not suggest that you try everything in this chapter as a way to avoid taking medication. Once you're diagnosed with ADD, it's important to consider what your health-care provider suggests.

In the next chapter, we'll explore why and when medication can be helpful, as well as how medication works to treat ADD symptoms. But the first step in getting treatment for ADD is finding out if you do indeed have ADD.

GETTING A DIAGNOSIS

Even if you're convinced that you have ADD, it's important to be evaluated by a doctor or therapist who has a thorough knowledge of adult ADD. Don't rely on self-diagnosis. Even if you're a professional, let another professional give you an objective diagnosis.

ADD is a diagnosis fraught with questions and controversy. Many media sources express concern that ADD is overdiagnosed. In some cases, this is true. It is critically important that people who are suffering from anxiety, post-traumatic stress disorder, manic depressive illness, personality disorders, thyroid imbalances, head injuries, and addictions not be diagnosed with ADD if they don't have it. However, as I've mentioned, ADD is much more of an inclusive than exclusive diagnosis. People with ADD are likely to have other coexisting conditions.

As with any misdiagnosed condition, treating the wrong problem, or only part of the problem, can lead to serious consequences. Therefore, it's essential that ADD does not become the all-encompassing label we slap on adults and children who may exhibit some of the symptoms. Each individual must be viewed in the context of his or her life. People in crisis or under stress can exhibit signs similar to ADD, but if these symptoms have not been present in some form during most of their lives, they are probably responding to their circumstances and do not have ADD.

On the other hand, many people who have ADD are not diagnosed. This is especially true of adults, women, girls, and those who are not hyperactive. When we look at the full spectrum of ADD, its subtypes, and how it is uniquely manifested in each individual, we can see why ADD is also underdiagnosed.

When we talk about over or underdiagnosis, we are really talking about misdiagnosis. Educating yourself about ADD is your best defense against misdiagnosis. I don't mean to sound like I lack faith in the medical profession, because I don't. It's just that so few health-care providers have training and experience in evaluating and treating ADD. The more you know, the better health care consumer you are.

While we are fortunate to have many fine professionals devoting time to one special illness or problem, including ADD, there is a downside to this specialization. An old saying goes something like this: "When all you have is a hammer, everything you see looks like a nail." Specialists who primarily treat survivors of sexual abuse, or patients with depression or ADD, may tend to see their patients' difficulties through the lens of their specialty. I have worked with many patients who have received a different diagnosis from each specialist they have seen. Coincidentally, the diagnosis matched the practitioner's specialty.

How to Get an Evaluation for ADD

The first step is to find a professional who has the experience and expertise to evaluate ADD in adults. Most treatment professionals are ethical and do not claim to specialize in areas where they don't have expertise. Unfortunately, some professionals advertise themselves as being experts in ailments that are more frequently diagnosed. Fifteen years ago, when our growing awareness of addictions made treating people with this disease a priority, some counselors, doctors, and therapists suddenly claimed to be addiction specialists, even if they had little experience.

Since ADD has become so high profile, ADD clinics and specialists are springing up all over. You need to look for a health-care provider who has had several years' experience treating adults with ADD. Since adult ADD has only really been recognized in the nineties, you will not likely find someone who has treated it for twenty years. This is okay, but you probably don't want to be evaluated by someone who has treated only a handful of adults with ADD. It is also helpful if the professional you choose treats conditions other than ADD. It's especially important to find someone who understands the link between ADD and addictions or is willing to consult with an addictions specialist.

Finding the right person to evaluate you can be difficult. The best recommendations usually come from patients or former patients. Ask around and you may hear the same names come up from different people. The last place to look is that full-page ad in the yellow pages or on billboards and shopping carts. Most clinicians who are exceptional do not have to advertise much. The excellent reputations they have earned among patients and fellow practitioners are an effective form of advertising.

Before you make an appointment to see someone for an ADD evaluation, consider asking him or her the following questions:

▶ What percentage of your practice is with people who have ADD?
▶ How often do you *not* diagnose ADD in people who think they have it?
▶ How long have you been evaluating and treating adults with ADD?
▶ Roughly how many adults with ADD have you treated?
▶ Roughly how many people have you treated who have ADD and addictions?
▶ What is your primary treatment for ADD? (You want to hear about ADD groups, coaching, help with organizing, and medication when warranted.)
▶ Is medication the only treatment I need? (Medication should be part of a comprehensive treatment plan when indicated.)

▶ What is your fee for the evaluation and for regular sessions? (Fees vary according to geographic location and type of practitioner you see. However, it's important to know ahead of time how much you will be charged for these services. It can take several sessions to make an ADD diagnosis.)

▶ How often will we meet for my treatment? (Due to related conditions, treatment plans can vary greatly. Your practitioner will have a better idea of the duration of treatment after an evaluation and several sessions.)

What to Expect
Many professionals, including myself, believe that in most cases ADD can be accurately diagnosed by obtaining a detailed history of the individual from childhood to the present. Whenever possible, other people in your life should also contribute information about your history. These people may be your spouse, parents, siblings, friends, boss, or coworkers. It is also helpful if you have someone in your life who can recollect information about you as an infant, toddler, and child. You can refer to the checklists in chapter five.

As I mentioned earlier, people with ADD are not always good at observing themselves and their behaviors. When I send questionnaires home with a client, I send an extra copy for significant others to fill out about that person as well. This way I get as broad a picture as possible of potential ADD symptoms throughout the person's life.

Doctors Hallowell and Ratey, in their book *Driven to Distraction,* say the following about using the patient's history as well as present behavior and problems to make the diagnosis:

"It is important to underline this point: the diagnosis of ADD is based first and foremost on the

individual's history or life story. The most important step in determining whether one has ADD is
sitting down and talking to somebody who is
knowledgeable in the field."[1]

Diagnosing ADD is similar to diagnosing clinical
depression. No blood test determines if you are biologically depressed or depressed because of an event in your
life. Your doctor makes the determination by asking you
about specific symptoms such as sleep and eating pat-
terns, concentration, sexual drive, energy level, and ability to have fun. The diagnosis is made by looking at your
family history of mood disorders, how you appear and
act, and your description of how you feel and function
now and in the past. Diagnosing ADD follows a similar
pattern.

Other diagnostic tools can be used, such as the T.O.V.A.
(Test of Variables of Attention)—a computerized performance test developed specifically to diagnose ADD, and
brain scans. These tools can be valuable in situations when
it's hard to differentiate ADD from other co-occurring conditions, or when the patient or family member wants to see
"proof" of the diagnosis. As of this writing, no definitive
test for ADD has been accepted by the medical profession.

Different experts will have preferred methods of diagnosing ADD. Be cautious of professionals who want to put
you or your child through thousands of dollars of psychological testing, brain scans, or diet programs, unless
you clearly understand why they need more information
than a comprehensive history provides. There are situations where ADD is just one of many problems; in these
cases it may be essential to have testing for related learning disorders, allergies, and physical, neurological, and
emotional problems. This is not to say that if a professional asks for additional testing you should say no. In
most cases, however, a thorough history, with input from
people in your life, should suffice.

Recognizing Recovery-Based Symptoms

It is complicated, but not impossible, to diagnose ADD during early recovery from addictions. If you are self-medicating your ADD with drugs, food, alcohol, or compulsive behaviors, your ADD is being treated. It's obviously not being treated in healthy ways or in ways that work; nonetheless, you may experience some relief from your ADD symptoms.

When you become abstinent, which is essential for your recovery from addictions, you will suffer from untreated ADD. By this I mean that your ADD symptoms will get worse as you are trying to get better. It is extremely perplexing and frustrating when you're trying so hard to do the "right" things, but you're actually functioning and feeling worse.

The other confusing part about ADD and early recovery is that many people without ADD will appear to have ADD symptoms during the first months of abstinence. They can be disorganized, restless, or unable to sit still; have difficulties concentrating and following through with commitments; and act impulsively. These ADD-like symptoms are referred to as recovery- or abstinent-based symptoms and are caused by early sobriety.

The differences between recovery-based symptoms and true ADD are many. First, the person without ADD will not have a history of attention, impulse, and activity level problems that go back to early childhood. Their symptoms appear when they get clean and sober. Second, these ADD-like symptoms go away within six months to a year of recovery. True ADD symptoms will not spontaneously disappear; instead they often become more pronounced and more noticeable in recovery.

Recognizing Acquired ADD

To make the diagnostic picture even more complicated, some people sustain permanent brain damage as a result of their substance addictions. It has been observed that cocaine and amphetamine addicts in particular can have

ADD symptoms with no history of childhood ADD. This "acquired" ADD is also seen in people who have suffered head injuries, especially in the frontal lobe.

More and more often I work with clients who were born after extremely long labors or with the umbilical cord around their neck or with forceps. I'm not saying that any occurrence of these conditions will automatically lead to ADD; however, I do note that the symptoms of ADD are very similar to those of a frontal lobe head injury which can be caused by trauma at birth, a blow to the head, or prolonged substance abuse. It is also more likely that high energy, risk-seeking childrenand adults are prone to hit their heads and injure their brains.

GETTING BETTER

Whether ADD is caused by genetics, or chemical or physical trauma, it deserves treatment. The most effective treatment for many is the combination of learning how to adapt their behavior, express feelings about their ADD, and balance brain chemistry through medication. Before we discuss medication in more detail, let's look at specific ways to change troublesome behaviors.

ADD affects each of us differently. Everyone with ADD will have difficulties with one or a combination of the following: attention, impulse control, and activity level. How we manifest these differences can be unique and paradoxical. This is why it's often difficult to diagnose ADD, especially in adults. Let's look at some of the specific problems related to ADD, such as the issue of personal boundaries, communication styles, and organization.

BOUNDARIES

Many of us have difficulty learning to create healthy physical and emotional boundaries in relationships. A physical boundary is the imaginary space around each of us. Have you ever had someone hug or kiss you, ask personal questions, or dump their problems on you? What would feel fine coming from someone with whom you have a close relationship may feel awful coming from someone you don't care for or don't know well. Boundaries have a lot to do with the context of the relationship. We all have comfort levels regarding how close we like others to get. You may not mind a stranger hugging you or joking with you, or you might feel violated by this behavior, because the relationship isn't close enough to warrant it.

Trespassing is violating property boundaries; rape is violating physical, emotional, and spiritual boundaries. These are obvious boundary violations. However, there are many subtle ways we disrespect the boundaries of others.

It's often easier to understand physical boundaries than emotional boundaries, which are like a series of fences, one inside the other, each with its own gate. We let in certain individuals, in specific situations, through some or most of these gates. By doing so, we bring them closer to our "true" self.

Another way of seeing these boundaries is to think of them as semipermeable membranes like those of the cells that make up our bodies. Semipermeable means that certain things are allowed in while other things are kept out. Our relationships with others function similarly to this basic cellular structure of the body. We can select the people we let in and how far we let them in, just as we choose who we will keep at a distance. We get into trouble when we let others get so close that they can harm us. We can also have boundaries so impermeable that no one can penetrate them, leaving us looking out at the world through our emotional fences and feeling like the outsider described in chapter five.

There are many ways to violate others' emotional boundaries. We trespass on others' emotions when we don't know where their boundaries are or when we do know but blatantly pass through them. We do this to each other in a variety of ways, such as asking for personal

193

information and not respecting "No" for an answer, inter-rupting, giving unsolicited advice, badgering, or coercing. We also trespass when we expect others to feel as we do and assume they feel as close to us as we do to them.

It is essential to honor our boundaries and the bounda-ries of others. The codependency recovery movement has helped millions to establish workable boundaries that enhance their relationships. Alanon and Codependents Anonymous (CODA) are two Twelve Step programs that are especially helpful in establishing and fine-tuning per-sonal boundaries.

How Do Boundaries Relate to ADD and Addictions?

Have you ever seen someone enter a social gathering with such a strong presence that they seem to suck the air right out of the room? They may be loud, disruptive, and domi-nate several conversations at once. Human beings, in gen-eral, are more apt to violate each other's boundaries when they are under the influence of alcohol and other drugs, because they lose control of their inhibitions.

People with ADD seem to consistently struggle with maintaining their own boundaries and with not violating the boundaries of others. The sad thing is, most people with ADD don't mean to be intrusive or disrespectful. Some-times they have no idea they have violated your boundaries. Sometimes they have no idea they have violated their own. Many people with ADD are always trying to guess what is the right or appropriate behavior. Their impulsiveness causes them to disclose more about themselves than is good for them. Some are used to being pushy, dominating, and controlling just to get through life. Many have such strong personalities that others are afraid to tell them how they come across. Without feedback, it's hard for them to change their behavior.

Let's look at some specific boundary difficulties you may have and explore behavioral changes that can help you relate to others in a more appropriate way.

Doorknob Conversations

Doorknob conversations are the ones that begin just as you're walking out the door. You may have spent several hours talking with a friend about all sorts of things. Then, just as you're about to leave, you say, "Did I tell you I'm moving to Texas next week?" You may even have your hand on the doorknob when you say, "Oh, by the way, did I tell you that Sally and I are getting a divorce?" It's quite difficult for your friend not to respond to information like this, even if he or she is about to be late for an important event.

Doorknob conversations can be quite frustrating for both parties. Your friend may not really have the time to go into the details at that moment and may feel guilty about that. And you have set yourself up, without realizing it, to not get the attention this important information deserves.

If you have the tendency to drop conversational bombs as you're walking out the door, you may want to consider an approach that will meet your needs better. It can be humiliating and unfulfilling to tell someone something very personal just as your time with them has ended. If you have something important you want to communicate, consider the following suggestions.

- ▶ Let the person know prior to your meeting what you want to talk about.
- ▶ Begin your time by telling your friend, spouse, therapist, or doctor what is on your mind.
- ▶ Let whomever you are talking with know that it's sometimes hard for you to stay on track.
- ▶ Ask for guidance to help you stay focused on your important topic.
- ▶ Practice finishing your important information before you detour to other subjects.

If you are the person lingering at the door with your ADD friend, setting boundaries for yourself is important; otherwise, you may end up resenting your friend's doorknob saga. Here's one way to handle this type of interaction.

"Gosh, Bob, I'm sorry to hear about you and Sally. I really want to hear more about this, but I have to leave right now. Will you be home later this evening so I can call you? Then I'll have the time to talk with you about what's going on in your life."

Most people with ADD do not intend to manipulate you by waiting until the last minute to tell you the most important news of their visit. People with ADD frequently get distracted and forget the important information they came to tell you in the first place.

Overstaying Your Welcome

Do you stay in relationships, jobs, and places long after their value is gone? Are you always the last one to leave the party? Does the hostess fall asleep in an upright position while you chat away, oblivious to her exhaustion? To you, the night may be young, but for others, it's over.

Knowing when to leave is extremely important. Many people with ADD do not pick up on subtle or even blatant cues to move on. They may be on the verge of being fired; yet, when given the option to quietly exit, they file lawsuits for wrongful dismissal to stay in jobs where they're not welcome. Fighting to keep a job can be far more stimulating than the job ever was, but win or lose they may have expended energy better spent on something else.

The same can be true with relationships. People with ADD may stay in them too long because of difficulty dealing with change and an inability to discern when the relationship is no longer serving either person.

If you have ADD, I know you don't mean to be rude or stay long after an event is over. You just don't know when to leave. Here are a few ideas to consider.

- ▶ Be aware of when others are leaving.
- ▶ Look for cues such as yawning, rhythmic head nodding, and watch peeking.

▶ Ask yourself or someone else if now is a good time to leave.

▶ If you are unhappy in a situation, consider your options. Staying may not be your only option.

▶ Consider setting time limits. "If my relationship isn't improving in three to six months I will talk about moving on."

▶ Set a time to leave social events. If you have a watch with a timer, set it too.

Telling Your Life Story to Voice Mail

Do you ever wish you could erase the message you just left on someone's voice mail? Do you find yourself leaving lengthy messages that are more detailed than necessary? If you have ADD, you may tell the answering machine what's on your mind . . . *everything* that's on your mind. Since your mind processes many things at the same time, you may mention all of them to a machine. This can be embarrassing for you and irritating or confusing to the person listening to your message. Here are some suggestions to consider when leaving telephone messages.

▶ Try keeping your message to the basics. "Hi, Susan, this is Paula. Please call me tonight. I'll be home after 8 p.m."

▶ Think about what you want to say before you call to leave a message.

▶ Consider writing the message down and saying it a few times to yourself.

▶ Decide before you call if this person is close to you and whether or not a personal message would be appropriate.

▶ If you catch yourself saying things to the machine that are not directly related, redirect yourself back to the basic message.

197

Just Say No

We all have trouble saying no at times. It's human nature to want to help and please others, but if you have ADD you may take this desire to the extreme. You may also be dealing with your unrealistic optimism, well-intentioned grandiosity, and impulsivity. How many times do you say yes when you really mean no? Do you ever overschedule yourself because you can't say no? Do the words, "Sure, I can do that," fly out of your mouth like hungry hummingbirds before you know what "that" is?

Learning to say no when you mean no takes practice, especially if you've spent most of your life saying yes. Practicing saying no will give you more control over your life. You will be less likely to overcommit and more able to adhere to your limits as a human being. Developing the ability to say no will also decrease your resentment toward those who expect so much of you.

Keep in mind that people in our lives may not always react positively to behavioral changes, especially if the changes affect them. Be aware that this may happen, but don't let it stop you from taking care of yourself. Your friends, family, and coworkers cannot afford your resentment. The better you take care of yourself, the less you will resent them.

Here are some tips to help you say no when no is what you want to say.

- ▶ Consider letting callers leave messages rather than answering the phone. This can give you time to think before you call back.
- ▶ If you answer the phone and the caller has a request, tell him or her you will call back in a few minutes. This allows you time to think through the request and what response you really want to give.
- ▶ If someone is asking you in person, tell him or her you have to think about it and will respond in a few minutes.

▶ Think each situation through. Do you really want to volunteer to make six dozen cookies for the home and school club?

▶ It's perfectly okay to decline invitations, extra work, good deeds, etc.

▶ It's better to decline than to feel overwhelmed or resentful.

▶ It's okay to change your mind and say, "I'm sorry, but now that I've thought about it, I realize I can't go to the movies tonight."

▶ Remember that you were not put on this planet to do everything for everyone.

▶ Cut yourself some slack when old voices tell you that you "should" do this or that.

Call a Plumber

Many years ago, my friend Maria shared with me some wisdom that would probably be obvious to most people, but I found it a revelation. Maria had been working on a home she rented out during the summer. She was extremely handy and could fix almost anything. She had spent two days struggling with the plumbing in the sixty-year-old house. Unfortunately, water pipes were breaking and leaking faster than she could fix them. When sewage erupted into the bathtub, Maria shouted, "Please, God. Tell me what to do." At that moment, Maria heard a voice in her head. "Maria," it said, "call a plumber." *What a novel idea!* she thought. And that's what she did.

What a revelation to the person with ADD who may not think of the obvious! Knowing our limits, whether or not we have ADD, is extremely important. Many of us with ADD feel we have to do everything, even the things we don't do well. I encourage people to capitalize on what they do well and find others to help them with the things they don't do well. Many people with ADD have wide varieties of skills, but if plumbing isn't one of yours, call a plumber. Here are some additional suggestions.

- ▶ Accept what you do well and ask for help when you need it.
- ▶ Remember that you can't and don't have to do everything yourself.
- ▶ Consider making trades with people you can help and who can help you.
- ▶ Give yourself permission to set realistic goals.
- ▶ Have the number of a good plumber or mechanic near the telephone.

COMMUNICATION

The "Gotta Go" Style

Someone near and dear to me starts every conversation with, "Gotta go." He'll call from Italy, Puerto Rico, or across town and say, "Hi, I gotta go." He'll talk on at an inaudible speed and then say, "Gotta go." After a few more gotta goes, off he goes.

Do you know people who walk into a room with "gotta go" energy? It's as though they're on their way out even as they're coming in. Their brain works so fast, they're already thinking about where they'll go next.

The "gotta go" style can be offensive. Others may feel that you don't value them enough to be present when you're with them. Your eagerness to move on to the next event can also create anxiety in those around you. Sustaining relationships can be difficult when you're rapidly going in several directions at the same time.

I know you don't mean always to be on the go, disregard others, or create stress. Here are some ideas to help you change a "gotta go" style.

- ▶ Set aside enough time for your conversation or visit.
- ▶ Try to be realistic about how long your conversation or visit will take. You may forget that it takes forty minutes to get to your friend's house and only set an hour aside for the entire visit.

▶ Recognize when you feel rushed to end phone conversations, interactions, or visits.
▶ Ask yourself if you really need to rush.
▶ Let friends and family know that you're working on this behavior and would like their help.
▶ Stop and take a breath or two when you're speaking.
▶ Remember to ask others questions about how they are. Make sure you listen to what they say.

The Quiet Type
Some people with ADD have had such bad experiences with saying too much of the wrong thing at the wrong time that they say very little. They overcompensate for their impulsiveness and talkativeness by being quiet. They may have a lot going on inside, but they can't always share it with others. They are sometimes judged as rude or snobbish when they're simply trying to follow the conversation. When you have ADD, it takes tremendous energy to focus on conversations or to interact appropriately in social situations. Sometimes, your brain just shuts down and you don't have the energy to say much.

People with ADD who are less verbal frequently have difficulties tracking conversations. It may also be hard for them to access information to join in conversations. Many people with ADD have a hard time recognizing or articulating their feelings. They aren't withholding; they just don't know how they feel.

Here are some things to consider if you want to improve your communication skills.

▶ Every once in a while ask yourself how you're feeling. This will help you practice labeling your feelings so you can share them with others.
▶ Recognize when you space out in conversations. Give yourself permission to say, "I'm sorry. I missed what you were saying."

▶ Give yourself permission not to be able to articulate every fact you know. There will be times when you just can't access information.

▶ If talking with several people at a time puts you on overload, try having a conversation with one person at a time.

▶ Accept that you will not be the Lily Tomlin or Chevy Chase of the party.

"Uh Huh" and Head Nodding

Oh, this can really get you into trouble! How often do you find yourself nodding and saying, "Uh huh," as though you're listening intently, even when you don't have a clue what the other person is saying? Your mind has spaced out, in, or ventured elsewhere. You've learned to act as though you're paying attention so well that not only do others think you are paying attention, you do too. Not hearing what is being said is an invitation to a host of communication problems.

Active listening is an art. However, many people with ADD are masters of another dangerous art: active listening without hearing. People in your life get upset when they find out you really didn't hear what they were saying; otherwise, you wouldn't have asked how their mother was when they've just spent five minutes telling you about her death from cancer. When people don't feel heard, they often feel demeaned or feel that what they're saying isn't important to you. It may be very important to you, but your attention drifts or leaps away while you say "Uh huh" and nod your head. Here are some suggestions to improve your listening skills.

▶ Practice becoming aware when you are in an "Uh huh" or head-nodding trance.

▶ When you become aware you're not listening, focus in on what is being said. It may be valuable information, or it may be boring.

▶ It's okay to ask questions about information you have missed.

▶ Try not to interact with people when the television, newspaper, or radio can distract you.

▶ Observe how many times you say "Uh huh." You may say it more than you realize.

▶ Stay engaged by participating without dominating the conversation.

▶ Breaking the pattern of brain shutdown is not easy, and not always under your complete control. Be patient and persistent.

Hey, You!

Do people's names flow through your mind like sand through a sieve with holes the size of silver dollars? Do you constantly call people by the wrong names? This is embarrassing on a good day and disastrous in certain business, social, and personal situations. Do you ever forget the names of your own children, spouse, or friends? You stare at them blankly, trying to pull a name from your brain to match a face you know only too well. If this person is close to you, they probably accept you as you are and it doesn't bother them. Some people, however, may feel offended because you've met them four times and still don't remember their name.

It's so frustrating and stressful to be talking with someone and not be able to access his or her name. Calling people by name has significance in our culture. People like to hear the sound of their name. We tend to be attracted to people who not only remember our name but use it during conversation. Hearing our names helps keep us focused and listening to whoever is using it. Listen to really good salespeople, teachers, politicians, business people, administrators, and public relations personnel. They will use your name several times during a conversation.

People with ADD forget many things. Names are just a few of the things that people with ADD forget. Here are some suggestions to improve your ability to recall names.

- ▶ Listen closely when you are introduced to someone.
- ▶ Repeat the name over and over until it builds its nest in your mind.
- ▶ Always look for name tags. This is a great way to remember a name.
- ▶ Write down the names of people you have met and refer to the list when you meet again.
- ▶ If he or she is willing, ask your partner or friend to help you remember.
- ▶ It's okay to say, "I'm sorry, I forgot your name." It's easy to miss names when first introduced, especially if the situation is distracting.
- ▶ If you're with a friend and someone approaches you, calls you by name, and you have no idea who they are, you can say, "I'd like you to meet my friend, Jill." (Hopefully you remember Jill's name.) The approaching person will usually say, "Hi, Jill, my name is . . ."

Verbal Diarrhea and Word Storming

Do you talk too quickly and say too much? Do people's eyes glaze over when you're talking to them? Do you ever realize that you're talking so much that you're breathless? Do you tend to give ten minutes of information to a question that can be answered with yes or no? If you can relate to any of the above, you may suffer from ADD verbal diarrhea, or word storming. I know you don't mean to talk people into a coma; it's just that you have so much to say and you want to be helpful. But are you being helpful or annoying? It's hard to listen when you're busy talking. Conversation means there is interaction between both parties. A monologue is when one person does all the talking.

If you feel inclined to change this style of communicating, here are some suggestions.

- ▶ Become aware of when you give more information than is requested. Some people with ADD tend to overexplain.
- ▶ Be aware of your tendency to dominate conversations. When you catch yourself, stop talking.
- ▶ Remember to ask others for their feelings and opinions.
- ▶ Stop and think about what you're about to say. Are you interrupting or changing topics?
- ▶ When you catch yourself drifting off the subject, stop and redirect yourself. It's okay to say, "Sorry, I got off track there."
- ▶ Practice listening and holding back your impulse to comment.
- ▶ If you're in a business situation, write down what you want to say. Then think about it before you start talking.
- ▶ Ask yourself, "What are the most important things I need to say?"

But, But, But!

WARNING: Defensiveness can be habit-forming and may be harmful to your relationships!

Many people with ADD become addicted to making excuses for their words and actions. After years of forgetting birthdays, offending others, being late, losing important documents, and making mistakes, defending yourself becomes a knee-jerk reaction. You may honestly forget important dates, deadlines, and paperwork, yet people in your life may accuse you of just not caring enough to remember. In school your teacher may have accused you of lying, when, in fact, you really did lose your term paper.

A defensive attitude is one way people with ADD protect themselves from feeling criticized, misunderstood, or ashamed. Without realizing it, they are constantly prepared to defend their honor, even when it doesn't need defending. If you were criticized all your life, your "criticism defender" is always on the alert. It will do anything to protect you, and often perceives criticism even in neutral situations. Add impulsiveness to this, and you can respond in ways that are harmful to you and others.

We all get defensive at times; it's one way we maintain our personal boundaries. But like most things in life, excess defensiveness can cause huge problems. It feels horrible to always be on the defensive, and it takes up an enormous amount of energy. Being defensive can make a bad situation worse. What starts out as a misunderstanding can escalate to argument, verbal fights, and physical violence.

It's okay to make mistakes; we all do that. However, a defensive attitude only creates more problems. Here are some ways to avoid reacting defensively.

- ▶ Be aware of your tendency to want to defend yourself.
- ▶ Be aware of your vulnerability about feeling criticized.
- ▶ Ask yourself, "Do I really need to defend myself?"
- ▶ Ask yourself, "Is this person upset with me or just upset?"
- ▶ Tell the truth. If you are caught double-dipping your tortilla chip, don't deny it.
- ▶ Count to five before responding to perceived criticism.
- ▶ The best way to end an argument, if you know you're wrong, is to admit it and apologize.
- ▶ Turn down the volume on (or turn off) your internal criticizer. Allow yourself to be human and make mistakes.

ORGANIZATION AND TIMING

What Time Zone Are You In?

Do you ever feel like you haven't adjusted to daylight savings time and are about an hour off? Perhaps you haven't adjusted to the three-hour time change from when you moved ten years ago. I know the feeling. Do you lose track of time, or underestimate how much time it will take to do things or get places? Or are you compulsively prompt to the point of feeling anxious if you think you'll be a few minutes late?

Like many people with ADD, you may have a very different experience of time than most people. Some people with ADD don't get going until the afternoon. Their preference is to work late into the night and sleep late in the morning. Not all jobs accommodate this time schedule, and it can be isolating to be awake when most people are sleeping and vice versa. For some, adhering to their own body clock works best. Their attempts to fit into a "normal" time schedule have been disastrous. Some people with ADD talk about a window of time at night during which they can go to sleep. If they miss that window, they may stay up all night. On the other hand, others are so tired after a day of intensity that they crash early and are up with the roosters.

Being in a different time zone can also cause problems in your relationships. For example, if you and your partner are in different time zones, you may miss quality time together. Have you ever convinced yourself that a project will only take a few minutes, only to find someone very upset with you for being two hours late? Steve is an example of someone who loses track of time. He has the habit of starting projects that "will only take a minute," while his family is waiting in the car to go on a picnic or vacation. Meanwhile, his wife, Muriel, heats up along with the car engine. When he finally reaches the car, Steve has no idea why Muriel, who has been waiting in a hot car for ten minutes with bickering kids, snarls at him. Working from a different experience of time can cause major problems with other people, with your work, school, mortgage company, and the IRS. Here are some suggestions that might be of help.

► Buy a watch with a timer you can set to beep hourly.

► There are also watches you can set to go off at specific times of the day to remind you to take medication, eat, or shift gears into another activity.

► If you work with computers, consider a program with an alarm you can set to let you know how much time has passed.

► Try not to get too stimulated and engaged in the evenings if you plan to go to bed at a certain time.

► Use calendars, appointment books, computer calendars, and pocket planners to remind yourself of appointments and deadlines.

► Before you start to do something, ask yourself, "Is it realistic to start this project now?"

► Set priorities and stick with them. For example, if your priority is to get to work on time, bypass cleaning the kitchen or watering the plants if you're already late.

I Can't Find My Tax Extension!

Do you ever get into a dither because you can't find something? It usually happens right when you need to leave for an appointment. There you are, late to meet your friends for a hike, and you can't find your hiking boots anywhere. Pretty soon you have your closet, bedroom, attic, garage, laundry room, car, and house torn apart.

What's even worse is when you already feel bad about not completing, mailing, or finishing something, and now you can't even find it. Agitation, aggravation, and condemnation fill the house with swirling black clouds as you turn into a raging twister. You rip and roar from room to room in search of the "blankity blank" tax extension form.

It will take time and patience to learn new ways of organizing your chaotic clutter. You will have to create systems suited for you. Some people make a living by helping others get organized. Some of these professional organizers often have the highly focused, organized type of ADD. You may consider getting help to create cus-tom-fitted organizational systems. You may never become the colored label file person who knows exactly where everything is. Progress, for you, may be having fewer piles in fewer places, thus limiting the square footage you will have to sort through to find that tax extension form. Notice we are not even talking about making the April 15 deadline yet. One thing at a time. Here are some tips for finding what you want when you want it.

- ▶ Have a specific place to leave your car keys when you come home; a hook on the wall can be helpful.
- ▶ Use sunglasses straps, keys that clip to your purse or belt, and fanny packs.
- ▶ Create a "priority" file or pile where you can see it.
- ▶ Avoid endless paper shuffling by dealing with paperwork as soon as it arrives. Stock up on envelopes and stamps to mail bills, etc.
- ▶ File folders in an accessible box or file cabinet decrease time spent hunting for what you need.
- ▶ Use color-coded files. They work well because you can see by glancing at the color which category you're looking for.
- ▶ Consider decreasing clutter by getting rid of things you really don't use or need. Try not to be impulsive when culling through your stuff.
- ▶ Keep all tax forms and receipts in files, a box, or a large envelope.
- ▶ Get clothes, lunches, briefcases, backpacks, coats, and keys out the night before.
- ▶ Accept your unique style of organizing if it works for you.

The Endless Mood Roller Coaster

Like many people with ADD, you may feel as if you're riding an endless roller coaster of mood swings. You may feel powerless to control your ups and downs. Your mood may change dramatically from one day to the next or from moment to moment. One moment you feel upbeat, brimming with self-confidence; the next moment you feel lower than a gopher snake's belly.

You may also suffer from volcanic eruptions of rage. You know your rage is disproportionate to the situation, but you can't seem to stop the lava once it starts flowing. Before you know it, you're standing knee-deep in molten rock, burning from the tremendous remorse you feel about the devastation you've created.

In a short period of time your mood may reflect depression, irritability, anger, joy, and shame. Such quickly changing mood swings can be quite perplexing to you and those around you. Your brain may misinterpret information and cause you to have intense reactions to people and situations. You may have difficulty managing your impulses, which contributes to what may be perceived by others as irrational responses or changes in mood. You may find yourself confused and feeling awful about your responses and actions and yet feel powerless to control them.

Your intense emotions and mood changes are based in your brain chemistry. However, there are some things you can do to balance your wild ride.

- ▶ Take two breaths before you act or speak (especially if you're angry).
- ▶ Practice listening without thinking about what you want to say next.
- ▶ Remove yourself from the situation before or during a rage attack.
- ▶ Allow yourself to break away from negative thoughts and moods.
- ▶ Be aware of what triggers mood changes.

▶ Before you make a major life change, discuss it with trusted friends or a therapist.

▶ Be willing to apologize when you hurt others' feelings.

▶ Recognize when you start spiraling down the shame tube; you don't deserve to go there.

▶ Try not to get too hungry, angry, lonely, or tired.

Whether you take medication or not, you will need to practice new ways of adapting to your ADD. Look for progress, not perfection. You've had ADD all your life and won't be able to change your ADD behaviors overnight.

ANOTHER NONMEDICAL SOLUTION

ADD Coaching

In 1994, Nancy Ratey and Susan Sussman cofounded the National Coaching Network (NCN) as a result of their belief that people with ADD need more than traditional counseling. A coach is a person who can assist you in the following ways:

▶ Create realistic short- and long-term goals and plans to accomplish them.

▶ Help you to create your own organizational system and work on time management and setting priorities.

▶ Provide support and encouragement.

▶ Help you to maintain medication monitoring logs if necessary.

▶ Help you to manage your ADD at work, school, and home.

Coaching differs from therapy in the following ways:

▶ Coaches do not help you work through past issues; coaching is meant to help you learn new behaviors.

211

▶ Coaching is oriented toward problem-solving rather than focusing on insight.

▶ Coaches can work with you alone or in conjunction with your physician, therapist, or Twelve Step sponsor.

Many people with ADD have found coaching to be a valuable part of their comprehensive treatment plan. Most coaches are flexible and understand that you may need to contact them daily or several times a week. It's important to ask your potential coach questions similar to the ones you would ask before proceeding with an evaluation or treatment for ADD.

Keeping an Open Mind

People have varying degrees of ADD, which impacts them in unique ways during different stages of their lives. If you have ADD, it may not be enough to change your thinking, emotions, and behavior. You may need to have your ADD treated at the chemical level. Try not to look at medication as your last resort. Please keep an open mind as you read the next chapter. You will be the one to decide if taking medication is right for you.

CHAPTER ELEVEN

HELP THROUGH MEDICATION
Why and When It May Be Right for You

Whether or not you decide to treat your ADD with medication is a difficult decision, especially if you're in recovery from drug and alcohol addictions. You may be thinking, "Drugs almost killed me. I've spent years trying to get off them, and now you want me to start taking them?" I know. At first it sounds pretty crazy, but bear with me as I explain why medication might help. It's your decision; I simply want to give you information to help you make that decision. I believe that people in recovery should be extremely cautious when taking medications in general, but being cautious doesn't necessarily mean abstaining from all prescribed medications.

Medication can be helpful for many ADD sufferers when used in conjunction with some of the following therapies: education, behavioral management, social skills development, ADD support groups, therapy, ADD coaching, addiction recovery groups, and Twelve Step programs. MEDICATION SHOULD NOT BE USED AS THE SOLE TREATMENT FOR ADD. Taking pills to rebalance your neurotransmitters is not enough. It is essential that recovering alcoholics and addicts with ADD get involved in ongoing treatment for their addictions and that all people with ADD take advantage of nonmedical treatments for their condition.

When it comes to taking medication to treat ADD during recovery, I tread cautiously and sensitively. However, I want to mention a tendency we all share that may influence our perceptions in any delicate discussion. In my experience I've found that human beings can slip into contempt for what they think they should disapprove of or for what they fear, even before they have enough information to truly understand what they are resisting. Herbert Spencer refers to this principle as "contempt prior to investigation."[1] Just as there are myths about ADD and addictions, there are myths about people in recovery taking medication to treat co-occurring problems.

If you are a member of a Twelve Step group, you may hear people at meetings say, "You just don't take anything, no matter what." You may also have a sponsor who doesn't support the use of medication to treat emotional and medical problems. However, Alcoholics Anonymous has become more accepting over the years of the need for some of its members to use medication to treat co-occurring conditions. The following excerpts are from the pamphlet, *The AA Member—Medications & Other Drugs*, printed in 1984.

> Because of the difficulties that many alcoholics have with drugs, some members have taken the position that no one in AA should take any medication. While this position has undoubtedly prevented relapses for some, it has meant disaster for others.
>
> It becomes clear that just as it is wrong to enable or support any alcoholic to become readdicted to any drug, it is equally wrong to deprive any alcoholic of medication which can alleviate or control other disabling physical and/or emotional problems.[2]

In spite of the opinions you may hear in Twelve Step meetings, Alcoholics Anonymous World Services, Inc., which writes AA approved literature, does not subscribe to the belief that alcoholics should abstain from medications to treat legitimate health concerns. Unfortunately, the people with the "Don't take anything" beliefs tend to be very verbal about their convictions.

I know from my work with hundreds of recovering alcoholics and addicts over the past two decades that there are many who take medication while they are in recovery programs. Due to the strong opinions of some Twelve Step members, therapists, and addiction specialists, those who take medication do not always speak up. This too is beginning to change. More and more people are talking with their recovering friends, sponsors, and at meetings about taking antidepressants, seizure medications, and medications to treat ADD. Please don't let the opinions of others keep you from getting the help you deserve.

With a greater understanding of how these medications work, and with more awareness of their low abuse potential when closely monitored, you will have the information you need to make your decision if you want to take medication on a trial basis. In any case, I hope you won't succumb to "contempt prior to investigation".

HOW MEDICATIONS WORK

It's only been since the early nineties that the medical profession has begun to accept that in approximately 70 percent of all cases, ADD does not disappear during adolescence. Treating adults with medication is a new practice for many doctors. The scientific community is quickly rallying to provide more statistically sound studies on the types and dosages of medications most effective for adults. Many physicians who work regularly with these medications have gained knowledge and experience by listening closely to what their adult patients say about how medications affect them.

The information you're about to read is based on recent research from physicians and scientists who are working on the leading edge of adult ADD treatment. Since information is growing so quickly, there will be new understanding about these medications before this book is printed. It's exciting to see the advances we've made in the past five years, and to wonder what the next five years have in store.

In Chapter Four we discussed neurotransmitters and how imbalances in these messenger chemicals are believed to cause ADD. Dopamine, one of these neurotransmitters, works to relieve symptoms of ADD in a way similar to the way antidepressants like Prozac work to rebalance serotonin, thus relieving symptoms of biological depression. Most of the medication used to treat ADD has focused on dopamine, but medicines that work primarily on serotonin levels are also being used.

Treating problems at the neurotransmitter level is still not an exact science. However, some physicians and their patients find that the medicine that works on serotonin relieves some ADD symptoms. Rebalancing serotonin alone is not always enough for other ADD sufferers, who find symptom relief only when they take medicine that works with dopamine. For others, the combination of both types of medicine is the best way to go. This is especially true if you suffer from depression as well as ADD.

Doctors Hallowell and Ratey, in their book *Driven to Distraction*, write, "For both children and adults with correctly diagnosed ADD, some medication will be effective about 80 percent of the time."[3]

Your prescribing physician will have a good idea of what medicine to start you on, but there is usually some trial and error involved. No one knows exactly which medication(s) will work best for each individual. It's not uncommon for a patient to try two or three different medications, at different dosage levels, to find what works best. Your doctor should also help you find the best time(s) of day to take your medicine. Taking medication in the afternoon or evening may keep one person up late at night, while another may find that taking stimulant medication prior to going to bed actually helps them sleep.

The following brief overview provides basic information about the different medications used to treat ADD. This is not meant to take the place of medical information provided by your physician. I will start with stimulant medication: Ritalin, Dexedrine, Desoxyn, Adderall, and Cylert. Then I will briefly mention antidepressants such as Serzone, Wellbutrin, Prozac, Paxil, Zoloft, and Effexor.

TREATMENT WITH STIMULANTS

When the subject of taking stimulants to treat ADD comes up, people naturally ask the question, "Am I going to be taking speed?" The answer is yes and no. If you and your physician choose to use Dexedrine, Desoxyn, or Adderall, you will be taking amphetamine medication.

Ritalin and Cylert, on the other hand, are stimulants but are not amphetamines. However, using stimulant medicines to treat ADD differs greatly from abusing speed. To begin with, the dosage of medication used to treat ADD is far less than what you would use to get high or wired with street amphetamines. Second, the dosage will not vary due to being diluted with baby powder, ephedrine, or who knows what. Third, you won't be smoking, snorting, or injecting your ADD medication. Finally, your ADD medication will be closely monitored by your doctor and other members of your support system. It is essential that your doctor understands your history of drug and/or alcohol addiction.

Stimulant medications have been used for over forty years to treat attentional problems, obesity, and narcolepsy, a condition where the brain spontaneously falls asleep. These medications, when used properly, have had a good safety record with few side effects. If you're taking stimulants to treat your ADD, you should not feel euphoric, wired, or zapped with energy. Sorry, no free highs. Instead, you should notice an increased ability to concentrate, focus, organize, and control your impulses and activity level. Among those who have a high activity level, many report feeling calmer, less restless, and less anxious when taking stimulants. For those who have low activity level ADD, many report feeling a more normal energy level.

If you're getting high, euphoric, or manic as a result of your ADD medication, something is wrong. Your dosage or type of medication needs adjustment; you may need to stop taking it, or you may have conditions other than ADD. Please consult with your doctor before you make any changes with your medication.

Let's start our discussion of specific stimulant medications with the one that has the highest profile and is the most controversial.

Ritalin®

The controversy about Ritalin (generic name methylphenidate) has increased over the past few years with television, magazine, and newspaper articles expressing strong negative opinions. The media has focused on the increasing use of Ritalin, and some people have been concerned that this drug has been used excessively or inappropriately to control children's behavior. In spite of all the fear-inducing media coverage, Ritalin has been used for decades with no long-term negative effects documented. In fact, the use of Ritalin has increased because of an increase in awareness of information about ADD in adults.

Ritalin is a mild central nervous system stimulant believed to increase the production of dopamine, which relieves or diminishes ADD symptoms. The most common side effects (decreased appetite, sleep disturbances, stomachaches, headaches, and anxiety) are usually manageable by changing the dose and time Ritalin is taken. Increased blood pressure is another possible side effect of Ritalin and other stimulant medications. Most doctors will monitor their patients' blood pressure during the first days and weeks of use. If there are no signs of high blood pressure, your doctor may only check it periodically.

This is not to say that Ritalin is 100 percent safe and everyone with ADD should take it. There are potential risks when we take any medication; even aspirin can cause problems for some of us. As with any medication, it is important to weigh the potential risks and potential gains and work closely with your doctor so that he or she can monitor your dosage to achieve the greatest level of effectiveness.

Adults seem to have fewer side effects from Ritalin than children. Many of my clients are disappointed to find that their appetite remains the same and is not suppressed by taking Ritalin, or any other stimulant medication, for that matter. Some clients also report that since taking Ritalin they sleep better, even though sleep disturbances are a side effect for some.

The biggest problem with Ritalin for some adults and children is the crashing or rebound effect that can occur between doses. Rebound symptoms occur when most of the medication wears off. At this point, ADD symptoms return, and sometimes, for a short period of time, they are even more intense than usual. Common symptoms of rebound include irritability, tiredness, impatience, emotional sensitivity, and intensified ADD symptoms. Rebound can be managed by adjusting medication dosage, timing, and, for some, switching to the slow release form of the medication.

Dexedrine®

Dexedrine (generic name dextroamphetamine) is an amphetamine stimulant that, milligram for milligram, is stronger than Ritalin and works a bit differently. Dexedrine works by blocking the reuptake of dopamine at the receptor site, where Ritalin works by increasing dopamine production.[4] We don't know exactly why, but some people respond better to one stimulant than to another. It's not uncommon to be given a trial of different stimulants if the first doesn't work well.

Dexedrine comes in tablets that work for approximately four hours, and time-released capsules called spansules, which work for six to eight hours. Rebound effects happen more often on the short acting Dexedrine than the longer acting spansules. People who do not do well on Ritalin often find relief with Dexedrine, or vice versa.

Desoxyn Gradument®

Desoxyn Gradument (generic name methamphetamine hydrochloride) is a sustained release amphetamine that also works to increase dopamine. There is very little written about the use of Desoxyn to treat ADD in adults. There seems to be greater fear of the potential abuse of this medication. Desoxyn is frequently not mentioned in professional journals, research articles, or at ADD conferences as a treatment option for adult ADD.

Since this medication is used by some physicians who treat patients I also work with, I have anecdotal information regarding the effectiveness of Desoxyn in a small group of adults. Patients on Desoxyn who have been on other stimulant medications report that Desoxyn has very few, if any, rebound effects and works in a consistent manner for six to ten hours. Most of the patients I work with who have histories of addictions have been taking Desoxyn for a year or more without any relapse issues. I wonder if the consistent long-acting effects of this medication may be less likely to create a craving to use more, because the person is not on a neurological rebound roller coaster.

Again, this is purely observational information from a sample of adults who are closely monitored by their physicians, participate in ADD-oriented coaching and therapy, and are involved in treatment for their addictions. Desoxyn, as with any stimulant medication, should *not* be used unless a doctor is closely monitoring a patient's responsiveness and emotional and physical reactions.

Warning: Your pharmacist may give you strange looks and lectures when you pick up your prescription for Desoxyn. Many pharmacists are not familiar with the use of Desoxyn as an effective treatment for ADD.

Adderall®
Adderall (generic name dextroamphetamine and amphetamine), also a long-acting stimulant medication, is a mixture of four amphetamine preparations. Adderall is fairly new on the market, and you may have to tell your doctor about it. Some ADD patients describe Adderall as providing up to eight hours of "smoother" and more consistent relief of their ADD symptoms than Ritalin or Dexedrine. Adderall seems to be comparable to Desoxyn for most sufferers of ADD, yet it costs about one-third less than Desoxyn. Again, the longer-acting preparations have less rebound effect, which may actually decrease its abuse potential.

The same pharmacy warning holds true for Adderall.

Cylert®
Cylert (generic name pemoline) is a stimulant drug that is considered to have no abuse potential. Cylert is not a "controlled" substance like stimulants used to treat ADD, which means it is easier to prescribe. The doctor doesn't have to write special prescription forms that are regulated.

As other medications come on the market, Cylert seems to be falling out of favor as the first choice of treatment for ADD. Although rare, Cylert can cause liver damage. If you take Cylert, your physician will order periodic blood tests to check your liver functioning. Cylert can also take two to four weeks to build up to a level that will decrease or relieve ADD symptoms. Cylert has the advantage of being taken only once per day.

Since Cylert is considered to have no abuse potential, it is frequently seen as the medication of choice for recovering alcoholics and addicts. The problem is that many recovering people already have fragile livers. Some physicians still prefer to use Cylert, when there is no evidence of liver problem, for fear that recovering individuals will be more likely to abuse prescribed stimulants.

Cylert works well for some, and may be the medication best suited for individuals with certain types of addictions; but like any of the medications, it may not be the one for everyone. The belief that Cylert should be used because a patient has a history of addictions has kept many recovering people from receiving more effective medications to treat their ADD when Cylert was not helpful.

ANTIDEPRESSANT MEDICATIONS

The longer antidepressant medications are used, the more we realize how effective they are in treating conditions other than depression. Wellbutrin, for example, works primarily with norepinephrine and dopamine, providing relief for some ADD sufferers. Antidepressant medications that work only with serotonin seem to help some people with ADD by improving their ability to control their impulses and feel more calm. They do not, however, seem to improve attention for most people.

It is becoming common practice among physicians to prescribe antidepressant medication along with a stimulant medication. Medications that were formally used to treat high blood pressure also can be helpful for some with ADD. The following is a list of some of the nonstimulant medications used to treat different aspects of ADD.

v Prozac
v Serzone
v Luvox
v Paxil
v Zoloft
v Clonidine

v Nortriptyline
v Wellbutrin
v Effexor
v Neurontin

STIMULANTS AND ADDICTIONS

One of the questions most commonly asked by individuals with histories of addictions is: "Are these medications addictive?" Stimulant medications have the potential to be addictive for those who are addiction prone, who are not receiving adequate treatment during their addiction recovery, and whose ADD medication is not closely monitored. Another way to put the question is, "Do these medications have a high potential for abuse when used to treat ADD?" No, they do not. Although rare, I have heard of several cases where amphetamine addicts abused Ritalin by taking more than prescribed, or by grinding it up to inhale or to mix with water to inject. These people had been given large prescriptions with no ongoing treatment for ADD or addiction.

You may be wondering, How can a drug be potentially addictive yet have a low potential for abuse? Good question. The answer has to do with several key factors: stage of recovery; desire to maintain recovery and treat ADD; close monitoring of medication; and involvement with addiction recovery support. When all of these variables are addressed, the chances of medication abuse is minimal. We will discuss each of these issues in detail in the next chapter. For now, let's look at a commonly asked question.

WILL I BE ON MEDICATION FOREVER?

Everyone responds to medication differently, depending on the type of medication, the severity of ADD, and what the person has to do in daily life. Some people do take medication for the better part of their lives because the consequences are so severe when they stop. Their ADD medication may contribute to keeping them clean and sober, employed, in relationships, and out of prison. Others find that after months or several years on medication, they are able to change troublesome behavior. The medication assists their brain in learning new ways to adapt to their ADD behavior. This is especially true for those whose ADD symptoms have not had a severe impact on their daily living. Some of these individuals are able to go off their medication.

A word of caution: *If you are taking medication for ADD, do not stop taking it.* You may not be a person who can function well without it, even after years of treatment. Before you even consider changing the dosage or discontinuing your medication, consult your physician. This is a decision that requires careful deliberation and must be made with your doctor's involvement.

Some individuals with ADD have functioned their entire lives without medication and can continue to function without it. What they find, however, is that instead of struggling to get through each day, medication helps them thrive in ways they never thought were possible. Taking medication greatly improves the quality of their lives and the lives of those around them. After functioning with a brain that works with them rather than against them, they usually choose not to go back to their former disabled ADD state.

People may choose to go off medication when they experience major life changes that don't require them to function at previous levels. This may be true if their children leave home, if they retire, if they move to a place where it's quieter and less overwhelming, or if they find a job that requires less focused attention and appreciates divergent thinking and high energy levels.

I Won't Take Anything, No Matter What!

Bob came to see me because he couldn't stop smoking pot, and he really wanted to stop. His wife had threatened to leave him if he relapsed one more time. Bob had been attending Narcotics Anonymous and Marijuana Anonymous meetings for two years. In spite of his best efforts, he couldn't stop smoking marijuana for more than five months at a time.

During our sessions Bob described how hard it was to pay attention during Twelve Step meetings. He talked about how marijuana was the only thing that helped him slow down and not be so "hyped up." Bob continued to smoke pot even though he was going to Twelve Step meetings and was trying to work the Steps.

Several of our sessions were devoted to evaluating Bob for ADD. He felt both confused and relieved by the diagnosis. Understanding his ADD helped him put together many pieces of his life and his recovery that had previously made no sense. On the other hand, Bob wasn't thrilled to have something else "wrong" with him.

Bob spent several months trying to digest information about ADD. He also worked his recovery program with the new behavioral skills he had learned to help him adapt to his ADD. After remaining clean and sober for six months, however, Bob was feeling more miserable than ever. Now he was acutely aware of just how difficult it was for him to show up for life every day.

When I brought up the idea of an evaluation for medication to treat his ADD, Bob resisted. Actually, resisted is an understatement. He gritted his teeth and in a low growl said, "No way! I'm not taking drugs." About a month later, Bob realized he was obsessed with wanting to smoke pot. It was then, as a last resort, that his desire to stay clean and sober and participate in his life outweighed his fear of taking medication.

Fortunately, Bob had an NA sponsor, Phil, who was willing to come to a therapy session with him. In our session, Phil learned about ADD and was able to say that if anyone had ADD, it was Bob. Phil felt reassured knowing that ADD medication would not make Bob high but would help him to focus better on his recovery program. Phil supported Bob's decision to take medication. The three of us developed a plan to help monitor Bob's progress and medication.

Bob has been taking Dexedrine for eighteen months now and recently celebrated two years of continuous recovery. He has gone back to school and is doing quite well in computer graphics. Bob had no idea that he is intelligent. He's enjoying the quality of his recovery, and he's working to improve his relationship with his wife.

Medication did not work magic for Bob, but his commitment to recovery and his willingness to work hard and get complete treatment for his ADD made all the difference. For him, the ultimate solution to a meaningful life lay in a balanced and comprehensive approach to treating his ADD and his addictions. Medication was necessary for Bob to be able to work on his other issues.

GETTING THE RIGHT MEDICATION FOR YOU

The first step in obtaining the proper medication is to find a physician who is well versed in treating adults with ADD. The ideal situation is to find a doctor who understands and treats ADD with corelated addictions. Depending on where you live, you may have to commit to driving to another city to find this person. Here are some places where you may be able to find information about physicians or clinics in your area.

▶ Attend meetings at your local chapter of Children And Adults With Attention Deficit Disorder (CH.A.D.D.). CH.A.D.D. is not in the business of making referrals, but you will meet people at the meetings who may share information about physicians.

- ▶ Talk with friends who have children with ADD. Pediatricians who treat children may also treat adults or be able to refer you.
- ▶ Visit online ADD chat rooms. People from all over the country share information about physicians and clinics that treat ADD.
- ▶ Browse the Web for information.
- ▶ Call the nearest college and talk with their Disabled Students staff. They should be able to give you information regarding where to get treatment for ADD.
- ▶ The process of finding the right physician may take some time. Most doctors with experience in this area may have a waiting list, so try to hang in there.

Once you've found a doctor you feel comfortable with, tell him or her about how you self-medicated your ADD. Be honest about your addictions. Since understanding the link between ADD and addictions is new, you may be the one to help educate your doctor. Many resourceful people with ADD have contributed to the higher education of medical professionals.

When taking prescribed medication, especially during the first month or so, it's important to have phone contact and/or a weekly appointment with your doctor. Some doctors may give you a simple chart with numbers ranging from one to ten. With this chart you can graph your mood, concentration, energy level, and impulse control. This gives you and your doctor important information about how your medication is working.

Depending on the effectiveness or any side effects, your doctor may want to alter the dosage and perhaps the type of medication you're taking. This is a fairly common practice. The important thing is that you're getting the best results with the least number of side effects. Side effects such as difficulty sleeping, anxiety, or stomach upset are usually remedied by changing the dose and time you take your medication.

A note of caution: Chocolate and caffeinated drinks, such as tea, cola, and coffee, may cause you to feel anxious and shaky if you're taking stimulant medication.

Now that you have a better understanding of the link between ADD and addictions, some tools to change your behavior, and you understand the role of medication, it's important to appreciate the potential for relapse. The next chapter provides you with practical ways to prevent ADD and addiction relapses.

∽◦◦∾

CHAPTER TWELVE

OH, NO! NOT AGAIN!

Preventing ADD and Addiction Relapses

Anyone can stop an addiction for the moment. But can you stay stopped? How many times have you said, "I promise I will never drink and drive again" or "God, if only you get me out of this, I will never smoke pot again." When you promised to quit drinking or using drugs, you absolutely meant it. You were dead serious and desperate to stop your addiction. You've tried your hardest, and yet you couldn't stay clean and sober. Before you knew it, you found yourself drunk or under the influence and feeling humiliated and demoralized. Your best efforts failed.

You are not alone. Millions of people stop their substance abuse or addictive behavior every day, only to fall back into it within days or months. Stopping isn't the issue. Staying stopped is. You may have tried to control or change your behavior by yourself, or you may have sought professional help. You may also be someone who has been or is involved in a Twelve Step recovery program. If you've given any of the above your best shot but are having trouble maintaining abstinence, there may be underlying issues that are preventing you from attaining and maintaining your recovery.

You may have an understanding of how the term *relapse* applies to addiction recovery but wonder how one can have an ADD relapse. We'll take a look at how the process of relapse affects ADD and addiction recovery, and I will provide suggestions and strategies to prevent this painful and life-threatening process. But first we need to understand exactly what a relapse is.

WHAT IS A RELAPSE?

Relapse is a term used to describe returning to a former condition. Relapse doesn't always mean that a person returns to drug or alcohol use. People with other medical illnesses have relapses when their conditions return to where they were after having a period of improvement or partial recovery.

Relapse was used to describe returning to addictions after a period of recovery in 1982, when Terence T. Gorski and Merlene Miller pioneered this concept in their groundbreaking book, *Counseling for Relapse Prevention*. Gorski and Miller tried to minimize the moral judgments regarding relapse by describing the physical, emotional, and behavioral aspects of this process.[1]

When we understand that having a relapse means returning to a former state of being, we can use this model when discussing ADD recovery as well. ADD and addictions are never cured, but there are many things you can do to maintain the improvements you make. Knowing what you can do to help yourself when you slide back into old thinking and behaviors is essential. You don't have to live with old behaviors and addictions that are harmful.

Relapse Is a Process, Not an Event

Relapse isn't an instantaneous event. Relapse, for most people, happens over time. Look at the Addictive Relapse Continuum that follows these next few paragraphs; it may help clarify what I'm about to say. Recovery and relapse are mutually exclusive states; in other words, when you're in recovery, you're not in relapse. You can't do both at the same time, just like you can't drink and at the same time be abstinent.

Relapse is, however, a temporary state, and it ends in two ways. One is by returning completely, and perhaps permanently, to the behaviors, substances, or illness you were recovering from. The other is by returning to your recovery. First let's look at addiction relapse and suggestions for continued recovery, then do the same for ADD recovery.

The Addiction Relapse Continuum

RELAPSE DYNAMICS		RECOVERY DYNAMICS	
●— The end of the relapse ←	—— isolation ←─┼─►	connectedness ——► with others	ongoing ──► recovery
drinking	old behaviors and old ideas	healthy relationships	freedom from addictions
abusing drugs			
abusing food	lying	spiritual connection	personal growth
compulsive behavior	obsessive thoughts		spiritual growth
attempting suicide	self-deception, denial	involved in ongoing support program	
death	compulsion to use drug or alcohol or engage in addictive behaviors		

You may want to take a moment and locate your position on the continuum. Be honest with yourself. Are you on the recovery or relapse side of the line? As you can see by the continuum, you may be in the process of relapse and not have taken a drink or a drug. Relapse is crossing over the imaginary line of recovery and returning to your old ideas and behaviors. Your denial may tell you that you're not really addicted. Your alcoholism may tell you that you can drink socially, even though you've always lost control when you drink.

If you find yourself on the relapse side of the line, you may be feeling isolated from others. Maybe you've stopped participating in your recovery program. You may find that your thinking has returned to old territory. You may have convinced yourself that you can eat sugar, even though you have a proven track record that you can't. You may also engage in dishonest behavior, rage attacks, and may feel ill at ease.

If not treated, your relapse will progress. If you don't get help to cross back into recovery, you risk feeling guilty, ashamed, isolated, depressed, confused, resentful, and all the other painful feelings you used substances to avoid.

The last step of a relapse is to punish yourself. You begin to seek relief in substances and behaviors that will hurt you and ultimately make you feel even worse about yourself. Many people have no idea they are in the process of relapse. They find themselves drinking, smoking pot, gambling, or binge eating, and have no idea what happened. You don't have to do this to yourself. If you're over the line, now is the time to get the support you deserve.

Living on the recovering side of the continuum means you feel connected with others—to family, friends, and community. You are growing emotionally and spiritually and living a clean and sober life. You feel a sense of belonging. You feel your pain without looking to drugs and old behaviors to soothe or mask it. You are developing a group of friends who enjoy their lives without participating in addictions. You practice principles of recovery in your daily living. Actively being in recovery does not mean that your life will always be smooth as glass or that you will never have adversities. Life happens, in and out of recovery.

It's common for people in recovery to hover near the dividing line between recovery and relapse. No matter how hard you work your recovery program, how many Twelve Step meetings, therapy sessions, and support groups you attend, there will be times when you cross into relapse territory. This happens to people with many years of sobriety, but it doesn't mean you have to take the relapse subway to the end of the line. You can switch directions as soon as you realize you're heading for a destination you don't want to go to.

WHY PEOPLE RELAPSE INTO ADDICTIONS

In my opinion, based on years of clinical observation, people relapse primarily because they are undertreated. People don't relapse because they are bad, stupid, or just don't care. They relapse because with addictions come other co-related problems, such as depression, abuse and trauma from childhood, emotional illness, ADD, learning disabilities, anxiety, obsessive compulsive disorder, posttraumatic stress disorder, and many more. Most people with substance abuse or dependency issues have a variety of complex challenges to work through. If these issues are not treated in a comprehensive way, it will be difficult to maintain abstinence from addictive substances and behaviors.

How ADD Contributes to Relapse

Chemical dependency programs used to focus primarily on helping people stay sober and work through issues directly related to their drinking or drug use. Today, as knowledge of what is called Dual Diagnosis is growing, most chemical dependency programs also treat depression, family issues, posttraumatic stress disorder, and other related problems.

Unfortunately, most chemical dependency specialists do not assess or treat ADD. Many function under the old idea that ADD is a fad or a disorder that children outgrow. There is also great fear among many chemical dependency treatment providers regarding the treatment of "emotional" problems with medication. What is often misunderstood is that many of these "emotional" problems have a medical or biological basis that must be treated as well. It's difficult to treat something you're not looking for or don't believe exists. And yet, treating ADD may be a large part of completing the puzzle of recovery for many people. If ADD is not treated, the puzzle has a huge hole in it. Untreated ADD may be keeping many people from a life of recovery, fulfillment, and serenity that is beyond their wildest dreams.

Sometimes people in recovery report being "struck drunk." They find themselves drinking in a bar or at a party without realizing what they're doing until it's too late. In most cases, however, those who return from a relapse can describe the sequence of events and the changes in attitudes and thinking that preceded their use of drugs, alcohol, or addictive behaviors. With help, and the aid of 20/20 hindsight, many individuals are able to gain understanding into the process that led them back to their addictions.

Some will describe feeling so good in their sober life that they drifted away from what was supporting their recovery. Others report convincing themselves that they could smoke pot on occasion and, before they knew it, they were smoking daily again. For others, it was an event, a crisis, the upsurge of painful memories, death of a loved one, or resentments they could not get over.

Untreated ADD may be making it even harder for you to remain abstinent from drugs, alcohol, or other addictions. While relapse is a process, for people with ADD that process can be an extremely short one. People with untreated ADD have a far greater chance to relapse due to a difficulty or inability to control their impulses. These people often truly feel they were struck drunk. They may be totally unaware of their relapse signals and impulsively return to substances, food, and behavioral addictions. For many the relapse process can take days, months, or even years; for some people with ADD impulsiveness, the process can happen in a blink of an eye.

Untreated ADD can make it impossible for you to follow any path thoroughly, let alone the path that the Twelve Step program and other programs of recovery suggest.

THREE KINDS OF ADDICTION RELAPSE

The Nontherapeutic Relapse

Relapse can be divided into two categories: the therapeutic relapse and the nontherapeutic relapse. A nontherapeutic relapse occurs when someone slips back into addictions and either never returns to recovery, or returns with no understanding about why they relapsed or how they will prevent another relapse in the future. They often deny the seriousness of their addictions during and after relapse. Even if they are fortunate enough to get back to recovery, they are at high risk of relapsing in the future. Not even the pain of relapse or its consequences are enough to help them change their attitude, thinking, or behavior.

The nontherapeutic relapse is common among people with ADD because they may not truly understand and accept the concept of cause and effect. It is hard for them to think through the consequences of a relapse and thus take the steps to prevent it. I work with individuals who are on probation or parole and who intellectually understand the consequences of drinking or using drugs again. They've told me they never want to be locked up again. Yet they run into an old friend and within minutes they're drinking, smoking coke or heroin, and, sometimes, committing impulsive crimes.

Many alcoholics and addicts do not have the chance to return to treatment after a relapse. Some live hopelessly stuck in their addictions, while others are institutionalized. And many die. It's tragic that they lose their lives, and the tragedy is compounded because their plight is misunderstood. They are disregarded by some as stupid, bad, or professional criminals with no sense of right or wrong. Their families and loved ones suffer feelings of guilt, shame, and powerlessness because they were unable to change the course of events.

The Therapeutic Relapse

A therapeutic relapse occurs when alcoholics and addicts are not only able to return to a recovery, but bring back with them valuable information about their relationship with food, drugs, alcohol, or addictive behaviors. A therapeutic relapse removes doubts about whether or not they can ever drink or use drugs without consequences. They are more accepting that their addictions make them feel worse rather than better.

With a therapeutic relapse comes surrender to the fact that old ideas and ways of living are harmful and potentially deadly. After a therapeutic relapse, the individual is more able to accept help from others. With a therapeutic relapse comes a stronger commitment to recovery and to life.

Suicide, the Ultimate Relapse

For some people, untreated physical, emotional, and spiritual pain becomes so intense that suicide feels like the only way to relieve their suffering. Some people take their lives by relapsing and accidentally or intentionally killing themselves with their addictions. Others make a decision to take their lives without returning to their addictions. These people are usually suffering from untreated problems such as depression, shame, ADD, PTSD, schizophrenia, or bipolar disorder.

The risk of a successful suicide attempt is greater when mind-altering substances are used. Drugs can inhibit the parts of ourselves that do not want to commit suicide. Untreated ADD can also increase the risk of suicidal thoughts becoming a reality, because ADD hampers impulse control in ways similar to drugs and alcohol. The most dangerous combination are the people with ADD who use substances. They can completely lose control of their impulses and end up dead, even if they don't really want to die.

Suicidal thinking in sobriety indicates that you are not receiving adequate treatment for all your problems. If you feel that your only choices are returning to your addictions or committing suicide, something is wrong. Help is available. Talk to someone immediately about your thoughts of suicide and seek professional help.

Clean, Sober, and Miserable

You may be one of the fortunate ones who is actively recovering from drug and alcohol dependency. Congratulations! You have a lot of courage and are on a path that will save your life. But what if the life you're trying to save feels worse than the drunken or stoned life you lived? Did you think all your problems would vanish when you gave up your addiction? Did you fantasize about the perfect life you would live if only you could get sober? How disillusioning to wake up sober and feel overwhelmed by the wreckage of your life. How discouraging to feel that daily life is still harder for you than those around you. How despairing to get sober, feel worse, and know that alcohol and other drugs are no longer an option to relieve your pain.

You are not alone. Almost everyone who lets go of self-medicating feels worse for a time. Simply stopping addictive behavior will not in itself treat the issues you've been attempting to deal with by drinking, using drugs, or acting in compulsive ways. Now you get to work through the underlying emotional and sometimes mental conditions that have been with you all along. Now you get to work through the trauma you most likely experienced throughout your life. Now you have the opportunity to learn to live life on life's terms. And now you don't get to medicate your pain with alcohol or street drugs.

No wonder people relapse. Early sobriety often doesn't feel good. It can be a time of great emotional pain, soul searching, grief, and, paradoxically, tremendous transformation. Some people enter recovery and float on what is referred to as a "pink cloud." They feel wonderful to be released from the bondage of addictions. Over time, though, many will fall through the pink cloud of early bliss and hit the reality of life.

Some people in recovery from their addictions continue to feel miserable, even after months or years of hard work and commitment. I know some alcoholics and addicts who have been clean and sober for years, are actively involved in their recovery programs, and have undergone years of psychotherapy to work through childhood trauma, family of origin issues, repressed emotions, and how they relate with others. They've been treated for conditions such as depression, anxiety, Obsessive Compulsive Disorder (OCD), and PTSD. In spite of all this treatment, much of which was necessary, they can't hold down a job, they move frequently, bounce checks, live in perpetual chaos, are always on the go, or they impulsively marry someone they met at an AA conference.

Not only are their lives unmanageable, they feel guilty, ashamed, frustrated, and desperate, because even with years of sobriety and therapy their lives are still a chaotic mess. After too many years of miserable sobriety, some look for the comfort they believe drugs, food, and alcohol will provide. Once they return to their addictions, their lives really crumble. Some make it back to try again, but too many end up incarcerated or dead.

Sinking in Recovery

When Geri entered a treatment program, she was living on a couch in a shooting gallery, where addicts bought and shot heroin and cocaine. Before her addictions had gotten the best of her, Geri worked on a fishing boat. She enjoyed the fast pace of commercial fishing and she loved the challenges of the sea. Geri was often late, sometimes forgetful, but she made up for that with her hard work and love for fishing. Angelo, the owner of the boat, hated to fire her, but she was a safety hazard when she came to work loaded, which was becoming a daily occurrence.

After Geri had been sober for a year, she got her old job back. Angelo was delighted to have her now that she was no longer drinking and using cocaine. What happened next was surprising for both of them.

Geri was frequently late to work. Angelo asked if she'd been drinking or using coke. Geri assured him that she wasn't. However, she kept making mistakes with the fishing nets and other gear. Over the next three months, Geri became increasingly depressed as she struggled with tasks that had once been second nature. Angelo continued to doubt Geri's sobriety. She reassured him that she was clean and sober and didn't know why she was having such a hard time paying attention, completing her duties, and living daily life now that she was in recovery. The day Geri spaced out and ran the boat aground, Angelo fired her. "You know, you worked better on cocaine than you do now," he told her angrily.

Geri had almost a year and a half of recovery but couldn't hold a job or pay her rent. She definitely felt worse than she did when she was drinking and snorting cocaine. She devoted herself even more to her Twelve Step meetings, but couldn't stay focused. She clung to her fragile sobriety until finally she slipped. Two days after celebrating two years of sobriety, Geri drank a beer. Within three days she was shooting and smoking coke. Geri disappeared. No one knows what happened to her. I wonder how Geri's recovery would have turned out if her ADD had been treated.

CAN ADD MEDICATION CAUSE ADDICTION RELAPSE?

This is a very important question, and one that people recovering from chemical addictions need to understand. Even though we talked about it in chapter eleven, it deserves further discussion. There are four important questions to answer before taking stimulant medication to treat your ADD:

▶ How strong is your commitment to maintaining your recovery and treating your ADD?

▶ How closely will your medication be monitored?
▶ Do you have a comprehensive treatment plan that addresses both your ADD and addictions, as well as any other co-occurring conditions?
▶ What stage of recovery are you in now?

Recognizing where you are in your recovery is critical to determining whether or when to try medication to treat your ADD.

Stages of Recovery

I have adapted the following stages from the work of Gorski and Miller.[2]

Pretreatment. This is the phase before alcoholics or addicts enter treatment. Their addiction is out of control and they don't realize they need treatment. This is *not* the time to initiate treatment for ADD, especially with medication. Using prescribed stimulant medication or antidepressants can have disastrous outcomes when the addict is not in treatment. They may mix and abuse medications in ways that become lethal. The priority of this phase is to move alcoholics and addicts into treatment for their addictions.

Stabilization. This includes a period of physical and emotional detox. During this stage alcoholics and addicts may experience withdrawal symptoms and can be quite ill. They may not be able to really understand the seriousness of their addiction or to commit to long-term treatment. Most individuals are confused, emotionally sensitive, perhaps volatile, and not clear enough in their thinking to benefit from cognitive therapy. The focus of this stage is to physically and emotionally stabilize the person so that he or she enters the phase of early recovery. This is also *not* the time to treat ADD.

Early Recovery. For many, this is a time of great confusion and turmoil. Alcoholics and addicts have made a commitment to their recovery but may still be in denial

about the seriousness of their addictions and feel ambiva-
lent about their decision to stay clean and sober. It's
difficult to get a complete picture of ADD and other co-
occurring conditions during this period. Signs of early
recovery, such as distractibility, restlessness, poor concentration, and impulsiveness can be mistaken for ADD.
Early recovery is *not* an ideal time to treat ADD unless
ADD is clearly hindering the person's ability to participate
in a recovery program.

I have worked with people who had a history of
relapse and whose ADD greatly impacted their ability to
get to treatment regularly, let alone focus enough to get
much from Twelve Step meetings, after-care groups, or
therapy. Their ADD impulsiveness also contributed to
their inability to avoid taking that first drink, puff, hit, or
line. For these people, treatment for ADD, including the
use of medication, was helpful, if not essential, in maintaining their recovery. In each case, the people were
extremely motivated to stay clean and sober and were
actively involved in a program of recovery. They worked
closely with a psychiatrist who carefully monitored their
medication.

Treating ADD with medications during early recovery
can prevent future relapse for some. The potential risk of
giving medication to someone who is newly sober must be
weighed carefully against the benefit. The key to successful treatment rests in a comprehensive treatment plan.

Middle Recovery. This is a time of accepting your
addiction and need for ongoing support and treatment.
Perhaps the toughest issues to work through in middle
recovery are shame and creating a sober identity. Middle
recovery is also the time when either the acute pain or the
pink cloud of early recovery diminish. It's time to create a
life based on recovery. For many, this means huge emotional, spiritual, relationship, living, and work changes.

Middle recovery is the time when you can clearly see
the effects of ADD. During middle recovery most people are

clear enough to sort out what are sobriety based issues and what are co-occurring issues that won't go away without help. Middle recovery is a time when many recovering people go to therapy. They know they need more help but are not always sure why. Assessing and treating ADD at this time can better enable them to work through their personal issues, stay sober, and increase the quality of their lives.

Ongoing Recovery. This is the stage where you continue to devote yourself to living clean and sober over the long haul. Your life and identity are expanding beyond your addictions. For many this is a time when life really begins to come together. They feel comfortable with their recovery and can feel serene even during stormy times.

On the other hand, this may be the stage when recovering alcoholics and addicts who have ADD are feeling more anger, self-loathing, shame, and confusion than ever because they're struggling with the same issues they've struggled with all their lives. They still impulsively quit jobs and relationships, can't concentrate, and are either too active or can't get started at all. And no matter how hard they try, they can't change.

If you can't personally relate to these feelings, just imagine for a moment how you would feel if every time you saw wood, concrete, asphalt, or metal, you slammed your head into it. No matter how much you bled, how much you hurt, and how hard you tried, you couldn't stop yourself. Now imagine that you've been doing this all your life. To top it off, you no longer self-medicate your pain. Recovering people with ADD are not masochistic; it's just that the pain of their addiction was even worse than the pain of uncontrollable head bashing.

I see many recovering addicts who have had years of psychotherapy and treatment for conditions other than ADD. Some are on the verge of suicide or relapse; others are depressed and feel vanquished. They are exhausted, spent, burned out, and tired of trying to live sober with a disability they may not even know they have. They deserve more from their recovery. They don't have to suffer from untreated ADD or become readdicted. They can have both problems treated.

For those who make it into ongoing recovery, their response to ADD treatment is usually quite remarkable and they are not at high risk to abuse stimulant medication unless they're already in the process of relapse. The problem isn't that they want medication; the problem is that many *don't* want to take medication. Recovering alcoholics and addicts are not beating down doctors' doors in search of stimulants. Most of them deny themselves treatment for fear they will jeopardize their sobriety.

RELAPSE PREVENTION

Comprehensive Treatment

The most effective relapse prevention is a comprehensive treatment plan. This means that both your ADD and your addictions are treated at the same time. If you stray away from your addiction recovery, you will be at greater risk to relapse. If you don't receive adequate treatment for your ADD, you're at greater risk for relapse. A comprehensive treatment plan is one that contains the following components:

- ADD treatment in the form of education, coaching, and support groups
- Regular visits with your doctor and close medication management
- Therapy or counseling regarding ADD and recovery issues
- Involvement in addiction recovery programs
- Family and relationship counseling when needed

Not everyone has the resources to get all of the above services. The bare minimum would be active involvement in addiction recovery such as Twelve Step programs, working with a sponsor who can support your ADD recovery, and close medication management from your doctor.

Medication

Research statistics regarding stimulant treatment for ADD and relapse are not abundant because the field is so new. However, experts who have treated adults with ADD and addictions believe in the efficacy of medication: "Studies by Wender and coworkers (1995) and Satel and Nelson, among others, demonstrate that most patients do not develop tolerance to, nor become dependent on, stimulant drugs."[3]

My anecdotal experience indicates that when people in recovery are properly diagnosed, and when their medication is closely monitored, they do not abuse their ADD medication. Most people in recovery respond to stimulant medication by feeling more in control of their thoughts and behavior, including those that can lead to relapse. They are able to concentrate and follow through with goals and tasks, which in turn increases their self-esteem. Many report feeling more alert, present, and aware of their feelings. Once recovering people experience the benefit of their medication, many do not want to even consider abusing it, because they enjoy feeling "normal."

HOW DO I KNOW IF I'M ABUSING MY MEDICATION?

You shouldn't consider taking medication unless you are clear about the following:

- ▶ Your sole motive is to improve your ADD symptoms.
- ▶ You are committed to being rigorously honest with your doctor, therapist, family member, and recovery support group or sponsor.
- ▶ You will only take medication as prescribed.

- ▶ If you do alter your dosage, you will consult your doctor.
- ▶ You will never give or sell your medication to others.
- ▶ If you feel high or wired on your medication, you will call your doctor immediately.
- ▶ You will not take medication to increase productivity, pull all-nighters, or function in superhuman ways.

If you are able to commit to the above, you will know you are using your medication correctly.

Superhuman Abuse

I have observed a subtle form of medication abuse among clients, friends, and colleagues with, but primarily without, histories of addictions. They don't take more medication than is recommended. They aren't scheming to get more or trying to get high or loaded. What they are doing is using their medication to increase their productivity in ways that become harmful to them. They become hyperfocused on projects and activities and become hyperproductive working machines.

I understand how seductive it can be when suddenly you are able to sustain your attention and have the energy to follow through and complete projects. This can be especially true when these abilities are new. Taking medication can initially feel like you've been given the brain chip you've been missing all your life. For some, their new ability to turn ideas and dreams into reality is so astonishing that they don't want to stop. They take their newly focused energy and throw themselves even harder into work, school, or parenting. Their frenzy is now more focused and productive, but they become unbalanced in other areas of life.

People are not machines. We weren't meant to produce like computer factories. We need to eat, sleep, have fun, rest, play, and connect with each other. If you find yourself locked into focusing on only a few things in life, talk with your doctor. This doesn't mean you have to stop your medication, but you will need help modulating your energy throughout different aspects of your life. ADD medication is not meant to make you superhuman.

ABUSING ADD MEDICATION

If you are an alcoholic or addict, you will, at some time, think about abusing your medication. If you are properly medicated, your ADD symptoms will be decreased, yet you will not feel high or euphoric. The sleeping addict part of your brain will wake up from time to time and want to get loaded. Your addictive brain will tell you to do all sorts of things that are harmful. However, you don't have to follow through with these self-destructive suggestions or obsessions. Besides, many people who do take more of their medication than is prescribed often feel ashamed, shaky, nervous, and guilty.

Here are some suggestions on handling the temptation to abuse your medication:

- ▶ Admit to yourself that you're thinking of experimenting or getting high on your ADD medication.
- ▶ Tell someone immediately. Call your doctor, therapist, sponsor, friend (who understands your addiction), or another person in recovery.
- ▶ Tell the truth about what you are thinking or what you have done.
- ▶ Do not let your shame keep you from getting help now. It's not too late to get help.
- ▶ Let your doctor help you create a plan to prevent future relapses.
- ▶ If you continue to abuse your medication, you need to strengthen your recovery program.

► Some addicts and alcoholics cannot use stimulant medication safely. If you are one of these people, you are not bad, you are an addict. There are other medications your doctor can prescribe that have no addiction potential.

Most people in recovery do not have problems with ADD medications. If you have problems taking only the prescribed amount, it isn't necessarily because you are self-destructive. It may just mean that you need more structure, supervision, and treatment for your addictions.

ADD RELAPSE

You may be wondering, "How can I relapse into ADD?" Since relapse is a return to a previous state, you can have an ADD relapse in a variety of ways. The first thing that can happen is that your ADD symptoms get worse. This can happen for a variety of reasons. If you're taking medication, the dosage or type of medication may need to be adjusted. Discuss this with your doctor. Sometimes a simple adjustment can get you back to where you were. If you forget to take your medicine or take it periodically, you are in relapse.

Relapse dynamics also happen when you're not getting enough help and support. As with addictions, you will feel isolated, intolerant of yourself, ashamed, and fall into old thinking and behavior. ADD relapse thinking occurs when you go into denial about ADD as a neurological difference and start to believe that you're just stupid and lazy like you've been told. You may even doubt you really have ADD, or wonder if ADD isn't just another fad the drug companies cooked up to make money. Before you know it, you've convinced yourself that ADD is a moral issue, that you are a rotten human being, and that you're unworthy of treatment and support. You may find yourself back in the grips of your out-of-control ADD symptoms.

Similar to the addictive relapse, the ADD relapse can

be a process that ends in two ways. One is that you move yourself to the recovery side of the continuum by getting help and support. The other is that your life gets so painful and chaotic that you either return to addictions, lose your ability to function, or become incarcerated or institutionalized. In some cases, ADD relapse ends in suicide.

It is essential to have someone in your life whom you trust to give honest feedback if you're moving down the ADD relapse continuum. Remember, denial can be powerful. It may take a tremendous amount of energy to stay grounded in reality. If you have ADD, the reality is that you will feel better, function better, get along better with others, and be a more productive member of your community when your ADD is treated.

ONGOING TREATMENT FOR ADD

While counseling that focuses on ADD can be valuable, especially during the early recovery stage, traditional therapy alone is usually not effective in treating ADD. You may find that a relationship with an ADD coach is helpful for a short period of time, or you may incorporate an ADD coach into your ongoing recovery program. The amount of support you need depends on the severity of your ADD and how you need to function in your life. The important thing is not to forget that your brain works differently from most people's and this difference can be disabling. Your ADD differences can become great assets if you are properly treated.

Ongoing treatment for your ADD can include the following:

- ▶ Taking prescribed medication when indicated
- ▶ Talking with others who understand ADD
- ▶ Joining an ongoing ADD support group
- ▶ Participating in online chat rooms with others who have ADD

▶ Attending ADD conferences
▶ Joining and attending Children & Adults with Attention Deficit Disorders (CH.A.D.D.) groups
▶ Working with an ADD coach
▶ Continuing to learn about ADD and how it affects your life

TREATING THE WHOLE PERSON

ADD and addictions do not usually travel alone; they are frequently accompanied by a variety of other biological and emotional problems. It's important to get help for everything that is hindering your ability to work, love, and enjoy life.

It's time to let go of the stigma and shame associated with ADD, addictions, and relapse. Unfortunately, we live in a society that is quick to make negative judgments about human conditions. The first step in changing these cultural attitudes is to change our own beliefs. We are all products of our culture. We will continue to perpetuate unrealistic standards, misinformation, and prejudices until we are able to accept our own humanness. When we accept our ADD, addictions, and any other co-occurring problems, we begin to let go of our judgments. By accepting who we are, we are better able to accept others as they are.

Some people have a difficult time accepting the help that Twelve Step programs provide. In the next chapter, we will look at specific ways to benefit from these programs when you have ADD.

∽∾∾

CHAPTER THIRTEEN

ADD AND ADDICTION RECOVERY
Your Unique Challenges with Twelve Step Programs

Twelve Step programs have become a household word. You may have friends or relatives who attend Twelve Step meetings. One of the characters on your favorite television show may be involved in a Twelve Step program.

Most people know something about programs like Alcoholics Anonymous, Alanon, Overeaters Anonymous, Narcotics Anonymous, Cocaine Anonymous, Gamblers Anonymous and the many other spin-off programs that have adapted the original Twelve Steps of AA. But have you ever been to a Twelve Step meeting? Do you understand how these programs work? You may know someone who has negative opinions of Twelve Step programs, or you may have had a negative experience yourself. On the other hand, you may have witnessed the transformation of a friend or relative who is involved in a Twelve Step program. You may be intimately familiar with the Twelve Steps yourself.

You've probably guessed that I'm biased in favor of Twelve Step programs. This may feel comforting to you, it may put you off, or it may not matter. If you're not fond of, or you dislike, Twelve Step programs, you might want to continue reading this chapter anyway, just to see if there are any principles or tools that might help you.

There are many ways to get clean and sober and maintain a life of quality recovery. Twelve Step programs are not for everyone who has an addiction problem. They may not be for you. However, over the past sixty years, millions of people worldwide have found recovery through their involvement with Twelve Step programs. Just as important, these individuals have discovered a relationship with a power greater than themselves and found fulfillment and serenity they never believed possible. Other recovering people find the help and support they need in treatment facilities, relapse prevention groups, their churches, therapy, and from family and friends.

Having ADD does not excuse you from the hard work of getting clean and sober and maintaining your recovery. Your ADD does not give you an excuse to slough off and avoid doing some of the uncomfortable and outright gut-wrenching work it takes to stay sober. Having ADD does not allow you to disregard the rights of others, talk instead of listening, or be less than honest with yourself and the people who offer you help. On the other hand, understanding your ADD will help you be more compassionate with yourself as you recover from addictions.

ADD provides a context for understanding why certain things are difficult for you. You may have had trouble following through with Twelve Step programs in the past. Maybe you've relapsed in spite of doing all the "right" things your program suggests. You may have stopped going to meetings due to negative experiences that left you feeling misunderstood and resentful. Or perhaps you're just learning about your ADD and trying to get clean and sober at the same time.

If you've tried Twelve Step programs prior to being properly treated for ADD, you may want to try again. Having ADD doesn't mean you can't benefit from Twelve Step programs. All you need is help adapting your ADD style to the program in ways that work for you. In this chapter you will be given practical suggestions about working the Steps, reading Twelve Step literature, dealing with your restlessness in meetings, and working with a sponsor. You're not a bad person who simply needs to become good. You are a person with addictions and ADD for which you need treatment that works.

WHAT ARE TWELVE STEP PROGRAMS?

When talking about Twelve Step programs, I use Alcoholics Anonymous (AA), the first, oldest, and largest of all Twelve Step programs for most of the examples in this chapter. Narcotics Anonymous is patterned closely after AA. Other programs that work with "addictions of doing," such as gambling (GA) or sex and love addiction (SLAA), are patterned slightly differently. Alcoholics Anonymous is based on several common beliefs:

▶ Admitting that you are powerless over alcohol
▶ Accepting that willpower alone cannot keep you sober
▶ Finding a power greater than yourself, who will help you to stay sober and enrich your life
▶ Recognizing that people with similar problems can understand and support each other
▶ Acknowledging that the twelve suggested steps of the program are tools to help you stay sober and guides for serene, meaningful living
▶ Understanding that anonymity is the spiritual foundation of the program
▶ Realizing that helping other alcoholics will help you to stay sober as well

Alcoholics Anonymous was started by Dr. Bob Smith, a physician from Akron, Ohio, and Bill Wilson, a stockbroker from New York. Bill Wilson realized that in order to stay sober himself, he had to help other alcoholics. He met Dr. Bob and later traveled to Akron to team up with him. The two worked with alcoholics at the Akron City Hospital during the summer of 1935. The first AA group was formed in the fall of that year. Over the next two years, groups of alcoholics seeking recovery sprang up in New York, Akron, Cleveland, and various parts of the country.

Here is the official definition of Alcoholics Anonymous.

> Alcoholics Anonymous is a fellowship of men and women who share their experience, strength, and hope with each other that they may solve their common problem and help others to recover from alcoholism.
>
> The only requirement for membership is a desire to stop drinking. There are no dues or fees for AA membership; we are self-supporting through our own contributions. AA is not allied with any sect, denomination, politics, organization, or institution; does not wish to engage in any controversy, neither endorses nor opposes any causes. Our primary purpose is to stay sober and help other alcoholics to achieve sobriety.
>
> Copyright © by the A.A. Grapevine, Inc.; reprinted with permission.[1]

In 1939, the book *Alcoholics Anonymous,* referred to by many as the Big Book, was written by a group of 100 sober alcoholics. While this book has been revised over the years, the Twelve Steps have become unchanging tools to live by that have helped millions of people, alcoholic or not.

How It Works

While the only requirement for membership in AA is a desire to stop drinking, most members find that working the Twelve Steps offers a practical strategy for turning that desire into an ongoing reality. Working the Steps, they believe, is essential not only for staying sober, but also for living a life of quality and serenity.

The Twelve Steps of Alcoholics Anonymous have been

reprinted thousands of times in books, articles, and magazines. They are valuable tools that have helped millions to recover from their addictions and living problems and find a Power greater than themselves that will help them solve their problems.

The Twelve Steps should be recognized as a statement of general spiritual principles rather than as a statement of specific religious beliefs and practices. Many people enter Twelve Step programs without a clear understanding of God. It is through attending meetings and working the Steps that many experience a spiritual awakening and begin developing their relationship with God.

THE TWELVE STEPS OF ALCOHOLICS ANONYMOUS

1. We admitted we were powerless over alcohol—that our lives had become unmanageable.
2. Came to believe that a Power greater than ourselves could restore us to sanity.
3. Made a decision to turn our will and our lives over to the care of God *as we understood Him.*
4. Made a searching and fearless moral inventory of ourselves.
5. Admitted to God, to ourselves, and to another human being the exact nature of our wrongs.
6. Were entirely ready to have God remove all these defects of character.
7. Humbly asked Him to remove our shortcomings.
8. Made a list of all persons we had harmed, and became willing to make amends to them all.
9. Made direct amends to such people wherever possible, except when to do so would injure them or others.
10. Continued to take personal inventory, and when we were wrong, promptly admitted it.
11. Sought through prayer and meditation to improve our conscious contact with God *as we understood*

Him, praying only for knowledge of His will for us and the power to carry that out.

12. Having had a spiritual awakening as the result of these steps, we tried to carry this message to alcoholics and to practice these principles in all our affairs.[2]

The Twelve Steps are reprinted with permission of Alcoholics Anonymous World Services, Inc. Permission to reprint the Twelve Steps does not mean that A.A. has reviewed or approved the contents of this publication, nor that A.A. agrees with the views expressed herein. A.A. is a program of recovery from alcoholism only - use of the Twelve Steps in connection with programs and activities which are patterned after A.A., but which address other problems, or in any other non-A.A. context, does not imply otherwise.

TWELVE STEP MEETINGS

Twelve Step meetings are places where people get together to talk about their common problems and help each other stay clean and sober or abstain from addictive behaviors. Sometimes a chairperson will talk about what life was like while he or she was drinking or using drugs; how he or she got clean and sober; and what life is like now. The meeting is then opened up for members to talk about a topic the chairperson has suggested, such as staying sober, developing gratitude, working the Steps, relationships, and so on. Members also talk about other things on their minds or problems they may need help with. In other meetings, called "speaker meetings," one person does all the sharing.

All Twelve Step meetings are similar in structure, but many differ in style. Some people who have never been to a Twelve Step meeting imagine a dark smoky basement full of scraggly old men who drink coffee and commiserate endlessly about their drinking experiences. There are, in fact, meetings all over the country where basements are full of scraggly old coffee-drinking, long-winded men. More often, though, Twelve Step meetings are held in churches, business buildings, schools, fellowships, and, depending on climate, outdoors. Men, women, and teenagers of all races and religions, educational backgrounds, and economic levels attend these meetings.

Some meetings have progressive and flexible ideas about the topics discussed and ways of working the Steps. Others are more traditional and can be rigidly structured. You will find meetings where people openly talk about depression and medications to treat medical and emotion conditions. You may also find meetings where some members believe that you wouldn't have any emotional problems if only you worked your program better. The good news is, there are many different types of meetings, and you get to choose the meetings that are right for you.

THOROUGHLY FOLLOWING THE PATH

The chapter in the Big Book entitled "How It Works" begins with this sentence: "Rarely have we seen a person fail who has thoroughly followed our path."[3] If you have ADD, you may have spent your life trying to follow many different paths, possibly all at the same time. The word *thoroughly* may not even be in your vocabulary. Or you may have the highly focused type of ADD and make yourself crazy trying to follow THE path as perfectly as it can be done. Having these ADD tendencies does not mean you will fail the Twelve Step program or that you will relapse into your addiction. It does mean that you must find the routes down the recovery path that work best for you.

The sentence that follows the one I just quoted is, "Those who do not recover are people who cannot or will not completely give themselves to this simple program." Wait a minute. Are they saying here that AA is a simple program? How can that be? You may have found the program to be anything but simple, and you may have given yourself to it completely, only to relapse. But that was before your ADD was acknowledged and factored into your strategy for recovery.

With a few minor modifications, we can keep the essence,

power, and structure of Twelve Step programs and make it possible for people with ADD and learning disabilities to work them. First, let's look at what kind of difficulties people with ADD have when it comes to working a Twelve Step program.

ADD Goes to AA

If you have ADD, you're probably aware of what trips you up. It may be hard for you to sit still for long periods of time—say for more than five minutes! You may have difficulty paying attention, even when you're interested. Is that an understatement? You may not enjoy writing a thank-you note, a letter, even a grocery list, let alone sitting down to write the fearless, searching moral inventory called for in Step Four. It may also be hard for you to listen when every cell in your body wants to pour out the waterfall of thoughts cascading through your brain.

You may never have felt comfortable being part of a group. Also, relationships and friendships may be as hard for you to sustain as keeping to a training program for running a marathon. Learning to trust is a big part of Twelve Step programs, but many people with ADD have difficulty trusting others. Don't despair. Most people, whether they have ADD or not, feel overwhelmed when they're newly sober and starting to live a whole new life of recovery. Your ADD may make some of these problems worse, but it can also serve as an asset in other ways. Let's look more closely.

Getting to Meetings

It may be hard for you to get to Twelve Step meetings, even if you've worked through your resistance and really want to go. Martin drove around for half an hour looking for a meeting. He was so frustrated and embarrassed by the time he found it that he didn't go in. He sat in the parking lot feeling ashamed for getting lost and being late. Martin was so angry with himself that he thought about getting drunk.

Instead he drove home and called his sponsor, who offered to take him to meetings until Martin was able to find them himself. Martin was relieved to hear how understanding and helpful his sponsor was.

Finding and getting to new places on time can be a nightmare when you have ADD. Since ADD is not an excuse for missing meetings, finding ways to adapt will help you attend the meetings you need. Here are some suggestions.

▶ Get several meeting schedules (in case you misplace one) and tack them up on your refrigerator or bathroom mirror. Keep one in your car.

▶ Even if you know where a meeting is held, it may be helpful to have a friend or someone you've met at meetings pick you up.

▶ Go into the meeting room, even if you're late. It's better to be late than miss the meeting and have a shame attack in the parking lot.

▶ Find meeting times that are compatible with your schedule.

▶ Allow plenty of time to get to the meeting. Getting a speeding ticket on the way can definitely be distracting.

▶ Make decisions not to engage in last-minute things as you're leaving for the meeting, such as watering plants or repairing the broken screen door.

▶ Accept that you'll be late and miss a meeting from time to time. Remember "progress, not perfection."

Now That I'm Here, How Do I Stay?

Now that you're getting to meetings, you may be experiencing difficulties sitting still and paying attention. Feel familiar? How often did you find yourself squirming in your seat, looking at the clock, and yawning when you were in school? Of course, meetings are not just like school. In fact, most meetings are very lively, interesting, sometimes funny, and often quite moving.

It's the not-moving part that may be hard for you. Do you ever feel like you might spontaneously burst into flames if you have to sit still another minute? You have never exploded into a fireball before—and you won't now. The key is to finds ways to be comfortable in meetings so you can get what you need from them. Consider these suggestions.

- Remember, you're an adult and you chose to be at the meeting.
- Remember that meetings are not re-creations of your nightmarish classroom experiences.
- There are no Twelve Step enforcers who will prevent you from leaving or from getting up once in a while.
- Allow yourself to sit near the exit in case you need to take a break or leave early.
- Give yourself permission to stretch, use the restroom, or get something nonalcoholic to drink.
- Try not to torment yourself mentally because you're feeling restless. It's okay!
- Fidgeting is allowed at meetings. Look around. You may see people as restless as you are, each of them secretly fearing he or she might be the next person asked to share.

Sharing in Meetings

You may be surprised to see how structured Twelve Step meetings are. People take turns speaking, sometimes waiting to be called on to talk by others. Once a person has spoken, it is another's turn. There is no "crosstalk"—expressing opinions or feelings after a person speaks. Some large meetings will ask members to adhere to a time limit when speaking so that everyone gets an opportunity to talk.

You may be the type of person with ADD who does well with this kind of structure. Or you may be the type of person who can hardly stop yourself from commenting on everything you hear that relates to you. You may even blurt out information about yourself that discloses more than you really wanted to share. You may find yourself feeling restless and anxious because you want to talk and talk and talk. If any of this sounds familiar, here are some ideas to consider.

- ▶ You don't have to say everything that is on your mind at meeting level. You can talk more with people after the meeting.
- ▶ Think before you speak. Is this something you really want to tell a whole room full of people?
- ▶ Err on the side of caution. If you're not sure you should say something in a meeting, wait and talk one-on-one with your sponsor or someone after the meeting.
- ▶ Allow yourself to go outside during the meeting. You may find others who have moseyed out to chat.
- ▶ It's always okay to "pass" if you don't want to talk.

Paying Attention

If you have ADD, paying attention in meetings may be difficult—even if the speakers and subjects are interesting and you can relate to what is being said. Your mind may wander through time, recalling events from your past and present, and thinking about the future. You may find yourself thinking about work or what you're planning for dinner.

Staying focused may be even harder if some people in the meeting seem to ramble on and on, repeating themselves. Who knows? Some of them may have ADD, too.

The first thing to do is accept that you won't hear and remember everything said at the meeting. Even people who don't have ADD space in and out during meetings. Cut yourself some slack. You may be gaining more from the meeting than you think. There's a saying heard around meetings: "Bring the body and the mind will follow." Most of us can absorb a great deal about recovery by sitting in meetings and being as present as we can. Here are some ideas to help you do that.

► Give your mind permission to drift, since it's going to anyway.

► Most places where meetings are held will have the Twelve Steps, posters, and interesting things on the walls. It's okay to read them if you get bored.

► If you're feeling bored, volunteer to talk.

► When people are talking, listen for similarities rather than differences.

► Try not to sit next to someone who distracts you. You may be attracted to other people with ADD and distract each other and those around you.

► Sit next to someone who has ADD. If this sounds like a contradiction, it is; however, do whatever helps you feel comfortable and stay focused.

► Ask yourself if you're feeling distracted and restless because people are talking about issues that are emotional or scary for you. ADD is not always the reason you're distracted.

Reading Aloud in Meetings

At the beginning or end of most Twelve Step meetings, volunteers are asked to read the Twelve Steps, Twelve Traditions, or other short pieces of information aloud for the group. Reading aloud is uncomfortable for some people. If you have ADD or a learning disability, reading out loud may be terrifying. However, please don't let your fear of reading aloud keep you from going to meetings. The addict part of you may be looking for excuses not to attend.

I know someone with ADD who could not read well, especially in front of people. Sherry had a near photographic memory and had memorized "How It Works" from the Big Book. Still, Sherry would hold the text in front of her as if she were reading along. This was a source of shame and embarrassment for her until one night when she was three years sober. The secretary of the meeting didn't show up. The members decided to have the meeting anyway, even though there was no literature to read.

Without thinking, Sherry volunteered to read "How It Works." She recited it perfectly. The meeting room was filled with applause, and her shame dissipated.

Here are some ways to handle reading aloud in meetings.

- Just say "No, thank you." Reading is not a requirement for Twelve Step membership. You don't need to explain.
- You're an adult now, and the whole class isn't waiting for you to make a mistake.
- Don't allow anyone to pressure you into reading if you don't want to.
- Remember, you have a right to be at the meeting whether you read or not.
- Try not to let your shame about your reading difficulties get to you. You can contribute to the meeting in other ways.
- Some people "forget" their glasses so they can't read.
- You may want to practice reading a piece at home that you will later read at a meeting.

More Reading

Reading may be fundamental, but it's not a requirement that needs to prevent you from maintaining and enjoying your recovery. Don't use reading difficulties as an excuse for not fully working your program.

It's important that you're able to understand the books and literature written for your Twelve Step program; that information will be invaluable for you. However, struggling to read it by yourself is not the only way to learn. Here are some options to consider.

- Share your reading difficulties with someone you trust.
- Ask people to read to you if this makes it easier

for you to stay focused and retain information.

▶ Find a sponsor who will support your efforts to improve your reading when you are ready and not make reading a major part of working your program.

▶ Reading isn't the only way to access information. Some Twelve Step books are on tape.

▶ If you have ADD, you may be eligible to check out books on tape at your local center for the blind or learning disabled.

▶ If you find yourself reading the same paragraph over and over, allow yourself to take a break.

▶ If you want to improve your reading ability, consider getting help from adult education, literacy programs, and community colleges.

▶ You may also consider being evaluated for learning disabilities, which are common in people with ADD and addictions.

▶ If reading is just not your best way to get information, accept it. Pursue the ways of learning that work best for you.

▶ Many people with ADD are experts at assimilating information from their surroundings. Meetings are great places to listen, observe, and learn from others.

Finding a Sponsor

If you've ever been involved or are currently involved in a Twelve Step program, you've probably had experience with a sponsor, who shares his or her experience, strength, and hope with you and guides you through the Twelve Steps. This experience may have been extremely rewarding, somewhat helpful, or horrible.

How will you know if a sponsor is a good match? You may think, "There's nobody like me, no one who will understand me or want to take time to help me." Well, guess what? Sponsors are like shoes. For every shoe there is another to complete the pair. Like a pair of shoes, you will find your match.

Some sponsors provide a tremendous amount of structure. They may ask you to attend ninety meetings in ninety days (90/90). The 90/90 format can be a lifesaver for most newly recovering alcoholics and addicts, as well as members with sobriety who want to strengthen their program. Some people with ADD respond well to this kind of structure because they know what to do each day. For others, however, 90/90 can be next to impossible to complete, especially if they have untreated ADD.

Some sponsors may request that you call them every day, while others will leave the calling schedule up to you. The key is to find a sponsor you can relate with and who has a style of sponsoring that will work for you.

I Have to Write?!
Just when you think it's safe to come out from under your reading shame, you may start feeling shame about your writing abilities. Some sponsors give writing assignments for each of the Twelve Steps. This practice can be very helpful for some, but frustrating and defeating for others. Everyone learns differently. It's hard enough to get clean and sober without having to carry around a suitcase full of bad feelings about your writing. Actually, writing is a very small part of working the Twelve Steps.

There are two Steps that refer specifically to writing, Steps Four and Eight. Step Four states: "Made a searching and fearless moral inventory of ourselves." The Big Book suggests that this inventory be written on paper. Step Eight says: "Made a list of all persons we had harmed, and became willing to make amends to them all." None of the other Steps mention writing or making a list. Here are some ideas about working these two Steps.

Making the decision to be willing to make amends is usually harder than actually making your list of the people you have harmed. Here are a few suggestions for working Step Eight.

► Have pen and paper with you whenever possible, and write down the names of people when you realize you owe them amends. This process can take a long time.

► Write down the names of everyone you've ever known, including yourself, and delete the people you feel you have not harmed.

► Talk your list into a tape recorder.

Here are some ideas that may help you work Step Four.

► Try writing your Fourth Step by using the example in the Big Book. The book provides columns that make it easier to record your inventory.

► Your Fourth Step does not have to be a dissertation. Keep it simple.

► No one need ever see what you write. You can read or talk about what you've written when you do Step Five.

► Consider taping your Fourth Step instead of writing it. Tape recorders were not household items in 1939 when the Big Book was written.

► Find someone who is willing to let you talk through your Fourth Step with them. Do not let your writing troubles prevent you from working this critical Step.

► If you can't seem to get started on your Fourth Step, get help from someone in the program. Try not to let this Step become an obstacle for you.

Picking Up the Phone

You may not always be near a meeting, but chances are you can find a telephone. Sometimes even a brief talk with another recovering alcoholic or addict is helpful. This is especially true if you're having a shame attack. Some people have a difficult time picking up the "thousand-pound" phone, while others can't seem to get off it. Here are some tips to make the phone a useful part of your program.

▶ If you can afford it, buy a portable phone that has a pager button. You can page your own phone when you misplace it.

▶ Think about what you want to say before you dial the number.

▶ Write down points you want to cover during the phone conversation.

▶ Give yourself a time limit on the phone. Consider setting a timer.

▶ Allow yourself to make a call even if you have no idea what you want to talk about. More may be revealed while you're talking.

▶ If you're easily distracted, turn off televisions, music, and the sounds of your family (try not to be rude) before you get on the phone.

▶ Find a quiet place to talk. You may end up taking your portable phone to the garage, car port, bathroom, basement, driveway, or car.

How to Keep from Falling Down the Steps

The Twelve Steps are tools for living. They were not written to make people feel bad about how they work them. There are no letter grades. There's no way to work them perfectly.

Taking the Steps helps you find principles to live by that enhance your life and the lives of those who love you. The Steps are straightforward, but our brains complicate them. At first, you will work the Steps, but soon you will live them. Don't drink or use drugs; do go to meetings, trust God, tell the truth. Do these and you will not fall down the Steps. Here are some handrail suggestions.

- ▶ Maintain a desire to live a clean and sober life based on spiritual principles.
- ▶ Choose a sponsor who will help you take the Steps in ways that work for you.
- ▶ Find a sponsor who will help you work the Steps in the order that works best for you and will be flexible with your not always linear style. Once you have truly worked Step One, the exact order of how you work the remaining Steps is not as critical as some may think.
- ▶ If you don't have a sponsor, find someone in the program who is willing to get you started on the Steps while you find a sponsor.
- ▶ Talk with others about their experiences working the Steps.
- ▶ You may want to consider using one of the many Step guide books that are available. The structure of these books may be helpful or may make you crazy. Look through the book before you buy it.
- ▶ Make working the Steps a priority in your life.
- ▶ Carve out periods of time for yourself to work on your Steps. You are making an invaluable investment in the quality of your life.

INVITING YOUR ADD OUT INTO THE OPEN

Do you feel comfortable telling your sponsor you have ADD? If you don't, you may want to ask yourself why. Do you feel ashamed of your ADD? Do you fear your sponsor will judge you or minimize the impact ADD has on your life? Discussing your ADD with your sponsor may cause you a great deal of discomfort. You get to sort out whether the discomfort you feel is your own or that of your sponsor. Keep in mind that you both may experience some degree of discomfort, especially if you're talking about medications to treat ADD. Ultimately, it's important that you have a sponsor who is able to understand this crucial part of you and who has the capacity to work with you effectively, based on who you are.

If you do decide to talk with your sponsor about ADD, give him or her time to digest what you say. They may know nothing about adult ADD, or they may have been exposed to old ideas or myths about your condition. Consider giving them articles, books, or tapes that will educate them about ADD. If, after a serious effort on your part, it doesn't look like the relationship will work, you may consider finding a sponsor better able to understand and support your ADD treatment. However, avoid impulsively bailing out on your present sponsor until you feel confident that he or she cannot support your full recovery.

Your ADD is a very important part of who you are and it will affect your involvement in the Twelve Step program. But don't let ADD become your primary or your exclusive focus so that you neglect your program. You must balance ADD and addiction treatment as you take each step along the high wire of recovery.

This brings us to another point. The reason you are involved in Alcoholics Anonymous, Narcotics Anonymous, Marijuana Anonymous, or Cocaine Anonymous is to deal with your alcohol or drug problem. People do not attend Twelve Step meetings to hear you talk about your ADD. Therefore, when you do talk about ADD, remember that some people will not understand. Members of Twelve Step programs as a whole are learning more about the variety of co-occurring conditions that alcoholics and addicts have. Many program members have an increased acceptance and sensitivity to the needs of some members who take prescribed medication. Still, misunderstanding, stigma, and fear cause some members to take rigid stances against the use of medication. Be careful that you don't open yourself up to undue criticism.

You may want to test the water before you talk much about ADD at a meeting. Listen for people who talk about depression, anxiety, manic depression, and other problems they've dealt with or taken medications to treat. These people may be more understanding and sympathetic to your ADD recovery. There are also meetings called "Double Steppers" or "Dual Diagnosis" where each member is dealing with addictions and other medical or emotional problems. Here, members talk openly about their experiences with medications in recovery.

Twelve Step meetings for people with ADD are also developing in some areas of the country. These meetings are for people with ADD, whether they have addictions or not.

Do It

You have nothing to lose. The meetings, coffee, and cookies are free. And to top it off, Twelve Step programs will refund your misery if you decide not to stay.

You may feel terminally unique and alone, but there are many people like yourself who have gotten clean and sober and stayed that way, even though they have ADD. Once you're in treatment for your ADD with skilled professionals, you'll be amazed at how much more you can get from Twelve Step programs. Drugs and alcohol will make your ADD worse. Untreated ADD will make your recovery more difficult and less fulfilling. Helen Keller said, "Although the world is full of suffering, it is also full of the overcoming of it."

Now is your time for overcoming. "Clear away the wreckage of your past. Give freely of what you find and join us. We shall be with you in the Fellowship of the Spirit, and you will surely meet some of us as you trudge the Road of Happy Destiny. May God bless you and keep you until then."[4]

CHAPTER FOURTEEN

❦

FEELING YOUR FEELINGS

Healing the Big Five

You have learned that ADD and addictions are no one's fault. You've had the opportunity to evaluate whether you should seek help for ADD and/or addiction. You've developed an understanding of why you, or someone you love, has been self-medicating all these years. You've also learned ways to change your ADD behavior, understand how medication can be helpful, prevent relapses, and work Twelve Step programs when you have ADD. If this sounds like a lot, it is.

Congratulate yourself for accepting that ADD is not a fad. Congratulate yourself also if you've made a commitment to get treatment for your ADD and addictions. You've taken huge steps toward your recovery. Some people never get this far. Congratulate yourself for your courage, even if you haven't yet been able to make the above commitments. You've still come a long way.

I wish I could say that accepting your need to treat your ADD and addictions was all you needed to do. However, there's more. You must also work through many feelings and experiences which, up to this point, may have been diluted or obliterated by chemicals, compulsive behaviors, or denial. Unresolved feelings can sneak around and bite you from behind, just when you think you're getting some stability in your recovery. You can't afford to ignore them.

WHAT AM I FEELING?

When we hold our feelings in, we deprive ourselves and those who love us of a huge part of who we are. We may not feel safe expressing our feelings, especially if we've internalized the concept of "good" feelings and "bad" feelings. I want to make it clear that there are no such things as "bad" feelings. We may prefer certain feelings and try to avoid others, but is the color blue "good" and the color red "bad"? Is a chipmunk "good" and a squirrel "bad"? Is one cloud better than another? Some things in life just are.

Feelings are feelings. More important, they are *your* feelings. They are a part of you; they belong to you. Take ownership of your feelings without judging them. This may be harder than it sounds. The first step is to sort out what is what. Put labels on your feelings so you know what to call them. Sometimes, just knowing what we feel in a given situation is liberating. Try these three word structures to label your feelings:

- ▶ I feel angry.
- ▶ I feel sad.
- ▶ I feel happy.

It takes only three words to express a feeling. Saying, "I feel that you're the biggest jerk I've ever met" is not labeling your feelings. Sometimes we confuse stating how we feel with what we are thinking. Starting a sentence with, "I feel" does not give us liberty to intellectualize our feelings or dump them on someone else.

You may start out with a small list of feelings, but over time you'll be able to identify many complex feelings that coexist. Imagine that you have a feeling muscle that is out of shape. As you practice identifying what you feel in various

272

situations, you are exercising a muscle that needs to work out often to get into shape. Keep in mind, as you work on naming your feelings, that it's possible to feel several feelings at once. For example, you might feel anxious, excited, and confident all at the same time when you're asked to speak in front of others.

If we don't express our feelings, they build up inside us. Expressing our feelings provides release and relief. Once we feel our feelings and express them, they go away. Have you noticed how rarely we have difficulty with repressed happiness and joy? We feel these pleasurable feelings, express them, and they pass. It's the feelings that we push, stash, stuff, or bury deep down inside that can haunt us.

You don't always make a conscious choice to stuff your feelings. You may have learned as a child that it wasn't safe to express your emotions. However, as an adult in recovery, you have the tools and support you didn't have as a child.

Want to make a feeling go away? Feel it. It won't likely dissipate by one quick feel, especially if you have many feelings all mushed together. This might be a time in your life to find a professional who can help you release feelings that may be knotted up inside. This may be the time when you're ready to work through the Big Five.

THE BIG FIVE

Five feelings in particular must be dealt with in order to recover from your ADD and addictions. These five powerful feelings are fear, anger, grief, guilt, and shame. It is my experience that if these five feelings aren't expressed in healthy ways, they can lead to relapse, depression, self-destructive behavior, violence, lost opportunities, and emotional and physical disease.

Fear, anger, grief, guilt, and shame are normal innate human emotions. Everyone experiences these feelings. You can see their expression in human infants, as well as other mammals. Have you noticed how pet dogs often respond when they've had a bladder or bowel accident on the carpet? They turn their head and body downward, giving no eye contact, and frequently act as though they will be hit or beaten, even if they've never been hit. They're expressing their shame, guilt, and fear.

It is not the feelings themselves that harm us, but how we express or don't express them. As human beings, we tend to spend more energy trying to avoid our feelings, especially the ones we think of as "bad," than learning how to express them in constructive ways.

You may be wondering why these five feelings are so important and powerful. Fear, anger, grief, guilt, and shame tend to come hand in hand with ADD and addictions. Most people with ADD and addictions have an abundance of these feelings. They also have difficulty expressing them.

Unresolved fear, anger, grief, guilt, and shame create more of the same feelings, which only grow more monstrous if we avoid or deny them, which only intensifies our desire to make the monsters go away. And so the cycle goes: Unresolved feelings lead to chemical and behavioral addictions, which lead to more unresolved feelings. Let's stop the cycle now by looking at what you can do to find relief from these bottled up feelings. We'll begin with fear.

FEAR

Fear is innate and instinctual. It is the body's fight or flight response to danger. Our ability to sense danger is essential for our survival as well as the survival of our offspring. Fear serves its purpose when it prevents us from walking through a dangerous neighborhood at night or getting into a car driven by someone who is drunk. Fear motivates us to take precautions that keep us safe. But what happens when fear becomes the basis of our life? What happens when we make decisions based solely on fear? This is when fear becomes limiting and even immobilizing.

Our fear is not healthy when we allow it to keep us in isolation, or when it prevents us from pursuing new interests, careers, relationships, or getting the help we deserve. Some of us fear change. We will remain in dysfunctional and painful situations because they are familiar to us.

Fear can also be expressed as chronic anxiety and panic attacks. This type of fear is often based in our neurochemistry and usually responds to a combination of medication, therapy, and learning skills to deal with our anxiety. Fear can also become a habitual response. This is especially true if we grew up in families where we lived in fear of physical, sexual, or emotional abuse. Living in intense or prolonged states of fear, whether you are a child or an adult, can cause your body to respond more readily with a fight or flight reaction.

Sometimes fear from past experiences is triggered by experiences in the present. Karen was shocked by the amount of fear she experienced when her toddler fell and cut his head. Karen became hysterical and almost paralyzed by her fear. She called her neighbor, who took Karen and her son to the doctor to stitch up the cut. Karen's fear turned into shame about how she reacted when she saw Jeremy bleeding.

The next day, when she was telling her mother how scared she had been, her mother told Karen a story of which Karen had no memory. When Karen was about eighteen months old, her father had lacerated an artery in his wrist while working on the car. Karen had seen blood pumping from her father's wrist and spraying all over the kitchen. She and her mother had taken him to the emergency room, where his wrist had been stitched. With this new information, Karen could now understand why the sight of blood was so frightening to her.

We can also be fearful of events even if we have no past history to influence our reactions. Sometimes we build up so much fear about going to the dentist, speaking in public, or taking a trip, that we're relieved to find the fear of anticipation far outweighed the actual event. Our minds, left unchecked, can convince us that all sorts of awful things might happen. At times, we get so carried away by our fear that we fail to deal with the actual facts of the situation. Some people in Twelve Step programs say that the letters F-E-A-R stand for False Evidence Appearing Real. Here are some suggestions to help you work with your fear:

▶ Acknowledge when you feel afraid.
▶ Ask yourself, "What am I afraid of?"
▶ If there is no apparent danger, ask yourself if your fear may be connected to past experiences.
▶ Make a list of all of your fears and share it with a close friend, therapist, or sponsor.
▶ Provide your mind with facts when it wants to take you on a fear expedition.
▶ Remember that anticipatory fear is often worse than the event itself.
▶ Continue breathing when you are frightened, and try to move into your logical thinking.
▶ Confront some of your fears when you're ready. Don't push yourself too hard.
▶ Don't allow your fear of change to limit your growth.

Since fear is such a gut-wrenching emotion, we frequently mask it by expressing other feelings, such as anger, shame, or guilt.

ANGER

We all feel anger. We may not outwardly express it, but it's there. At times, we do feel and express our anger, and sometimes we rage. Rage and anger are not the same. Anger is feeling indignant, resentful, and hostile, and is frequently a defense against feeling our fear. Rage is loss of control over your expression of anger. Fires rage, hurricanes rage, and so do people.

We tend to describe our behavior as an expression of our anger, even when it is actually rage. Rage attacks are explosions of anger that often come on without warning.

We've talked about how if you have ADD, you're prone to spontaneous rage attacks. We also know that substance use can decrease a person's ability to control anger. What could be a disagreement with some hurt feelings turns into destructive and annihilating rage.

Rage can also implode—be directed inward. Imploded rage leads to more substance abuse, depression, self-mutilation, and, in some cases, suicide. Since you've come this far, you may as well deal with your rage. Understanding and expressing anger and rage in a safe way is a part of the process of recovery.

Falling Through the Pink Cloud

"Pink cloud" is a term used to describe the initial feelings of relief and bliss that often follow the acceptance of having ADD or addictions. You feel wonderful because you're getting help and you can see that the light at the end of the tunnel is not a train heading straight for you. However, the pink cloud of early recovery usually dissipates eventually, leaving you falling from the sky. When you hit the ground, you feel the pain of your fall, and then you feel angry because you've had to cope with ADD all by yourself. You feel angry because no one helped you as a child. You may feel furious with those who teased and humiliated you. You may feel enraged by the thought of never drinking or using drugs again.

Getting help for your ADD and addictions will help you be more present in the moment and aware of *all* your feelings. It's as if your feelings are thawing out after being in the deep freeze. You feel all of your feelings more intensely—more joy, more gratitude, more happiness, more pain and sadness. You may be surprised and shocked at the depth and power of your anger and rage. You may feel furious and not even know why. You may even fantasize revenge toward those who misunderstood and abused you. These types of fantasies are a normal way to release anger. They become problematic only if you dwell on them or act them out.

So What Do I Do With All This Rage?

You talk it out, walk it out, scream it out, run it out, pound it out, and throw it out. Anger is mobilizing. You can't feel angry and depressed at the same moment. Also, your anger doesn't have to be self-destructive or harm others.

You won't be able to discharge all your anger at once. It has taken a long time to build up and it will take a long time to let it out. Don't expect all your anger to dissipate in one therapy session of rage reduction. If you stay clean and sober, you'll have plenty of time to work through your anger.

Physical exercise is essential for many people who are recovering from ADD and addictions. Exercise allows the body to relieve stress, aggression, and excess energy. For some people, regular workouts become a part of their recovery program.

Physical exercise increases endorphins in the brain. Endorphins, which occur naturally in our brains, have a chemical structure similar to morphine. They are considered the body's natural pain relievers. In addition, endorphins are thought to help regulate the body's response to stress and mood. Increasing your level of endorphins contributes to the feeling of well-being you may experience after exercise. Some researchers believe that addiction to drugs such as the opiates and alcohol actually suppresses the body's natural production of endorphins.

Relaxation training can also provide relief from anger and pent-up stress. Many fine relaxation tapes are available. These tools not only help with anger management but can also help with sleep problems common among people with ADD and addictions. Some tapes offer soothing background music or the sound of ocean waves. You may hear affirmations or be led through a calming guided visualization. Some tapes focus on releasing tension from the muscles of your body. You may then be able to calm yourself, decrease stress, relax, and manage your anger.

We've talked about how people with ADD may be impulsive. The ADD brain doesn't allow a person time to think through the consequences of his or her actions.

The combination of anger and impulsiveness can cause great harm to you and those around you. Buy yourself some time to deal with your anger by asking yourself the following questions:

- ▶ Is he or she intentionally trying to irritate me?
- ▶ Am I feeling threatened or afraid?
- ▶ Am I feeling overly sensitive?
- ▶ Do I really want to respond in anger?
- ▶ What will the outcome be if I respond in anger?
- ▶ Is this my business or someone else's?
- ▶ Do I really want to take this one on?
- ▶ What will I gain by getting angry?
- ▶ What will I lose by getting angry?
- ▶ What other ways can I respond to this person or situation?

Buy yourself some time by doing some of the following:

- ▶ Take some deep breaths.
- ▶ Go for a walk.
- ▶ Go for a run.
- ▶ Shoot baskets.
- ▶ Pound meatloaf.
- ▶ Pull weeds.
- ▶ Take a few more deep breaths.
- ▶ Excuse yourself and leave the room.
- ▶ Leave the room without excusing yourself.
- ▶ If you're calm enough, go for a drive.
- ▶ Call a friend, family member, your ADD coach, or sponsor.
- ▶ Roll up all the windows in your car and scream.

▶ Hit a punching bag, pillow, or other object you won't harm.

Just taking the time to ask yourself a few of the above questions may help alleviate your knee-jerk anger response. Finding replacement behaviors for rage attacks can eliminate a whole other set of problems. If you can stop long enough to follow the event in your mind to its conclusion, you may decide to alter your impulsive response. Learning to choose your battles is one of the great lessons of life.

Resolving Conflict Without Injury

Conflict is a natural consequence of human interaction. Many of us spend a lot of time trying to avoid conflict with others; sometimes we avoid others altogether. Some of us intimidate and even traumatize others as we seek to "win" disagreements. There are three primary ways to deal with conflicts: passivity, aggressiveness, or assertiveness. The conflict resolution continuum shows each style and the associated behaviors.

Styles of Conflict Resolution

PASSIVE	ASSERTIVE	AGGRESSIVE
■ Solves conflict by giving in ■ Self-sacrifices ■ Harms self ■ Disregards own needs	■ Ask for needs directly ■ Negotiates ■ Respects self and others	■ Solves conflict by taking what he or she needs ■ Harms others ■ Others are sacrificial ■ Disregards others' needs

We learn to solve conflicts by watching those around us. If you grew up in a family where angry words were rarely spoken, chances are there was a lot of unexpressed anger floating around your home. You had no role models to show you how people deal constructively with conflict. If you grew up witnessing how aggression doesn't work well to solve conflict, you may have developed a passive or avoidant approach to conflict.

On the other hand, if you grew up in a family where arguing or fighting was the norm, you may meet conflict with aggression. Some people with ADD seek conflict. They seek out fights with others as a way of stimulating their under-active frontal lobes. The energy produced by the conflict is painful, but it's also activating. Alcohol and other drugs can increase aggressive behavior and decrease impulse control.

Aggressive behavior is rarely an effective way to handle conflict. Even if you get what you want, the cost is almost always too high. However, avoiding conflict leads to distance and disengagement.

Meeting conflict with assertion leads to energy, contact, and the chance to work through the inevitable confrontations we encounter. Becoming more assertive will help you feel more empowered and less angry.

Dinner for Two

Let's use the example of you and a friend deciding where to go for dinner. Your friend asks, "Would you like to go to the rib place for dinne r?" You'd rather go somewhere else. The passive way of conflict resolution is to give in, to sacrifice your needs to avoid conflict.

"Oh," you say, "you want to go to the rib place for dinner? Okay." Meanwhile, you're stewing, "Why does she want to go to the rib place; doesn't she remember I don't eat meat? Oh well, I guess I can get a salad. It will be okay." Your friend has no idea that you aren't happy about the decision, and you end up feeling resentful as you sit in the restaurant, smelling all that red meat.

When you're passive, you solve potential conflicts without having to risk a confrontation. However, by not asking for what you need or by failing to state your preferences, you set yourself up to harbor resentments. When you're passive, you can get hurt.

When you're aggressive, on the other hand, you get what

you want at the other person's expense. If you're an aggressive person, the same dinner scenario could go like this.

"Would you like to go to the rib place for dinner?"

"No!! Don't you remember I don't eat meat? What a stupid idea! Take a vegetarian to a red meat factory for dinner! I want to go to the salad place or no place."

You not only state your demands, you shame the other person. You leave no room for negotiation. You may have gotten your way this time, but there may not be another time. The person who felt powerless and shamed may find another dinner partner.

Being assertive is somewhere in between. Again the question, "Would you like to go to the rib place?"

The assertive response: "Not really. I don't eat meat and the rib place doesn't offer much else. Is there another place you would like to go that also has vegetarian dishes or a salad bar?" In this case you're clearly stating your preference, giving a reason why, and offering a compromise. This can bring you and your friend closer as you learn more about each other.

Letting Go of Resentments

It's hard to stay clean and sober if you've built up unexpressed resentments. And it's impossible to live a life with ADD and not have resentments. If you're not aware of any resentments now, continue with your recovery and they will surface. Trust that your resentments will not harm you if you allow yourself to express them. Only when we hold onto old hurts and wrongs, real and imagined, are we further injured.

Holding onto resentments can keep you feeling like a victim. In some cases, you were victimized by others. You may have grown up in a family where you were verbally, physically, or sexually abused. You may have been horribly neglected by the adults who were supposed to care for you. These abuses caused damage and you need help to move through the pain you've experienced. You didn't deserve to be treated in these ways. No child deserves abuse. But you can't be a survivor until you accept that you were a victim.

One of your challenges is to heal these wounds so you can eventually let go of the resentments you may still carry. You can express your anger by blaming others, or you can use the energy from your anger to propel yourself into making necessary changes. It's important to acknowledge and feel your anger toward those who misunderstood your ADD. It's essential to feel your anger toward those who teased and humiliated you. You have many reasons to be angry, and it's important to feel it. But don't get stuck there.

Your resentments toward others hurt you. I once heard someone say that to carry a resentment toward someone is like "letting that person move into your mind and live there rent free." It's time to kick them out! Get rid of them and use the space they took up for more positive and productive things. Just about anything is more positive and productive than allowing those dinosaurs to trample the fertile grasslands of your mind. Some of your resentments may come from present circumstances. You will have the opportunity to work through them as well.

There are many ways to let go of resentments. To let go, you must first acknowledge your resentments and then be willing to put them behind you. Since letting go is a process, allow yourself all the time you need.

Recovery is more than staying clean and sober and getting treatment for your ADD; it's a lifelong process of new awareness, life-altering events, spiritual growth, maturation, and transformation. Part of this transformation comes by working through unresolved feelings of grief.

GRIEF

Grief is the pain of loss. Grief is a process rather than a one-time feeling. Grief is like the ocean waves that move in one after another. Sometimes we feel that we've experienced all of our grief only to be hit by another wave when something reminds us of how much we miss what we no longer have.

Loss is painful, whether it's the loss of loved ones, relationships, pets, jobs, capabilities, opportunities, possessions, lifestyles, or dreams. Most grief can be attached to a specific loss, but sometimes our grief is a build-up of losses we may not be able to identify. The more willing and available we are to experience our feelings of grief, the more likely we are to heal from our losses. Feeling our grief enables us to experience the pain of our losses and move on with our lives.

Dr. Elizabeth Kubler-Ross pioneered the concept of grief as a process of feelings. Dr. Kubler-Ross outlined these feelings in her five stages of grief—denial, anger, bargaining, depression, and acceptance. These five stages have become a basis for understanding the healing process of grief. No one moves through each stage in perfect order. Most people will move in and out of these stages, at times needing to revisit a specific stage. The one thing that remains consistent about the stages of grief is that acceptance is the end of the process. It is only after we deny our loss, express our anger, bargain to have it be different, and feel our depression, that we're able to accept what we've lost or, in some cases, never received.

Grief is a profound emotion for those of us with ADD and addictions, because we've experienced so much loss in our life. You may have lost your self-respect, dignity, and integrity as a result of your ADD and addictions. You've probably lost opportunities, dreams, and relationships because you couldn't be emotionally present or follow through with commitments.

Types of Grief

I know this is an over-simplification, but I view grief in two forms. The first is acute or immediate grief. We know why we grieve when our pain and sorrow are attached to a specific loss. Grieving can take months and years, even under the best of circumstances. I believe there are some losses we never completely get over. I've worked with parents who have lost children, and they always feel this loss. Their grief no longer keeps them from living their lives, but at some level, their pain never goes away.

The other type of grief comes from what I refer to as "The Well." The well is a deep place within us where years' worth of unexpressed grief resides. We all have a well of grief; for some, it's deeper than for others. The depth and fullness of our well depends on the type and numbers of losses we've had. It also depends on our ability to express our grief at the time. It is difficult to grieve losses effectively in childhood, especially when we're very young. It's also impossible to grieve losses we don't know occurred. Frequently, only when we're adults, and possibly in treatment for addictions, ADD, and other problems, do we realize how full our well is.

Our well of grief is tapped into when we experience a loss. The deeper our well is, the more intensely we may feel our present loss and thus the more deeply we may grieve. Many people are baffled when they lose someone they're not very close to and experience profound grief. What they're experiencing is a combination of present grief and old grief, which is being drawn up from the well.

Your Grief Won't Kill You

Grief can be so painful that many try to avoid feeling it by either denying its existence or using substances and behaviors to push, mash, stuff, and stash it deep inside. This unexpressed grief causes problems, because the only way to process it is to feel it.

The thought of feeling your deep well of grief is probably overwhelming. The good news is that you don't have to feel it all at once. As a matter of fact, your psyche will not allow you to feel a lifetime of grief at one time. It would be too much for any human being. Our unconscious mind doesn't give us more than we can handle. This is when denial can be helpful; we are able to experience our feelings only when we're strong enough to feel them.

Most people in recovery do not have to do a lot of tapping to feel their grief. I think it's important during early recovery from addictions and ADD that you don't try to tap into your grief. Allow yourself to stabilize in your recovery. Your grief isn't going anywhere, and it will reveal itself to you when you're ready.

You may be the person whose grief overflows when you stop self-medicating or are no longer living in ADD survival mode. Your emotions now have the opportunity to surface; in fact, they may seem to flood you. Here are some tips on staying afloat while you experience your grief.

- ► Remember, feeling your grief will not kill you, even when you feel like you're dying from the pain.
- ► Crying is a normal human expression for men, women, and children.
- ► Crying is a primary form of communication when we are babies.
- ► Allow yourself time and space to cry.
- ► Write about your losses in any way you like.
- ► Express your grief into a tape recorder.
- ► Find friends, family members, a sponsor, or therapist you can talk to about your losses. It's okay to feel your pain with others.
- ► Consider attending a grief recovery group. Being with others who are grieving can be healing.
- ► Allow those who love you to be there for you.

I frequently work with clients who, after months of working through issues, find themselves remembering and feeling pain from their past. Their first response is usually to feel that they are backsliding or emotionally unstable. I tell them what I absolutely believe to be true: "The reason you are feeling these feelings right now is because you're more emotionally healthy than you've ever been. Your psyche is providing you with this information because you're strong enough to handle it now. You're in a place in your life where you have the support and safety to feel your feelings. You are more spiritually connected. You aren't feeling these intense emotions because you are unstable. You're feeling them because you are very stable."

Be patient with yourself and your grieving process. There is no "right" way to grieve and no time limit as to how long you should feel your feelings. If you feel your grief is overwhelming, or if you feel stuck, consider getting help and support. You don't have to go through this alone.

It is common for people to complicate their grief process by feeling guilty or ashamed if they are grieving longer than they think they should. Let's look next at guilt and shame.

GUILT AND SHAME

I often hear people say they're feeling guilty about something, when in fact what they are describing is shame. We tend to use the words *guilt* and *shame* interchangeably, but they are two distinctly different emotional and physical responses. Guilt is the feeling that you did something wrong. Shame is the feeling that you *are* wrong. Guilt is a feeling about your behavior. Shame is your judgment of your soul.

You can take action to relieve feelings of guilt. Shame, on the other hand, can be a hopeless prison because there's no one to make amends to since you didn't harm anyone. More accurately, someone harmed you by shaming you. If you have ADD or addictions, the chances are you've experienced plenty of shame and guilt. Unresolved guilt and shame can lead right back to addictions.

Getting Rid of Guilt

If I do something wrong, I have the ability to make amends. If I cause you pain, I can apologize and acknowledge my wrongdoing. If I take something from you, I can give it back. If I break something of yours, I can replace it.

It's helpful to understand the context of the behavior you're feeling guilty about. Again, guilt is about something you feel you've done wrong.

I often work with clients who have tremendous guilt about how they parented their children. When they're able to accept the reality of their situation, it's easier to let go of the guilt.

Your ADD and addictions may have made it impossible for you to be the kind of parent you feel your children deserved. You may have had your children at a young age, or you may have grown up without healthy parenting models. Your willingness to forgive yourself for your past behavior can set you free from your guilty feelings. Self-forgiveness will also make you more available to make amends and be more emotionally present for the people who are in your life today.

A byproduct of making restitution to those you have harmed is that you may be better able to let go of your guilt. Holding on to your guilt will not only punish you but all the people who want to be close to you.

If you are clear about the difference between guilt and shame, I think you will find that guilt is actually easier to remedy. So let's spend a little more time discussing shame reduction.

Reducing Shame

Healthy shame is a natural human emotion. Healthy shame helps us to acknowledge and accept out limitations as human beings and is necessary for us to live in connection with others. Our healthy shame warns us if we intrude on another's boundaries. It tells us when we're compromising our own values. Shame in itself is not bad. Shame, like other human emotions, is a necessary part of us.

John Bradshaw, in his book *Healing the Shame That Binds You*, defines the difference between healthy shame and what he refers to as toxic shame. "Toxic shame is so excruciating because it is the painful exposure or believed failure of self to the self."[1]

Toxic shame is the belief that you are broken, damaged, flawed, and worth less than others. When shame turns toxic, it no longer acts as a way of setting healthy limits and helping you maintain your balance in relationships with others. Instead, it is internalized and becomes part of your core identity.

We don't just feel shame, we become shame-based. We *are* shame. Shame can be triggered from within or from outside of ourselves. The feeling of shame is so powerful that in some cultures it is considered better to kill oneself than to shame one's family. Shame is the response of lowering the head, averting eye contact, rolling the shoulders forward, and wanting to disappear.

Many of us come from families where our parents used shame as a form of discipline. For some minor infraction our parents told us, "You should be ashamed of yourself." We induce shame in our children when we call them names or give them labels. Attention Deficit Disorder is a label that is shame-inducing.

Shame severs our emotional connection with others. Shame will isolate you and leave you alone with your feelings of self-loathing. When you're feeling ashamed, you feel unworthy to be seen by others, let alone spend time with them. Shame prevents you from letting in the caring and love that others give.

Drinking and drug abuse will increase your feelings of shame, which will increase your need to isolate. Shame is an emotion we feel ashamed to feel. Also, many of us feel ashamed to talk about our shame. A downward spiral of shame and isolation, fueled by alcohol and other drugs, can be a killer. Shame makes it hard to reach out for the help you need.

Four Ways to Heal
Talk about your shame with someone who will not abandon you. Talking about your shame with someone who cares can heal old wounds as well as new ones. Your ADD, compounded by your addictions, can create a junkyard full of wreckage. As a result, you may be living in

heaps of broken and discarded interactions and relationships. People, places, and things that were once beautiful now lie rusting and in pieces. Talking about your shame dissolves feelings of isolation and creates intimacy.

I have spent many hours listening as others talk about and express their feelings of shame. I've spent countless hours talking to my therapists and friends about my shame. When I hear others talk about their shame, it allows me to accept my humanness. It allows me to feel less shame for doing, feeling, thinking, and being human. Sharing our shame with others takes the power out of it. Feeling ashamed of our shame fuels it.

For those in Twelve Step programs, the fifth step, "Admitted to God, to ourselves, and to another human being the exact nature of our wrongs," is an extremely powerful way to reduce shame.

Connect with others who understand your problems. We are social beings. Humans have always lived together in caves, tribes, villages, cities, or neighborhoods. Our most basic needs for love, physical touch, security, companionship, and belonging are met largely by connecting with others. Affiliation, belonging, and being a part of a larger context, provide us with the interpersonal connections that help us get our needs met.

You don't have to die of cancer to empathize with someone who is dying. In the same way, many caring people can empathize with your shame even if they have never experienced ADD or addictions. They will be able to share their shameful feelings as well.

There is, however, a joining on a different and deeper level when you know that someone else has really been where you've been. There's an understanding and resonance that happens when people share honestly about problems they have in common. Hearing others confess to doing and saying things you do and say can ease your sense of isolation. In addition, shared humor regarding ADD and addictive behavior can be healing.

Shame is a bit like mold in a petri dish. If you keep the top on the dish, mold will grow. If you uncover the dish and give it sunlight, the mold dries up. It becomes powder that is eventually blown away by the wind. Opening up and sharing your shame with those you feel connected to will help reduce disabling shame feelings to harmless dust.

Find out where your shame came from and give it back. Shame is passed down from generation to generation. Shame can snowball. Understanding where your shame came from will help you give it back to those people, institutions, and belief systems that dumped it on you.

In some cases, a court of law gives victims permission to confront their perpetrators, thus giving them the opportunity to return their shame where it belongs. For most of us, however, giving back our shame is a process that doesn't include those who passed it on to us. We release our shame by understanding its origins, feeling it with someone we trust, and becoming willing to let it go.

Challenge your core beliefs. We all have beliefs about who we are. We may believe that we're smart, attractive, and easy to get along with; or that we are stupid, ugly, and unworthy of the attention of others. We have hundreds of conscious and unconscious beliefs about the core of who we are, most of which we've gathered from others. We internalize, or "own," what others tell us about ourselves. We're especially susceptible to internalizing what our parents or others in authority tell us about who they think we are.

Some of your core beliefs about yourself had some validity when you were a child. But as you've grown up and changed, those core beliefs are no longer accurate. Some were never valid; they were the projections or feelings others had about themselves, which they put onto you.

A challenge in recovering from ADD and addictions is to sort out for yourself what you know to be true about you. By challenging your core beliefs, you determine which ones are valid and which are not. This is the process of redefining who you are. You get to rid yourself of everyone else's beliefs about who you were.

Consider this brief exercise. Find a private place where you are not likely to be interrupted. Take a piece of paper or tape recorder and complete the following sentences.

I am _____

I am _____

I am _____

Record or write the first thoughts that come to mind. Don't worry about the content, spelling, or grammar. Just allow your thoughts and feelings to emerge without censoring them. You may finish the sentence with a word, several words, or a paragraph. Try not to write a book right now. You can do that later, if you wish. Once you feel you've finished, put what you've written away for a while in a safe place. When you're ready, look it over and ask yourself the following questions about each sentence.

- ▶ Where did I learn this about myself?
- ▶ Was the belief I have about myself ever true?
- ▶ Does this belief hold true today?
- ▶ Is this belief one I have internalized from someone else?
- ▶ Does it serve me to hold onto this belief about who I am?
- ▶ Do I want to change this core belief?
- ▶ What is a more accurate belief about who I am today?

It can be very helpful to share your core beliefs with a trusted friend, Twelve Step sponsor, ADD coach, or therapist. People with ADD are notoriously poor self-observers. It is often quite helpful to hear others' feedback about how they experience you. You will often realize that many of the core beliefs you hold to be true are erroneous.

I have a friend who was told by her father that she was a procrastinator. Her father made her write this long word one hundred times. As an adult, she would tell people that she was a procrastinator, until one day a coworker said, "What are you talking about? You never wait until the last minute to do things. You plan out your projects and pace yourself well." My friend gave this coworker's observations some thought and realized he was right. Further investigation led my friend to conclude that she, in fact, did not procrastinate. She could see her history of completions that were well paced. Then she realized something chilling: Her father put things off until the last possible minute. Her father, not she, procrastinated.

Working productively with the Big Five emotions can become a part of your life to the point that you don't have to consciously think about them. You express your fear, anger, grief, guilt, and shame in constructive ways as you become aware of them.

There's one last thing I'd like to say about healing, and that is about the power of humor.

HEALING LAUGHTER

If you've ever been to a Twelve Step meeting, ADD or addiction recovery or support group, you may have been surprised by the laughter you heard. ADD and addictions are serious problems that negatively impact people's lives, and recovery is hard work. Not everyone in recovery feels joyous and filled with merriment and good humor. Yet there is often a lighthearted atmosphere of humor and laughter when people with ADD and addictions get together.

The ability to laugh at ourselves and with others is healing. However, humor is not funny if it comes at the expense of others. Some people confuse teasing with humor. These people may also use "joking" as a way of expressing hostile messages. How many times have you heard someone say, "Hey, it was just a joke"? If it truly was a joke, the teller shouldn't have to explain why the "joke" was funny; the humor should be obvious.

Also, humor is not healing when it is used to avoid feeling other feelings. There are things that happen to us that will never be funny. We can't laugh and joke our way through the pain of life, but feeling the pain can help us to see the humor in some experiences.

We can find humor in our experiences when we realize they are common to being human. The ability to laugh at our humanness helps us connect with others. Some of the best comedians are funny because they joke about themselves and about the common human thoughts and behaviors we all experience.

I've observed over the years how alcoholics, addicts, and people with ADD in particular utilize the healing properties of laughter. The shame and humiliation of addictions and ADD are reduced by expressing the sometimes ironic and funny aspects of both. Some of the funniest, wittiest people I've ever met are recovering alcoholics and addicts with ADD. Their humor can be quick, tangential, poignant, understated, and brilliant in its simplicity. Take Clark's story, for example.

The Postman Has a Problem

Clark, whom I met in an ADD support group, had kept the secret of his ADD from the world, or so he thought. Most people in his life knew that something was very different about him. One night he shared with the support group how ashamed he used to feel for not being able to get his bills to the post office on time. As he related the following story, group members broke out into laughter. Spurred on by their laughter, he became even more animated and funny. This is what he said:

> I have the hardest time getting my bills to the post office. First, I have to find them somewhere in the

mountains of paper I call my filing system. Once I locate them, I have to force myself to sit still and write them out. I would rather clean the cat box than pay my bills.

Once I finally write them out, I usually don't have stamps for the envelopes. I tear my house apart looking for stamps, which leads to several hours of poring through old magazines or other urgent tasks, such as putting my CDs in alphabetical order. After I've put my house somewhat back together, I accept that I am out of stamps. This is especially hard for me. You see, I work at the post office.

I put my bills in my car so I'll remember to get stamps and mail them from work. The other day, while driving, I became engrossed in thoughts about noses. Do you ever wonder why people's noses are so different? I do. The screeching of car brakes broke my spell and I realized the car in front of me had stopped. I had to slam on my brakes and swerve to avoid ending up in their back seat. Months of unstamped mail slid out from under the passenger seat in my car. I guess I'm lucky that panic stops are a part of my routine; otherwise, I would be in collections.

Group members were laughing because they could absolutely relate to what was once a shameful secret for Clark. As he shared his shame about working for the post office and not being able to mail his own bills, it was the laughter, the connection with others who understood Clark, that was healing for everyone in the room.

YOU DESERVE RECOVERY

Each day I understand more about how pervasive ADD is in my life. My clients, friends, family, and colleagues are my teachers. I know I will gain more knowledge, insight, and understanding of ADD and addictions long after this book is published, and so I accept that the end of this book is the beginning of a new phase of discovery and growth. I hope this is the end of some of your pain and suffering, and the beginning of more recovery and healing. You deserve the best.

Cherish yourself, including your ADD and addictions, for they are as much a part of you as your hair and eye color, ideas, feelings, and unique sense of humor. You wouldn't be who you are without your experiences. I wouldn't wish ADD and addictions on anyone, but if these are the genetic cards you were dealt, your life can still be fascinating and fulfilling.

I wonder if our complicated lives don't boil down to some very simple principles.

- ▶ Tell the truth to yourself and others.
- ▶ Never give up on your dreams.
- ▶ Trust that God has not brought you this far to abandon you.
- ▶ Accept that without help it can be too much for you.
- ▶ And, of course, every ending is a new beginning.

For More Information on ADD and Addictions

Books

Alcoholics Anonymous: The Story of How Many Thousands of Men and Women Have Recovered from Alcoholism. New York: Alcoholics Anonymous World Services, Inc., 1976.

CH.A.D.D. Educators Manual *Attention Deficit Disorders: An In-Depth Look From an Educational Perspective.* A project of the CH.A.D.D. National Education Committee written by Mary Fowler.

Friends in Recovery, The Twelve Steps: A Key to Living With Attention Deficit Disorder. San Diego: RPI Publishing, Inc., 1996.

Gorski, Terence T. and Merlene Miller. *Counseling for Relapse Prevention.* Independence, Mo.: Herald House-Independence Press, 1982.

Hallowell, Edward M., M. D. and John J. Ratey, M. D. *Answers to Distraction.* New York: Pantheon Books, 1994.

Hallowell, Edward M., M. D. and John J. Ratey, M. D. *Driven to Distraction.* New York: Pantheon Books, 1994.

Kelly, Kate, Peggy Ramundo, and D. Steven Ledingham. *The ADDed Dimension—Daily Advice for ADD Adults.* New York: Simon & Schuster, 1997.

Kelly, Kate and Peggy Ramundo. *You Mean I'm Not Lazy, Stupid, or Crazy?* Cincinnati, Ohio: Tyrell and Jerem Press, 1993.

Kotulak, Ronald. *Inside the Brain: Revolutionary Discoveries of How the Mind Works.* Kansas City, Mo.: Andrews and McMeel, 1996.

Latham, Peter S., J. D. and Patricia H. Latham, J. D. *Attention Deficit Disorder and the Law: A Guide for Advocates.* JKL Communications, P.O. Box 40157, Washington D.C. 20016.

Ledingham, D. Steven. *The Scoutmaster's Guide to Attention Deficit Disorder: For Adults Working With Attention Deficit Disorder in Scouting and Other Youth Activities.* Tucson, Ariz.: Positive People Press, 1994.

Lehmkuhl, Dorothy and Dolores Cotter Lamping. *Organizing for the Creative Person.* New York: Crown Trade Paperbacks, 1993.

Mellody, Pia. *Facing Love Addiction: Giving Yourself the Power to Change the Way You Love.* San Francisco: HarperSanFrancisco, 1992.

Miller, David and Kenneth Blum, Ph.D. *Overload: Attention Deficit Disorder and the Addictive Brain.* Kansas City, Mo.: Andrews and McMeel, 1996.

Nadeau, Kathleen G., Ph.D., ed. *A Comprehensive Guide to Attention Deficit Disorder in Adults: Research, Diagnosis, Treatment.* New York: Brunner/Mazel, Inc., 1995.

Narcotics Anonymous, 3d ed., rev. Van Nuys, Calif.: World Service Office, Inc., 1986.

Sheppard, Kay. *Food Addiction: The Body Knows*, rev. and expanded Deerfield Beach, Fla.: Health Communications, Inc., 1993.

Soldon, Sari, M.S., M.F.C.C., *Women with Attention Deficit Disorder,* Grass Valley, Calif.: Underwood Books, 1995.

Somer, Elizabeth M. A., R. D. *Food and Mood: The Complete Guide to Eating Well and Feeling Your Best.* New York: Henry Holt and Company 1995.

Weiss, Lynn Ph.D. *ADD on the Job: Making Your ADD Work You.* Dallas: Taylor Publishing Co., 1996.

Weiss, Lynn Ph.D., *Attention Deficit Disorder in Adults.* Dallas: Taylor Publishing Co., 1992.

Weiss, Lynn Ph.D. *Give Your ADD Teen a Chance.* Colorado Springs: Piñon Press, 1996.

Pamphlets

The A.A. Member—Medications and Other Drugs. New York: Alcoholics Anonymous World Services, Inc., 1984. Box 459, Grand Central Station, New York, NY 10163.

Questions & Answers on Sponsorship. New York: Alcoholics Anonymous World Services, Inc., 1983. Box 459, Grand Central Station, New York, NY 10163.

Understanding Anonymity. New York: Alcoholics Anonymous World Services, Inc., 1981. Box 459, Grand Central Station, New York, NY 10163.

Newsletters and Publications

AA Grapevine:The International Monthly Journal of Alcoholics Anonymous
P.O. Box 1980 Grand Central Station
New York, NY 10163-1980

ADD-VANTAGE
P.O. Box 29972
Thornton, CO 80229-0972
(303) 287-6944

The Challenge Newsletter
P.O. Box 488
West Newbury, MA 01985
(508) 462-0495

Sober Times
P.O. Box 31967
Seattle, WA 98103

Journal Articles

Blum, Cull, Braverman, and Comings. "Reward Deficiency Syndrome." *American Scientist*, (March-April 1996): 143.

Comings, Muhleman, Ahn, Gysin, and Flanagan. "The Dopamine D2 Receptor Gene: A Genetic Risk Factor in Substance Abuse." *Drug and Alcohol Dependence*, 34 (1994).

Hooper. "Targeting the Brain." *Time*, (Fall 1996).

Zametkin, Nordahl, Gross, King, Semple, Rumsey, Hamburger, and Cohen. "Cerebral Glucose Metabolism in Adults with Hyperactivity of Childhood Onset." *The New England Journal of Medicine*, 30 (1990): 1361-1366.

~∞~

RESOURCES: ADD, ADDICTION, AND LD ORGANIZATIONS

AIEN (ADDult Information Exchange Network)
P.O. Box 1701
Ann Arbor, MI 48106
ADDinfo@ADDien.org
(313) 426-1659
(Information, support groups, books, and conferences)

ADDA (The National Attention Deficit Disorder Association)
P.O. Box 972
Mentor, OH 44060
Voice Mail: (800) 487-2282 Office: (216) 350-9595
(Annual conference, Web page)

CH.A.D.D. (Children and Adults with Attention Deficit Disorders)
499 NW 70th Avenue, Suite 308
Plantation, FL 33317
(305) 587-3700
(Annual conference, extensive information on children and adults with ADHD)

LDA (Learning Disabilities Association of America)
4156 Library Road
Pittsburgh, PA 15234
(412) 341-1515
(Annual conference, LD information)

A.D.D. WareHouse
(800) 233-9273
(Free Catalog of ADD books, videos, and audio tapes)

Alcoholics Anonymous World Services, Inc.
P.O. Box 459 Grand Central Station
New York, NY 10163
(212) 870-3400
(Pamphlets, publications, books)

Twelve Steps Meetings
(Your telephone directory has the number of the central office nearest you or a recording of meetings in your area. Look up phone numbers by the name of the specific Twelve Steps group—Cocaine Anonymous, Gamblers Anonymous . . .)

Notes

Chapter 2

1. Edward M. Hallowell, M.D., and John J. Ratey, M.D., *Answers to Distraction* (New York: Pantheon Books, 1994), p. 11.
2. Schubiner, Tzelepis, Isaacson, Warbasse III, Zacharek, and Musial, "The Dual Diagnosis of Attention-Deficit/Hyperactivity Disorder and Substance Abuse: Case Reports and Literature Review," *The Journal of Clinical Psychiatry* 56, no. 4 (1995).
3. Maureen Martindale, "A Double-Edged Sword," *Student Assistant Journal* (November/December 1995): 1.

Chapter 3

1. Conversation with T. Dwaine McCallon, permission to print granted.
2. Eyestone and Howell, "An Epidemiological Study of Attention-Deficit Hyperactivity Disorder and Major Depression in a Male Prison Population," *Bulletin American Academy Psychiatry Law* vol. 22, no. 2 (1994): 181.

Chapter 4

1. Daniel G. Amen, M.D., *A Clinician's Guide to Understanding and Treating Attention Deficit Disorder (Childhood Through Adulthood)* (Fairfield, Calif.: MindWorks Press, 1995).

2. Ronald Kotulak, *Inside the Brain: Revolutionary Discoveries of How the Mind Works* (Kansas City, Mo.: Andrews and McMeel, 1996), p. 90.
3. Quoted in Kay Sheppard, *Food Addiction: The Body Knows*, rev. and exp. ed. (Deerfield Beach, Fla.: Health Communications, Inc., 1993), p. 45.
4. Kotulak, p. 71.
5. Blum, Cull, Braverman, and Comings, "Reward Deficiency Syndrome," *American Scientist* (March-April 1996): 132.
6. Comings, "Genetic Factors in Substance Abuse Based on Studies of Tourette's Syndrome and ADHD Probands and Relatives. II. Alcohol Abuse," *Drug and Alcohol Dependence* 35 (1994): 17-24.
7. Hallowell and Ratey, *Answers to Distraction*, p. 210.
8. David Miller and Kenneth Blum, Ph.D., *Overload: Attention Deficit Disorder and the Addictive Brain* (Kansas City, Mo.: Andrews and McMeel, 1996).
9. Blum et al., "Reward Deficiency Syndrome," p. 143.
10. Zametkin, Nordahl, Gross, King, Semple, Rumsey, Hamburger, and Cohen, "Cerebral Glucose Metabolism in Adults with Hyperactivity of Childhood Onset," *The New England Journal of Medicine* 30 (1990).
11. Kathleen G. Nadeau, Ph.D., ed., *A Comprehensive Guide to Attention Deficit Disorder in Adults: Research, Diagnosis, Treatment* (New York: Brunner/Mazel, Inc., 1995), p. 4.

Chapter 5

1. *Diagnostic and Statistical Manual Of Mental Disorders: Fourth Edition* (Washington D.C.: American Psychiatric Association, 1994), p. 82. Note: The DSM manuals are used by doctors, psychologists, psychotherapists, and insurance company employees to label human behavior. The official diagnostic label for ADD in 1997 is Attention-Deficit/Hyperactivity Disorder (ADHD). There are, however, three subtypes of ADHD:
   ▶ Attention-Deficit/Hyperactivity Disorder, Predominantly Inattentive Type
   ▶ Attention-Deficit/Hyperactivity Disorder, Predominantly Hyperactive-Impulsive Type
   ▶ Attention-Deficit/Hyperactivity Disorder, Combined Type
For the purpose of simplification and to decrease confusion, I use the term ADD in this book.

2. Sari Solden, M.S., M.F.C.C., *Women with Attention Deficit Disorder* (Grass Valley, California: Underwood Books, 1995).
3. Colin Wilson, *The Outsider* (Great Britain: Picador, 1978).

Chapter 6
1. William Carlos Williams, *Imaginations*, Webster Schott, ed. (New York: New Directions Books, 1970), p. xviii.

Chapter 7
1. Kotulak, p. 106.
2. Kotulak, p. 107.
3. *Alcoholics Anonymous: The Story of How Many Thousands of Men and Women Have Recovered from Alcoholism* (New York: Alcoholics Anonymous World Services, Inc., 1976), p. xxvi.
4. Miller and Blum, p. 102.
5. Blum et al., "Reward Deficiency Syndrome," p. 143.

Chapter 8
1. Blum et al., "Reward Deficiency Syndrome," p. 143.
2. Kotulak, p. 106.
3. Blum et al., p. 143.
4. Zametkin et al., "Cerebral Glucose Metabolism in Adults With Hyperactivity of Childhood Onset."
5. Lynn Weiss, Ph.D., *ADD on the Job: Making Your ADD Work for You* (Dallas: Taylor Publishing Co., 1996).
6. Scott D. Lindgren, Ph.D., "Sugar, Aspartame and Hyperactivity," *ADHD Report* (August 1994).
7. Heather Ture, M.A., M.F.C.C., "The Big Burn," *The Sun* vol. 2, no. 18 (1988).
8. Document 002522, American Cancer Society, printed on 7/10/96.

Chapter 9
1. *DSM-IV* (Washington, D.C.: American Psychiatric Association, 1994).

Chapter 10
1. Hallowell and Ratey, *Driven to Distraction*, p. 195.

Chapter 11
1. Herbert Spencer, as quoted in *Alcoholics Anonymous: The Story of How Many Thousands of Men and Women Have*

Recovered from Alcoholism (New York: Alcoholics Anonymous World Services, Inc., 1976), p. 570.
2. The pamphlet *The AA Member—Medications & Other Drugs* (1984),
p. 13.
3. Hallowell and Ratey, *Driven to Distraction*, p. 237.
4. Kate Kelly and Peggy Ramundo, *You Mean I'm Not Lazy, Stupid or Crazy?* (Scribner: New York, N.Y., 1995), p. 334.

Chapter 12
1. Terence T. Gorski and Merlene Miller, *Counseling for Relapse Prevention* (Independence, Mo.: Herald House-Independence Press, 1982).
2. Gorski and Miller, pp. 48-54.
3. J. Kreisman, M.O., "Who's Afraid of ADD?" Special Report: Attention-Deficit Hyperactivity Disorder, *Psychiatric Times* (July 1996): 46.

Chapter 13
1. *A.A. Grapevine: The International Monthly Journal of Alcoholics Anonymous*, P.O. Box 1980, Grand Central Station, New York, NY 10163-1980.
2. *Alcoholics Anonymous: The Story of How Many Thousands of Men and Women Have Recovered from Alcoholism*, Alcoholics Anonymous World Services, Inc. New York City, 1976, pp. 59-60.
3. *Alcoholics Anonymous*, p. 58.
4. *Alcoholics Anonymous*, p. 164.

Chapter 14
1. John Bradshaw, *Healing the Shame That Binds You* (Deerfield Beach, Fla.: Health Communications, Inc., 1988), p. 10.

INDEX

A

Abuse:

    physical, 161, 177-78

        in family background, 275, 282-83

    substance, 132-33

        associated with ADD traits, 35, 103

        evaluation check list, 107-18

        medication abuse, 244-47

        See also Self-medication

    verbal, 153, 177-78

        in family background, 275, 282-83

        insults from others, 32-33, 87

Activity level, 82-83

    high activity level:

        physical exercise for, 17, 20, 42, 90

        restlessness, 41-43, 60, 161

        See also ADD traits; Hyperactivity

    low activity level, 43-45, 77, 85-88

ADD:

    in infancy, 68-72

    in childhood, 72-77

    in adolescents, 77-79

    in adults, 29-33, 79-84

        men, 89-92

        women, 85-89, 186

    assets:

        adaptability, 98-99

ADD, assets (continued)
    creativity, 105-06
    curiosity, 64
    expansive, divergent thinking, 80, 102-04
    honesty, uncensored, 101-02
    intuition, 49, 100-01
    sense of humor, 94, 96, 294-95
    tenacity, 64
    thinking and talking on your feet, 90, 104
  culturally induced symptoms, 52-54
  without hyperactivity, 43-45, 85-88, 186
  See also ADD traits
ADD coaches, 211-12, 248-49
  coaching groups, 87, 163
  in comprehensive treatment program, 213, 243
ADD and correlated conditions:
  depression:
    biological, 22, 190, 216
    chronic, 19, 23, 89
    in dual diagnosis, 233
    with low energy ADD, 44
    and neurotransmitters, 58, 216
    self-medication for, 140
    as a spectrum disorder, 61
    treatment outcomes, 238
  eating disorders, 35, 159
    and neurotransmitters, 58, 59
    as spectrum disorders, 61
ADD and correlated conditions (continued)
  learning disabilities (LD), 46-47, 190, 233
  manic depression or bipolar, 26, 140, 236
  obsessive compulsive disorder (OCD), 58, 238
  posttraumatic stress disorder (PTSD), 123-24
    and addiction relapse, 233, 236
    and neurotransmitters, 59, 60
    treatment outcomes, 238
  See also Addictions; Anxiety; Food
ADD and criminal behavior, 31, 40, 58
  alcohol and drug related, 31, 114-16, 143-44
  relapse into, 235

ADD traits, 34-35
See also Attention; Impulsivity; Organization
Adderall, 217, 221
Addictions, 137-38
consequences of, 107-18, 133, 146-47
obsessive thoughts, 133, 135-36, 176
tolerance, 133, 134-35
withdrawal, 135, 161-62, 163
symptoms during, 26-27, 127-28, 240
Addictions to:
amphetamines, 157-59, 191-92
caffeine, 125, 162-64
cocaine, 24, 31, 159-60, 191-92
marijuana, 23, 138, 156-57
narcotics, 125, 161-62
nicotine, 125, 134-35, 164-65
Addictions to: (continued)
prescription medication, 88, 138, 166-67
See also Alcoholism; Food
Addictive behaviors, 59, 140
exercise, 181-82
gambling, 138, 147, 170-71
Internet and Web browsing, 173-75
sexual, 138, 175-80
spending, 138, 171-72
work, 138, 180-81
ADHD, 40, 151
Adolescence, 42, 77-78, 86, 131
Alcoholics Anonymous (AA), 253-56
and ADD medication, 214-15
definition and beliefs of, 253-54
Alcoholism, 107-38, 124-27, 154-56, 161
as a disease, 119, 138
genetic transmission, 62, 121-22
treatment for, 240-44, 249, 251-57
See also Addictions
Anger:
occurance and management of, 276-83
rage, as ADD trait, 33, 34, 161
spontaneous attacks of, 29, 45-46, 65, 92, 210

F

Fear, 161, 274-76
See also Anxiety
Food, 121
    anorexia, 150-51, 182
    binge eating, 58-59, 128, 149
    bulimia, 58-59, 128, 149-50, 151
    compulsive overeating, 59, 148
    self-medicating with food, 20-21, 88, 147-54
    sugar addiction, 138, 147, 151-52

G

Genetics, 56
    receptor site studies, 59-60, 60-61, 122
    spectrum disorders, 61
Grief, 283-87
Guilt, 287-88

H

Hyperactivity:
    childhood history of, 62-63
    gender differences, 85, 90
    and glucose absorption, 62, 149, 151-52

I

Impulsivity:
    as an ADD trait, 34, 38-40, 83-84
    biological factors, 18, 33, 57-59, 61-63
    consequences of, 65
        criminal behavior, 31, 235
        drug experimentation, 131
        relapses, 27, 234, 235
    and drugs, 156, 165
    moodiness, 97-106, 210-11
    and social interactions:
        anger response, 279-80
        disruptiveness, 33, 194
        interrupting, 39, 91-92, 204-05
        verbal outbursts, 30, 104
    See also Organization

L
Learning disabilities (LD), 46-47, 77, 190
Learning styles:
    auditory, 48
    kinesthetic, 49-50
    visual, 48

M
Medication, 213-28
    in comprehensive program, 188, 213, 226, 243-44
    How it works, 215-22
    management, 211, 223, 243-45
    medication and relapse prevention, 239-40, 244-47
    See also Antidepressant medication; Self-medication
Memory, 23, 33
    enhanced for details, 47
    impairment of, 29-30, 46-47, 156

N
Narcotics Anonymous (NA), 19, 225
    See also Twelve Step programs
Neurotransmitters, 33, 56-60, 119
    dopamine, 59-60, 149, 216
      receptor sites, 58-60, 61, 122
      reuptake inhibitors, 219
    imbalance in, 33, 216
    serotonin, 58-59, 148, 149, 216

O
Organization, 33, 34, 45-46, 208-09, 211
    time, problems with, 34, 206-08, 211
    See also Activity level

R
Relapse, 229-49
    ADD relapse, 247-49
    addiction relapse, 19, 135
      multiple instances of, 27, 118
      rationalizations, 128
      underlying problems, 145
    prevention of, 243-44

About the Author

Wendy Richardson M.A., LMFCC, is a Licensed Marriage Family and Child Counselor, and Certified Addiction Specialist in private practice. Over the past twenty-two years, she has acquired extensive experience while working with juvenile and adult offenders, in school-based intervention, and chemical dependency programs.

Wendy has devoted much of her time to educating medical and chemical dependency professionals, teachers, and parents, as well as treating people with ADD and co-related addictions. She is a consultant, trainer, and is a frequent presenter at national ADHD and LD conferences. Wendy is motivated by her personal and professional passion to help others whose lives have also been affected by ADD and addictions.

Wendy lives with her husband and two children in a rural area of California. She and her family travel whenever possible. They enjoy walking and hiking on beaches, in deserts and forests, and finding new trails wherever they go. This also gives Wendy time for her other passion: wildlife and nature photography.

DEAL WITH ADD AT ALL LEVELS.

Adult ADD

Reader-friendly and designed for the ADD reader, *Adult ADD* examines at least four of the current controversies surrounding ADD: diagnosis, symptoms, treatment, and the question, "Is ADD a legitimate disability or just an excuse?" It also brings a better understanding of adult ADD to professional care-givers and the families, friends, and coworkers of those adults who suffer from ADD.

Adult ADD
(Thomas A. Whiteman, Ph.D., and Michele Novotni, Ph.D.) $14

Give Your ADD Teen a Chance

Give Your ADD Teen a Chance provides parents with expert help by showing the difference between ADD behavior and "normal" teenage development. It offers specific help for the academic challenges ADD teens face, and enables parents to look objectively at their ADD teen by giving guidelines for discipline, guidance, and responsibility.

Give Your ADD Teen a Chance
(Lynn Weiss) $15

Get your copies today at your local bookstore, or call (800) 366-7788 and ask for offer **#2350**.

Pinon Press

Prices subject to change.